Stand Alone, Inventor!

Robert G. Merrick

SNP
Panpac

Copyright © 1997, 1998, 2000, 2002, 2004 Robert G. Merrick

This edition is published by
SNP Panpac Pte Ltd
97 Ubi Avenue 4
Singapore 408754

First published in 1997 by Lee Publishing Co. (USA)
Reprinted in 2000, 2003 and 2004

Project Editor – Wong Wan Ling
Cover design by Dan Teo – NestComm

ISBN 0-9643832-0-9

Printed by SNP SPrint (M) Sdn Bhd

To Letha

"*Is there any more feverish dream of glory in the world, outside of Islam, than the dream of being an inventor? Certainly not in the United States; and probably not in Japan or any other industrial country. An invention is one of those super-strokes, like discovering a platinum deposit, or a gas field, or writing a novel, through which an individual, the hungriest loner, can transform his life overnight, and light up the sky. The inventor needs only one thing which is as free as the air: a terrific idea.*"

— *Tom Wolfe*

whose renowned works include *The Bonfire of the Vanities* and *The Right Stuff*.

Reprinted by permission of the author.

CONTENTS

Disclaimer

This book is intended to provide certain information within the subject matter covered. It is sold with the understanding that the author and the publisher are not engaged in rendering legal, accounting or other professional services. If legal or other expert assistance is required, you should seek the services of a competent professional.

It is not the purpose of this book to reprint all the information that is otherwise available, but to complement, interpret, amplify and supplement certain texts from the standpoint of the author, and relate to you some of his first-hand experiences. You are urged to read all the available material, to learn as much as possible about inventing and marketing and to tailor the information to your individual needs. For additional sources, see the many references in the Resource Section.

Stand Alone, Inventor! is not a surefire, get-rich-quick book. Anyone who decides to try to invent for profit must expect to invest not just money, but a lot of time and careful effort. For many people, not necessarily the majority, self-venturing a patented product with one's own company can prove to be more lucrative than selling or licensing it to another. Many have built solid, growing, rewarding businesses—some quickly, some very slowly.

Every effort has been made to make this book as complete and as accurate as possible. However, there may be mistakes, both in typography and in content. Therefore, this text should be used only as a general guide and not as the supreme source of information on how to profit from an invention. Furthermore, this book contains certain changeable information on the subject matter covered, and is up-to-date only as of the printing date. The purpose of this book is to educate and entertain. The author and Lee Publishing shall have neither liability nor responsibility to any person or entity with respect to any loss or damage caused, or alleged to be caused, directly or indirectly by the information contained in this book.

Pronoun Notice

In most of the text of this book the author follows the traditional editorial practice of using the pronouns "he", "his" and "him" when referring to persons in general, who may be either male or female. When he does this it is for the purpose of keeping the text easier to read compared to text with the more precise references, "he or she", "his or her", and "him or her". (Luckily, for author and reader alike, the word "inventor" is not gender-specific.)

Acknowledgments

Even a stand-alone inventor can use a little assistance and encouragement along the way. These are the people (in addition to my entire family) who helped me in one important way or another to succeed with my inventions, my company, and my start and finish of this book. To them I am truly grateful. Thanks!

Ron Alley*■Lynn Bachman*■Roger Borovoy*■Bob Brennan■Kevin Bruce■ El Brown■Buck Buchanan■Jerry Burch■Susan Burlison■Tony Campbell ■Barbara Carey■Randy Carling■Remberto Carranza■Troy Challenger*■ Bob Chaney ■Wanda Chirichigno* ■Bob Condon■Rick Crandall■Stuart Crump■Bob Darling■Mike Davidson■Jerome Davis■Wally Dean■Don Dible ■ Mike Dikas ■ Dikran Ekmekji ■ Dave Estes ■ Bob Farmer* ■ Dick Franklin ■ Dale Frase*■Jean Fuller*■Rocky Furukawa■Gary Gairaud ■ Bill Gilmartin ■ Phil Goodman ■ Michael Guerra ■ Dave Guthery ■ Fritz Haas*■Sharon Hall■Harry Hambly■Sam Harding■Dick Harmer■Judi Harper*■Tom Healy■Dick Heyman■Mary Ellen Hills■Ted Hittell■Poul Hoegh■Jack Hokanson■Jerry Humpal■Knox Hurst■Chris Jones■Lisa Kanarek*■Linda Kawasaki■Wendell Keene*■Martin Keller■Donald G. Kelly■John L. Komives■Bob Krolick*■Steve Lang■Guy Lee■Alan Leeson ■ Bob Legge*■Glenn Littlefield■Robert G. Lougher■Alan MacPherson*■ Walt Madden■ Jorge Marcondes■Bill Martin■Wint Mather■Stan McCarthy ■Mark McColl■Regis McKenna■Waldemar Mehlig*■Gene Merrill■Ron Messenger ■ Roy Nishi ■ Bob Noyce* ■ Barrie O'Brien ■ Ward Osward ■ Eduardo Pacheco■Fred Patton*■Ray Piontek■Dan Poynter*■David Pressman ■Joe Presti■Minor Rasmussen■John Ready*■Bob Reed*■Martha Regan■ Ben Ridge■Jo Anne Santos■Stu Schneider■Richard Scott■Bill Seidel■ Dick Selberg■Aziz Shariat■Kim Shepard■Bob Sherman*■Terry Short■ Ed Shriber■Yuh Shuan*■Hal Shuster■Vanessa Singer■Rick Singson■Hal Smith■Keith Strom■Vince Thomson■Gene Torske■Larry Udell*■Chuck Vanderwege*■Jeff Vinson*■Dr. Eugene Wagner■John Waters*■Erik Werner ■Jim Woodbridge*■Geri Wyatt■Larry Yurkonis■Carla Zilliox■Kent Zilliox*

*A Special Thanks

FOREWORD

When inventor-entrepreneur Bob Merrick showed me his latest creation, his "how-to book" for start-up inventors and entrepreneurs, the book's title gave me pause. *"Stand Alone, Inventor!"* is a phrase that encourages one to become the independent entrepreneurial type that I so often cautioned my audiences *not* to emulate. In lectures and writings for more than a quarter century, I've advised inventors and entrepreneurs that they should *not* try to face a tough world on their own. Instead, I've always called on them to seek the sage advice and capable assistance of those who have (as the kids say today) "been there, done that."

"No man is an island," I implored, recalling the oft-quoted observation of 16th Century author John Donne. And to make that point with some audiences, I sometimes drew upon the street-wise wisdom of modern day philosopher Harry Calahan, better known as Hollywood's Dirty Harry. In the movie, *"Sudden Impact,"* Police Inspector Calahan intones: "A man's gotta know his limitations."

The term *"Stand-Alone"* could hardly apply to those I've counseled, or so I thought. But then I read Merrick's manuscript. I get his point, and it's a good one.

Inventors and entrepreneurs, imbued with the knowledge and wisdom that ebb from Merrick's engaging experiences, *can* break away from the crowd. And, armed with the resource guidance his book contains, they most certainly *can* rise to levels of power and independence. While we don't always agree one hundred per cent, I found a great deal of commonality in our messages, Merrick's and mine; especially when it comes to engaging professional assistance in some key areas. For struggling inventors everywhere, we both advise: "Do what you do best, let others do the rest."

For example, start-up inventors can and should do their own research on product needs, on the state of the technology, capital availability, manufacturing options, and self-promotion. Homework, bookwork, network, legwork. But, when it comes to complex legal work, including drafting patent claims or threatening legal action for infringement, it's best to call in the "suits." Even so, Merrick teaches that inventors can venture much further on their own than they might have thought possible.

Using his own experiences as a setting, Merrick paints a mural along the hallways from workbench to marketplace. What he did first. What he did next. What he wished he had done; or hadn't done. The inventions he uses as examples are as easy to grasp as his easy-going, often entertaining dialogue. And, when Merrick pardons himself for editorializing about one side issue or another, his readers aren't lost; they hang on to see what he has to say. After all, Merrick's "been there; done that."

Perhaps the best lesson of the book, naturally from my point of view, is that the ownership of intellectual property is the great equalizer for the start-up inventor. Merrick shows this time and again. The protection offered by patents, trademarks, and copyrights can make a decided difference in the marketing jungle.

Hopefully, many fledgling patentees will pick up a copy of this book and find themselves leaping far beyond their dreams to the level of independence that Merrick promises. Just as hopefully, among those who read this book will be those thousands who never thought of themselves as inventors or entrepreneurs, but once learning how it's done, will be passionately inspired, and successfully motivated.

Perhaps the sense of accomplishment that the reader can anticipate by putting Merrick's lessons to use is best summed up in the words of another author, John Godfrey Saxe in his 19th Century poem, "The Game of Life."

> **In battle or business, whatever the game,**
> **In law or in love, it is ever the same;**
> **In the struggle for power, or the scramble for pelf,**
> **Let this be your motto — Rely on yourself!**
> **For, whether the prize be a ribbon or throne,**
> **The victor is he who can go it alone!**

Donald G. Kelly
Director
United States Patent &
Trademark Office, Washington, DC

INTRODUCTION

By Professor Robert S. Krolick

I asked my friend Bob Merrick why he decided to write this book, and why he gave it the "commanding" title. He told me that when he speaks at workshops and seminars he meets many people who want to invent for profit, but who lack proper guidance about how to proceed with the best chances for success. Also, during three years as President of the California Inventors Council, he had seen too many creative people with little or no idea what to do after the inventing. "Often, because of this," he says,

As a tenured Professor in the Department of Design and Industry at San Francisco State University, Professor Krolick created and taught an innovative course that covered the invention, protection, development and marketing of new products. The effectiveness of this course won him the highest award of the Freedom Foundation, the Meritorious Award for Excellence in Private Enterprise Education. He has appeared on TV's *Good Morning America*, *Evening Magazine* and *CNN*. In 1992 Professor Krolick retired from teaching to devote full time to his company, Westedge, of San Rafael, CA. Westedge is a successful one-person venture that makes and sells a very simple product that Professor Krolick invented and patented. (See Ch. 2)

"many inventors got mixed up with the wrong partners, slick promoters or unfair licensees, only to end up in a loss situation." That's why he exclaims in the title of his book, *Stand-Alone, Inventor!*

Bob told me that if readers retain only one thought from his book, he hopes it would be: "Inventing, like life, is an individual pursuit; the more control you have over yours, the better". He said that aspiring inventors, and those who have stumbled, need the basic training found in this book, because it will teach them not only what's best to invent, but the correct steps to take for a successful outcome.

When I met him about fifteen years ago, Bob Merrick already had a reputation for inventing and bringing to market simple consumer products. At the time, I was teaching various college courses in product innovation, design and marketing. Often, I got Bob to speak to my classes. He taught my students some valuable lessons on how to get a new product made, promoted and sold at a profit.

Eventually, I incorporated some of Bob's ideas in into my course materials. Over the years we kept in touch, often to compare notes about our respective inventions and enterprises.

I asked Bob how he happened to get started as an inventor/entrepreneur. He told me that he had taken a managerial job in the marketing department of a young semiconductor company in Palo Alto that manufactured transistors. Soon after he was hired, his marketing duties called for him to help introduce to the world his company's groundbreaking invention, the first production integrated circuit. He was greatly impressed by this historic event.

Bob served six years in the exciting high-tech environment, and was a first-hand witness and participant in the earliest beginnings of what is now called Silicon Valley. But, instead of luxuriating in a corporate position, Bob wanted to be his own boss, and market his own inventions. Although he did not believe his future would be in the high-tech arena, he felt a calling to start a company of his own. But first he would need a product.

He says he set a goal to dream up a unique product, a suitable vehicle for launching a business. Soon he reached that goal, and the resulting product was the centerpiece of his new sideline business. By the time his career as an inventor unfolded, he had introduced more than a dozen inventions, including a series of four simple consumer products that were very successful. These four products have kept his company running smoothly and profitably for more than 25 years. He calls them his "Million Dollar Ideas."

The Author's Four "Million-Dollar Ideas"

1. The Military Pay Calculator

Bob's first idea was a simple invention to help the Department of Defense organize the monthly pay tables for its military men and women. Having been on active duty in the Navy, he was aware that the individual GI's pay was quite complex, because there were many types of pay.

Each type of pay was administered by a different bureau, which meant that there were many different printed pay schedules to refer to if one wanted to figure the total pay of an individual. Bob felt that a combined schedule was needed that would pull together all types of pay for easy calculation. So he went to work and devised a small paperboard slide chart, a military pay calculator for the Army that he called, "Pay-Rule."

Over the next few years his Pay-Rule idea would yield more than a million dollars in product sales—which became Bob's definition of a *million-dollar idea*. He would tell my students, "To large companies a new product having the potential of grossing a scant million dollars or so in sales—over a few years—is of little or no interest." Usually, this level of sales is considered too insignificant to bother with." But, Bob points out, "This set of circumstances leaves the door wide open for the individual, someone like you. Because if you, as an inventor/entrepreneur invent a product that can accumulate a million dollars or more in sales—even if it takes you a few years—it would provide you with an income that could make you financially independent. Further, since the 'big boys' aren't interested in such pint-sized sales, you would probably end up with the market all to yourself!"

Early on, the Pay-Rule enabled Bob to quit his regular job and devote his time to producing more Pay-Rules for the other service branches. Pay-Rule produced a substantial income for Bob and his company for more than ten years.

2. The Crystal-Date® Watch Calendar

A lot of individuals in business would be perfectly content with the volume of sales Bob was doing, but Bob wasn't. For one thing, his sales weren't diversified. He was totally dependent on just one customer—the United States Government. Bob felt it was time to see if he could come up with another product.

On the band of his wristwatch Bob wore a small metal clip-on calendar that showed the current month. During a sales call in Washington, one of his military customers admired his watch calendar and asked him to submit a quote on a quantity of 10,000 such watchband calendars. Bob said he would be happy to do so.

When he returned to his office, he did a source study and was amazed to find a thriving industry: There were more than thirty companies engaged in the production of metal clip-on watchband calendars! Bob was also surprised to find that 10,000 sets of metal clip-on watchband calendars cost so much that to make a decent profit, he would have to sell them for $0.35 per set, which struck him as rather high. Bob's customer also believed the cost was excessive. No sale. So, even at a time when the media was slamming the Pentagon for paying contractors "$500 for a hammer." at least one military buying office was showing some restraint!

Because of this experience, Bob felt that watch calendars might offer him an interesting new product challenge. During several weeks of pondering the problem, he was racking his brain trying to think up a less-costly calendar for the watch. Nothing occurred to him until one weekend, while he was watching a baseball game on television. The network superimposed the scores of some other ball games right over the picture of the game he was watching. Suddenly, Bob says, he got his "second *million-dollar idea!*"

Although he was aware that information could be displayed in this way, he had not appreciated its relevance to his problem. He now realized that people were becoming accustomed to seeing one image displayed right on top of another. He imagined a monthly calendar, printed on a transparent substrate affixed to the outer surface of a watch crystal. A transparent, pressure-sensitive label was the answer! The watch owner could focus his eyes either on the watch dial for the time of day, or on its crystal for the calendar dates. Removable adhesive would be used to permit the calendar to be peeled off and replaced at month's end.

Bob surmised that the pressure-sensitive labels were sure to cost a lot less than the metal calendars. He also believed that it would not take much money to get into production. He could take advantage of the label making industry, which could offer almost any description of label he needed.

He knew that if his new product turned out to be acceptable to existing consumers of metal watchband calendars, the market would be substantial. And, he knew there was at least one buyer (in the Pentagon) who would want to see this new product!

Bob told me he was too excited to watch the rest of the baseball game. He put a piece of transparent Scotch® tape over the crystal of his watch. Next, he took some india ink and drew a crude calendar on the tape. He wore this "prototype" model for several days just to see if it was practical, and he found it was indeed quite useful.

He said he was most impressed, however, with the fact that while he wore the calendar many people, seeing it on his watch, would ask, "Hey, what's that on your watch?" Thus, Bob felt his new invention had enough novelty value to catch on quickly. Actually, with this test Bob had conducted the market research he needed for his new product idea.

And he was particularly elated when he realized this was a product he could sell to someone other than the U.S. Government! Bob told me that in a few years—after his watch calendar had become a success—more than 90% of his sales volume came from hundreds of commercial accounts. He estimated that of the top Fortune 500 companies about 300 were quantity buyers of his Crystal-Date® calendars.

Having satisfied himself that his new invention had great potential, Bob met with a patent attorney. He was very pleased when, six months later, he was granted a 17-year United States utility patent on the watch calendar. A small one, but a legal monopoly! The watch calendar grew to account for the major part of Merrick Industries' sales volume for more than 12 years. It was produced in thirteen languages and was covered by additional patents in England and Spain, with others pending.

3. The Lint Mitt

Could there be another new product idea even simpler than the watch calendar? Let's take a look.

One day a label salesman called on Bob and suggested that he come out with a lint remover. It would be a large, flat pressure-sensitive label—to be made, of course, by the salesman's company—cut out in the shape of a whisk broom. The salesman explained that the user would simply peel off the backing sheet and pat his clothing with the sticky side to remove lint and dust. Bob didn't care for the idea. He said he thought a large "label" would be too floppy to handle, and not very useful. Bob asked the salesman if he himself would ever use such a lint remover. The salesman admitted, "Actually, around the office we use an ordinary packing list envelope. We stick our fingers in it like a mitt, peel off the backing and pat our clothing. Because it goes on the hand like a mitt, the user can pat his or her clothing repeatedly with the sticky side. It works great!" Bob thought to himself, "Could this be another Million Dollar winner?"

The next day Bob did a source search for companies that made packing list envelopes. Before long, he entered into an exclusive agreement with one of them to manufacture to his specifications what he called the Lint Mitt® lint remover. (Unfortunately, for the salesman who gave Bob the spark for this idea, his employer did not make packing list envelopes!)

Bob's specifications called for a mitt that was larger than a packing list envelope (to better fit one's hand), and that had a flap to make it easy for the user to open. It was printed with his trademark and how-to-use instructions. Some mitts would be printed in color with the logo of a hotel or dry cleaner.

He tried to get a design patent on his Lint Mitt structure, but he was turned down by the patent office, because it was too similar to the packing list envelope. Bob gave his design a certain measure of protection, with a registered Lint Mitt® trademark, and with copyrighted how-to-use instructions.

Bob's marketing efforts resulted in the Lint Mitt® becoming a standard room set up amenity in quality hotel chains such as Hyatt, Marriott and Westin, as well as hundreds of independent hotels around the country and overseas. Eventually, the Lint Mitt became his third *million-dollar idea*.

Bob tells me the Lint Mitt is alive and well today at age 16. Sales to hotel chains and others are conducted by letter, telephone, FAX and personal calls. "We know hotel guests love this useful amenity", says Bob, "because we hear from many of them who want to buy a supply for use at home."

4. The Business Card Punch

Noticing in the 1980's that most of his sales were going to just one industry—hotels—Bob began getting nervous again. He realized his company needed still another new product.

He flipped through his inventor's notebook—the place he recorded random ideas and improvements for products—to see if he had any good ideas stockpiled in it. He came across an entry from years earlier: Under a rough sketch of something that looked like a hinge, was a description, "A punch for notching business cards to adapt to Rolodex files."

Like a lot of people in the course of business, Bob collected the business cards of various individuals and companies. He wanted to file some of the cards for future reference. Rather than transcribe the business card data onto pre-punched blank rotary file cards, it seemed quicker to trim the business cards to a smaller size, and paste or staple them onto the blank file cards.

While using the "cut and paste method", it occurred to Bob that the manufacturers of rotary card files, such as Rolodex Corporation, *must* sell a punch that cuts notches in business cards to fit the rails of their files. So Bob called four leading rotary card file manufacturers, but could find none that was selling such a punch.

A lady who took Bob's call at one company told him she was sorry to say, but they didn't offer such a product. When he asked why, she said she guessed that it was because pre-punched blank cards were such a big part of her company's business, "We probably don't want people punching cards!" After that call, Bob felt that he had uncovered an opportunity for another *million-dollar idea!*

Within a year Merrick came out with a hand-held, punch made of molded plastic that—with one squeeze—chops two notches "that will make business cards work like Rolodex® brand cards", to quote his advertising.

Offering it at $8.95, Bob set up distribution of his punch into the office products market, where right away it became a big hit. Patented, and dubbed the "Merrick™ Punch," it can be found today in the stores of

Staples, Office Depot, OfficeMax, and many other office supply outlets, as well as in catalogs such as Quill. Bob also exports his punch to Europe and Asia.

In addition, the punch lends itself very well to the promotional products market, where he calls it the Personal Punch™ and offers it custom imprinted with company logos for corporate recognition.

Within four years the business card punch became Bob's fourth *million-dollar idea*. Bob reports today that he has manufactured and sold more than three million business card punches.

Now that I have introduced the author to you, I will turn the book over to him. Bob will devote the rest of this book to teaching you the nuts and bolts of how to get your product made and marketed at a profit.

CHAPTER 1

Ten Rules for the Stand-Alone Inventor

Making money from your own ideas is almost assured if you learn to use my rules for the Stand-Alone Inventor. But before you review these rules, you may be wondering, what do I mean by a "Stand-Alone Inventor?" The expression first came to my attention in a conversation with my patent attorney several years ago. He mentioned something about a particular inventor he knew. When I asked him if the inventor worked for a corporation, he replied, "No. He's a 'Stand-Alone Inventor,'—like you." This is the handle, I learned, that patent attorneys use for the non-corporate inventor.

In this book I greatly expand the "legal" definition. I believe a term is needed to describe the self-actualizing individual with moxie who is willing to find out and do everything that is needed after the inventing to make it a success. Over the years many people have made a success of their inventions in this way, but they have never been singled out and given a name. I call these people *"Stand-Alone Inventors."*

> ❝ The motto of the Stand-Alone Inventor is: If I keep my invention simple enough, I can finance and promote it myself, and I can get it produced and distributed at a profit—all by myself. ❞

The motto of the Stand-Alone Inventor is: "If I keep my invention simple enough, I can finance and promote it myself, and I can get it produced and distributed at a profit—all by myself."

Even if your preference is to simply license your invention, you will find it much easier to sign up a licensee if you first develop your invention into a commercial product in the manner of the Stand-Alone Inventor. But, my most important advice to you is to try to stand alone. Do your best to stay away from partners, venture capital firms, invention marketing scams and licensees. More about why in the chapters to follow.

I assume because you are reading this book, you have an interest in independent inventing. You have taken step one. But—

If you want to join the ranks of Stand-Alone Inventors, you must take an additional step: Venture your project alone, rather than defaulting to a partner, financier, or licensee.

As one who has produced a continuous cash flow for many years bringing consumer inventions to market, I have devised certain rules that I apply whenever I contemplate an idea for a new product. I have found these rules greatly increase my chances to succeed—and I know they will help you, too. I call them *My Ten Rules for Stand-Alone Inventors.* Your new product won't necessarily fail if you break a few of them. But in my opinion, the more of these rules you keep, the more likely you are to reach a profitable outcome.

> ❝If you want to join the ranks of Stand-Alone Inventors, you must take an additional step: Venture your project alone, rather than defaulting to a partner, financier, or licensee.❞

Here are ten rules for you to use as a checklist against your next idea for an invention:

1. Go With What You Know.
2. Think Up Products for Big Markets.
3. Invent Products That Can Be Patent Protected.
4. Create Products That are Physically Small.
5. Design Simple Products That are User-Friendly.
6. Develop Products That Offer Repeat Sales.
7. Devise Products with a Low Manufacturing Cost.
8. Keep Your Initial Cash Investment Small.
9. Have Others Do Your Manufacturing.
10. Price Your Product to Yield a Good Profit.

> It has been said that, "To invent is to choose:" First, you choose what problem needs solving, and then you choose ways to try to solve it. If you discover a good solution, you choose to try to license or sell the solution, or you choose to try to develop and market the solution on your own.

1.   Go With What You Know.

Draw from your own special experience and try to invent in a field that you know something about. It's tough enough to develop an invention into a profitable new product; but it's almost impossible to do it in a strange environment where you don't even speak the language. The Wright Brothers used their experience as bicycle mechanics to unlock the secret of flight. In their early attempts at flying, their test crafts would slip sideways and crash. But their background in cycling taught them that balance and control were essential. Likewise in an aircraft, they reasoned, these elements had to be conquered before sustained flight could happen.

It's unfortunate that so many inventors who decide to go into business for themselves do so with virtually no previous experience in the area of their invention. Many times the proper experience would have told them their new product would probably not succeed in the first place. I believe an inventor could take a sensational new product, approach a strange industry with it and still be turned away because of lack of grounding and proper contacts. But if you stay within your own field you can draw help from your existing knowledge and relationships to accomplish your goals.

Stand-Alone example: My previous experience in the Navy gave me insight into some of the aspects of military pay, and into some of the problems of armed forces recruiters. Later, in my civilian job, I had gone through all of the steps, from idea to product realization, to produce a paperboard slide rule device. And, in doing so, I had developed a relationship with a company that later would be my supplier. As a result, it was a relatively easy undertaking for me to develop and market my first product, the military pay calculator, which I sold for many years.

2.   Think Up Products for Big Markets.

Be honest with yourself when you size up the market for your invention. You'll want it to appeal to a very large segment of the population. For example: All adults. All computer owners. All homeowners. All automobile owners, and so on. All these are big markets worth going after. But, if you think your product will be of interest only to math teachers, piano players, or sky divers, think again before you spend much time or money on it. Why? Because at best, you may not sell enough product to cover your cost to make and promote it. But, do your homework carefully, because some rich markets are well hidden: Who would have thought that Professor Krolick's idea for a plastic hinge for supermarket pasta bins

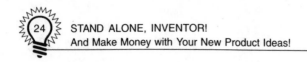

would enable him to live like a Lotto winner? (See Chapter 2)

3. Invent Products That Can Be Patent Protected.

It doesn't take a Harvard MBA to appreciate the value of a small monopoly. And that's what you get by patenting. You also get a certain measure of similar protection with copyrights, trademarks and trade secrets. These protections will help you deter or stop competitors from bringing out a knockoff, or otherwise copying your creations. Obviously, by blocking competition, you can enjoy a higher price and a bigger sales volume for your product.

The trick, however, is to come up with products that are sufficiently novel that none of your competitors can devise anything remotely similar or cheaper without infringing you. My business card punch enjoys this kind of monopoly. More about this in Chapter 5

4. Create Products That are Physically Small.

Less is more. The primary advantage of physically small products is their ease of storage and handling, which makes them relatively inexpensive to keep in inventory. My first inventory of 5000 military Pay-Rules could be kept at home in our hall closet. Just think if I had invented something the size of a shoe box and had to store 5,000. It would probably have taken a space the size of my garage!

It's not only convenient to store products that are physically small, it's also easier and cheaper to send samples to prospects and to ship orders. Customers appreciate compact products, too. Keep in mind that it's much easier to carry a small product to a potential buyer for a demonstration. People always want to see the actual product; not just a catalog sheet or a video. Whenever I pioneered a new product (they were always small), I was never without a few samples in my coat pocket or in my brief case. I recall making a substantial product sale at 30,000 feet to the guy sitting next to me on a business flight to the East Coast. Try doing this without a demo!

Finally, if you invent a retail product that takes up only a little space, you greatly increase your chances of getting it accepted into stores, where shelf space is always at a premium.

5. Design Simple Products That are User-Friendly.

Simple is smart. Usually the simpler the product, the more user-friendly it is. So, develop your new product to be as simple as it can be.

Remember, as the inventor, you can execute simple products faster and cheaper, compared to complex products. Simplicity will not only help make manufacturing easy, but it usually results in an easier-to-promote product because it's easier to use. User friendly is more than just a computer buzzword. It's your customer's first impression of you, your product and your company.

Do your best to make it quick and easy for your customer to figure out how to use your invention. Print brief how-to-use instructions on your package. Don't hesitate to halt work on a product idea if it's turning into a "Rube Goldberg" in complexity. Deep-six any product you invent that is hard to demonstrate, or that requires a lengthy education period before customers can use it. People will say, "It's a nice idea, but...."

Finally, when you launch your product, try to offer it in only one color and in one size. Remember Henry Ford's Model T offer: "They can have any color they want, as long as it's black!" Years later, he offered his Model A in a few other colors. Lesson: Consider adding options only after you prove your basic product will sell, and only if and when you find you need to.

6.   Develop Products That Offer Repeat Sales.

If your product won't get used up, wear out, go out of date, or spoil after the customer buys it, you'll never hear from him again. This is why you should try to invent something that will need to be replaced. My military Pay-Rules had a built-in obsolescence factor that was wonderful. Whenever GIs got a raise, all of the Pay-Rules in use automatically became obsolete. I was then in the enviable position of being able to sell large numbers of up-dating or replacement units.

My Crystal-Date watch calendars also delivered guaranteed product obsolescence. Nothing goes out of date with more reliability than a calendar! One corporate buyer set his computer to automatically issue us at the end of each year a re-order for 100,000 sets of my Crystal-Date watch calendars for use in his Christmas mailings. His orders kept coming for more than a decade!

Also, as thousands of hotel guests all over the country use my Lint Mitt lint removers and dispose of them, it means that before long the hotels will be sending me replenishment orders. Lint Mitt re-orders which began in 1979, continue to come into my company to this day.

Many big corporations have used the "repeat-sale" strategy for years. Gillette has made millions selling blades that wear out. Razor companies

Figure 1-1. Launched in 1979 (when hairstyles looked like this), my Lint Mitt® disposable lint remover for hotels and dry cleaners still produces repeat orders today.

even decided to add throw-away razors to their lines. And, by the same principle, in the long run, camera makers would rather sell you film.

So, if possible, try to deal in consumable or disposable products when you invent.

7. Devise Products with a Low Manufacturing Cost.

If your idea for a product requires holographic printing, for example, the set up and manufacturing costs will be very high, This can be a problem, because you may end up having to charge more for your product than your customers are willing to pay. The same is true if your product idea includes a custom electronic chip or other sophisticated technology. Your potential sales volume for these types of products needs to be huge if you are to end up with a unit price that is reasonable. You'll need to penetrate a big market with big sales. Big preparation costs need to be amortized over big quantities to get a profitable return on your investment.

> I marveled at the fact that a single sheet of watch calendars that was physically smaller than a dollar bill, and that I printed for $0.15, would sell at wholesale for more than a dollar. Was this better than printing money? You better believe it was! And, it was perfectly legal!

Getting started with an invention that has a low manufacturing cost means that it will take you less risk money to develop it to find out what you have. All of this means that you must categorically reject any product ideas that have big up-front costs, or high unit costs to make. One of my secrets to keep costs low is to try to use existing technology whenever possible. I always avoid re-inventing the wheel. For example, I borrowed the format for my Pay-Rule from a 20-year old structure, the paperboard slide rule. My watch calendar is a custom design that uses proven label-making techniques. My lint remover mitt is a modified packing list envelope. If your product requires a push button, for example, try to find one that already exists as a component in another product. Track down the maker, and have that company or its competitor supply you. This approach will save you the time and expense of tooling up and making the component yourself.

When I was marketing my transparent calendar for the watch, my cost to print and package a 12-month calendar sheet was less than $0.15. Yet consumers were paying $2.98 at retail for this product. Nearly 20 times cost. This is called a "low-mass, high-information" product. Consumers pay for the value of the solution, not for its size, weight or perceived cost.

8. Keep Your Initial Cash Investment Small.

Without a super high-tech product, it is difficult to raise investment capital in today's financial environment. So, don't waste time hunting down venture capital firms. Unless your project needs several million dollars, it's not likely to interest them, anyway.

It is best to get started with a new product using only your own cash. If you can do this, you will retain complete ownership and control of your enterprise. Having autonomy with your venture is a nice way to live— no one's looking over your shoulder and/or asking for reports.

But, keep in mind that it's common for new products to fail. Unless you have a sizable cash surplus, it's more prudent to start out playing with small chips. Limit yourself to several months' pay. Don't mortgage the farm! Work off your kitchen table, and keep your costs down. By being conservative in this way, if your new product fails, the financial hit will not wipe you out. And, you will have left the way open to try another invention later. (See Chapter 6)

My Crystal Date watch calendar, was so simple, it took only about $500 to buy the initial trial inventory. I took samples from this inventory to test the reaction of people in the market to this new product. A positive or negative reaction would be used as the basis of a "go"-"no-go" decision for the project. A "no-go" decision would have meant that I risked and lost $500 on the idea. The "go" decision that I actually made, meant that I could now proceed with full confidence that I would not *lose* any money on the project. Why? Because the positive reaction I got from the market test convinced me that if I invested more money in a larger inventory, I could sell enough of it to at least cover my costs and break even. As it turned out, the idea was a smash hit that was a money machine for me for more than a decade.

9. Have Others Do Your Manufacturing.

Far too many novice inventors rush out to purchase machinery so they can go into production. Usually the equipment they want is quite costly in terms of initial outlay, operation, overhead and maintenance. This approach is to be avoided in the beginning, because there is a much cheaper and less-risky way to go.

The best solution to getting your invention manufactured is to subcontract, or outsource, the work to a qualified vendor. No matter what you invent there is a company somewhere that can produce it for you. When you sub-contract, you are still seen as the "manufacturer," which could be important to your company's image in the marketplace. More importantly, you keep your risk low, by not putting cash into machinery that you may not need all the time.

Outsourcing means you are paying someone else for the cost of materials, for manufacturing time, i.e., running a machine, and perhaps for assembling your product—plus profit. The economy is evident when you realize that you only need to be "manufacturing" a few hours per week, or a few days per month. And, of course, if your product bombs, you won't need *any* manufacturing time. By outsourcing you are buying only the materials and manufacturing time you need—when you need them. It's ideal.

> **❝The economy of outsourcing is evident when you realize that you only need to be "manufacturing" a few hours per week, or a few days per month.❞**

In some instances, however, it may be wise to outsource only the mechanized portion of the production. Bring the hand assembly operations under your own roof, and use part-time labor that is cheaper than the manufacturer's.

10. Price Your Product to Yield a Good Profit.

Your product must be able to command a price high enough to return a decent profit. Begin pricing your product at a level higher than you think you'll need. In doing so, you will: a) test to see how high a price the market will bear, and b) restrict sales volume until you make sure your manufacturing capacity can keep up with demand. All too often, inventors will launch a new product at a ridiculously low price thinking they will stimulate sales. Don't try this. You must set your price as high as possible to allow for a comfortable net profit after numerous trade discounts and expenses. Someone once advised, "Price yourself to happiness!" More specifics about this in Chapter 11.

Summary

There you have my Ten Rules for the Stand-Alone Inventor. These rules are intended to help you make intelligent choices. Especially for your first few inventions. Later, after you have succeeded as an inventor and have accumulated greater financial resources, you can attempt more complicated projects and play with bigger chips. But when you are starting out as an inventor, you should always carry a card with these ten rules printed on

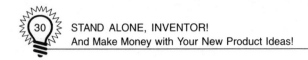
it. Then, whenever an idea for an invention pops into your head, you can use the card as a checklist to see if the idea is a good one. If it measures up, it's probably a "keeper," and worth pursuing.

Note: The Resource Section begins on page 259 and is arranged by chapter to make it convenient for you to find related references.

CHAPTER 2

Some Successful
Stand-Alone Inventors

Before getting into the "basic training" part of this book, I want to tell you the stories of a few individuals who followed most of the ten rules of the Stand-Alone Inventor. These inventors took control and made it big. In early attempts, some of them had ignored these rules and failed. In the end they all succeeded by developing simple inventions they could manage essentially by themselves. After their stories, I will tell you my own story of how—using the ten rules—I found the road to self-employment with my first invention.

Escape Your Shape!

Meet Barbara Carey Stachowski, slender, early thirties, married, and the mother of a twelve-year-old son. On a recent January 1st she was watching a TV "infomercial" on which some people were touting exercise equipment. The program was pushing the New Year's resolution thing about losing weight, and Barbara recalled her unpleasant experiences with yo-yo dieting. Many times she had gained weight, dieted to lose it, only to end up gaining it back again. A familiar story for many.

> **❝At that moment Barbara realized that she possessed a valuable formula for getting weight off and keeping it off.❞**

However, in the previous 12 months things got much better for Barbara. She had thirty pounds to lose to get back to her target weight, which she did. But this time she had been successful in maintaining her target weight. She was through yo-yoing because this time she did something different.

At that moment Barbara realized that she possessed a valuable formula for getting weight off and keeping it off.

She analyzed how she had accomplished her goal in the previous 12 months. She realized the formula she used not only included a certain amount of good diet and exercise, but a unique motivational component. She called the component her *secret mirror*, and here's how she discovered it:

Two years earlier while she was re-decorating her house, she purchased a mirror at a department store. She thought the mirror, which measured about 1 by 4 feet, would be perfect for her to hang vertically in her dressing area, which she did. "When I first looked at myself in that mirror," she said, "I couldn't believe what I saw. I was taken back like I was in school again; that's the way I *used* to look!"

Barbara took a closer look at the mirror itself and discovered it was flawed; it had a slightly convex shape to its reflective surface, something like a "fun house" mirror that makes one look skinny. She decided not to return the mirror to the store because she liked the good feeling she got looking at herself as a slender person. After about a week she found she was habitually checking her appearance in the mirror, because she saw herself as a slimmer more attractive woman.

"I felt that the person in the mirror, the lean person I'm looking at, must be doing things different from what I do, because I was doing the things that fat people do: Physically, I was relatively inactive. I was eating for emotional reasons, rather than eating when I was hungry; I was not listening to my stomach. I neglected my needs for breakfast, which made a starving person at lunch, and I would go the refrigerator and over-eat.

"These are a lot of the things people do who are overweight. So I did some research and made a laundry list of all the things that lean people do, and I discovered that there are very different habits between lean people and overweight people. Since my image of myself was now that of a leaner person, I found myself changing my habits gradually, making simple improvements day after day.

"I started eating low fat food, I started really caring about the things I ate and I started eating foods my body loves. I increased my activity level, I started walking fifteen minutes a day, and then I started some indoor exercise on a stair climbing machine that I could stay with. As I began to lose weight, each time I looked in the mirror I continued to see myself about 10% slimmer, and I got a very good feeling - a continuing reward - which was really the motivation that made me stick with what I was doing."

"When I summed it all up, what I really had was a brand new *motivational system* that wouldn't compete with Richard Simmons' books, that wouldn't compete with Jane Fonda's, or Cindy Crawford's videos, but would actually complement all other programs out there and give people the repeated motivation they need to stay with their program for a long time."

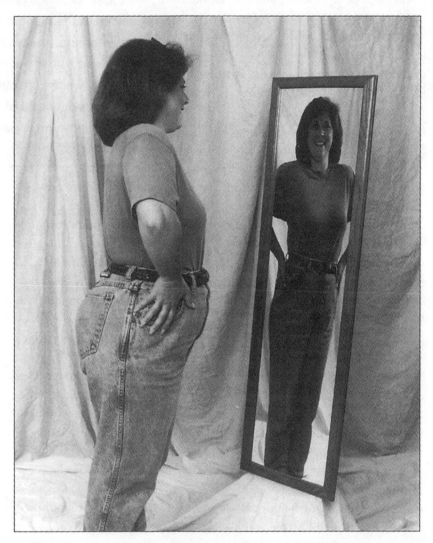

Figure 2-1 A model demonstrates Barbara Carey Stachowski's Motivation Mirror™ that was sold on a major home shopping TV network. The mirror was accompanied by an audio tape she called *Escape Your Shape*. Thousands were sold on TV at $39.95. Barbara told me she is proud to call herself a Stand-Alone Inventor.

On January 2nd, the day after Barbara assembled her product idea in her mind, she called Steve DeVore, the founder of Sybervision, and told him about it. He liked the idea and encouraged her to do something with it. He suggested she contact his writer, Stew Nohrnberg, which she did, and they worked out a script together. "On the 5th of January I rented a recording studio and hired a female narrator to do the talking. The result was a twenty-four minute audio tape telling customers how to use the mirror to help motivate them in their weight reduction program, whatever it was." Barbara's complete package, designed to sell for $39.95, would include the Motivation Mirror and the audio tape that she called, *Escape Your Shape.* Meanwhile, she had found a Southern California company she could sub-contract to manufacture, pack and ship her product for her.

> ❛Today Barbara is proud to call herself a Stand-Alone Inventor and she wouldn't have it any other way. She will only work on relatively simple products that she can manage and control—by herself! ❜

Next, Barbara flew to New York by herself and talked to the producers at a major TV home shopping network. They bought the product immediately and gave her a purchase order with Receipt of Goods, or ROG terms (payment three days after shipment) for 5000 units on the condition she would appear on live TV to help pitch the product. Soon after the 5000 units were delivered, Barbara flew to New York and showed the Motivation Mirror on TV for the first time. After a few airings it was clear: At $40 a pop, sales were dramatic.

Let's take a look at how Barbara was able to put this program together and make it work. Barbara needed to find a unique financing scheme. After all, the order would involve a considerable sum of money, and she would need to convince her manufacturer in Southern California that he would be paid. First of all she required her customer to pay within three days upon receipt of goods at their dock. Payment was made by electronic transfer to a special trust account Barbara set up for the purpose at her bank. Next, she issued a purchase order to her manufacturer whom she can now assure will be paid first—out of the special bank account—as soon as the goods are received. This clever financing arrangement worked, and it precluded Barbara having to apply for a time-consuming bank loan or credit check.

Barbara is to be congratulated as a full-fledged Stand-Alone Inventor. After all, she dreamed up an idea on January 1st, put together a salable product, and by January 27th put a check in the bank that was about the equivalent what a rookie pro athlete makes in a year!

Barbara says it really took more than 27 days, because she really has to count several years of previous experience working with a much more complex invention (Breaking Rules 6 and 8). Barbara had designed a unique watch for children that incorporated what she calls "interactive visual technology." This is a new way to perceive time using the sense of touch. This project necessarily involved investors. It needed costly development, and it would need to be licensed to a watch manufacturer. After five torturous years, the project so far has yet to find a licensee. Barbara concedes now she should have been doing something much simpler.

Barbara and her mirror are a classic example of successfully following many of the Ten Rules listed in Chapter 1.

Today Barbara is proud to call herself a Stand-Alone Inventor and she wouldn't have it any other way. She will only work on relatively simple products that she can manage and control—by herself!

I've Got Rhythm

Eight years ago, vivacious Vanessa Singer was near death with a massive brain hemorrhage. It was so bad that doctors were reluctant to touch the case, and she was not expected to live. Her family had to search the entire country for a doctor who was willing to help. Finally, they found Dr. Gianota at the University of Southern California who told them he would have to operate immediately or she could die within two months. Eight hours of surgery later the good doctor had located and removed an abnormal blood vessel formation.

Today, at the age of 27, Vanessa Singer is not only alive, she is living the American Dream! She invented a product for guitarists that is taking the music industry by storm. She calls her product the Rhythm Pick™, which is now sold in music stores in 42 states in the US, and in 24 other countries.

It all started in August of 1994. Something happened that would change Vanessa's life forever. She was playing a song on her guitar and she decided that she wanted some rhythmic accompaniment. She tried playing the guitar while holding a "shaker egg," a miniature percussion "rattle" shaped like an egg, which is used as an accompaniment to various instruments. She found this "juggling act" awkward while trying to play. Vanessa thought the shaker egg and the pick might work together

Figure 2-2. Vanessa Singer shows off her patented invention, the Rhythm Pick™, a big seller that enriches guitar music. She kept her product simple and manageable in the manner of the Stand-Alone Inventor.

in an interesting way if they were combined as one piece. So she went to her kitchen and using a knife, sliced a slot in the egg that would hold the pick. Next, she tried her new invention and she was amazed at the unexpected result. It sounded like the playing of maracas, the gourd instrument that goes, "cashush-a-cashush-a-cashush-a" when shaken. It works especially well with an acoustic guitar.

Vanessa was at once very excited about the prospects of what she had discovered. "It was the biggest dynamite blast that I ever felt!" she says.

Vanessa believed immediately that her combination product idea could be made if it were molded into a single-piece shaker egg/guitar pick. She reasoned that the advantages of such a product would be two-fold: It would add a new percussive background to the sound of guitar music, and it would help guitarists improve their feel of rhythm. Vanessa was correct, because her Rhythm Pick™ took off like gangbusters to become one of the hottest new products on the music market today.

> **❛ Vanessa was at once very excited about the prospects of what she had discovered. "It was the biggest dynamite blast that I ever felt!" she says. ❜**

To get started, she put together a corporation she calls Take Your Pick, Inc., which is located in Canoga Park, CA. She made the product a reality, by working with designers and molders and finally investing in an injection mold. Her invention was awarded US Patent #5,483,859. She promotes the product through publicity and advertising and she uses endorsements by guitarists such as Wolf Marshall, whose instructional tapes and CD's are distributed worldwide. He says, "By listening to yourself play with the Rhythm Pick, you develop a better pulse, a better sense of rhythm, and you can really improve your timing."

By 1996 Vanessa had added two more products to her percussive line: "The Rhythm Bag" and "The Rhythm Thang," both of which, she says, are being received in the music market with great enthusiasm.

Congratulations to Vanessa for overcoming adversity, and enriching the music world. She is a true Stand-Alone Inventor!

It Takes a Mirror

A publicity squib in the March, 1996 issue of *Mademoiselle*, the national fashion magazine, reads:

"**Lip Trick**- Instead of reapplying lipstick at the table using a compact mirror (bad form) or doing it in a cab without any mirror (bad news), try this little gizmo. Just stick the teeny Dazzle Dot Lipstick Mirror on a lipstick cap and you can have instant, discreet reflection. $1.99 for a two-pack at drugstores."

And, in the March 1996 issue of *New Woman* another squib, this time showing a color photo, reads:

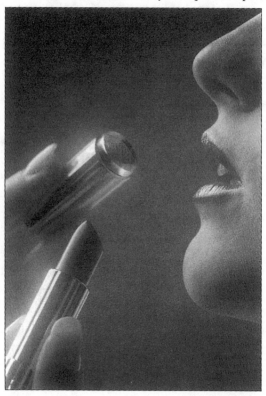

"**Mirror, Mirror**- Turn your lipstick cap into an instant looking glass with the Dazzle Dot Lipstick Mirror (below) from Hills Industries. This dime-size, self-adhesive mirror attaches to most caps and ends the frustration of rummaging through your purse for a mirror or peering into a blurry spoon to touch up your lipstick. The tiny invention has a tiny price, too: $1.99 for a pack of two. For more information, call (800) 573-1760."

This extremely valuable free publicity was the payoff from a press release sent out by a Stand-Alone Inventor in Belmont, CA.

This release, the inventor's very first, resulted in publicity notices running in these

Figure 2-3. Mary Ellen Hills' Dazzle Dot® lipstick mirror caught the attention of the fashion world and became a big hit overnight. She has more products waiting in the wings ready to debut when the time is right.

and several other major women's magazines around the country. The originator of the release (with the help of a friend) and creator of the Dazzle Dot mirror is Mary Ellen Hills, thirty something, who one year earlier, had no clue she would be running her own company. Although she and her husband had frequently discussed various ideas for new products, neither had ever pursued any of them until....

Wanting to freshen her lipstick before leaving a restaurant, Hills searched in her purse unsuccessfully for her compact. Grabbing her dessert spoon, she touched up her lipstick aided by a blurred reflection from the spoon. Turning to her husband, she said: "Somebody ought to put a little mirror on the end of lipstick caps." He replied, "Why don't *you* do it?"

> ❛ This extremely valuable free publicity was the payoff from a press release sent out by a Stand-Alone Inventor in Belmont, CA. ❜

In the months to follow, Mary Ellen's life would change. She would still work with her husband in the family-owned auto repair business, but she would spend increasingly more time on her new sideline venture that she named Hills Industries. Because she was a neophyte, she knew she would need a lot of help and did not hesitate to ask for it.

Hills took her first prototype to the Service Corps of Retired Executives (SCORE). "I got an incredible amount of help from them," she said. They referred me to several sources of supply I would need. After a few months her product was in its blister package, ready for market.

Although she was told of the importance of market research and test marketing, she opted to skip the scientific approach. Rather, she immediately hired a sales rep in the cosmetics field to take her product directly to a buyer at a drug chain. The buyer's response was disappointing to say the least. The

Figure 2-4. Stand-Alone Inventor Mary Ellen Hills created a professional-looking blister card package for her Dazzle Dot® lipstick mirror. Look for it in your favorite drug store.

sales rep said he found no interest, and that he did not believe he could sell Dazzle Dot™ into this market.

Although Mary Ellen was quite discouraged, a few weeks later she asked a salesman friend of hers if he would give it a try, even though his sales experience was in an unrelated field. Surprisingly, he found enthusiasm for the product everywhere he showed it, and even came back with a few orders. Mary Ellen took his success story to a national tradeshow and lined up more sales reps, orders, and distribution. Before her third year her sales of Dazzle Dot™ went into six figures.

Mary Ellen is a true Stand-Alone Inventor because she took the initiative by herself and got her product manufactured and launched. Today she has two additional products and an employee to help with the phones and the shipping. Although her extra income from her venture is not enormous—yet—she's in the black, sales are growing and she has several new ideas that she believes will increase the size of her portfolio of products and her profits.

What? A $10 Toothpick?

Meet Dr. Eugene Wagner, a dentist of Bronx, New York, who realized he'd rather invent and sell than drill and fill. His first invention, called 'DenTemp', was a temporary replacement material for fillings for home use by consumers. Cost to develop: $5,000. Dr. Wagner admits he was naive when he sold the rights to his DenTemp to a big dental manufacturing company for a total amount of $37,500 that was to be paid to him on a provisional basis over 5 years. Only if the buyer was satisfied with the volume of sales, would an annual payment be made to Dr. Wagner. Hindsight tells Dr. Wagner it's too bad he didn't patent the invention himself and for seventeen years collect royalties based on sales, especially since sales after the fifth year had expanded five-fold!

> **Often patients in his chair would ask to borrow one of his dental instruments, namely the sharp stainless steel examining probe, which had always been the dentist's exclusive tool.**

Dr. Wagner did not enter the ranks of Stand-Alone Inventors until he developed his next invention. After many of his patients complained of not being able to remove plaque and food particles stuck between their teeth using ordinary toothpicks, matchbooks or paper clips, he believed he was uncovering another need in the consumer marketplace.

Often patients in his chair would ask to borrow one of his dental instruments, namely the sharp stainless steel examining probe, which had always been the dentist's exclusive tool.

As Dr. Wagner complied, it hit him that he was getting a clear signal from the market that people would be willing to purchase and use such a device.

Before long Dr. Wagner had developed (and was producing by hand) a stainless steel instrument with a fishhook-shaped head. A "personal" toothpick. To make it safer, he dulled the sharp point slightly and mounted it into a fountain pen casing with a cap. Dr. Wagner wisely avoided costly development by borrowing this casing from existing pen manufacturing technology. He bought custom stainless steel points from a dental instrument maker, and stock fountain pen cases from a pen company. The combined result was a very 'high end' toothpick for pocket or purse. Hence, the $10 toothpick. This time Dr. Wagner applied for his own patent.

Having sold the rights to his previous invention, he presented his new toothpick, which he trademarked ORAPIK®, to Johnson & Johnson and others. But, all these companies turned ORAPIK® down. The big corporations said they didn't believe it was the type of product that 'fit in' with what they currently sold, etc., etc.

Dr. Wagner observed that the big dental manufacturers are primarily interested in disposable items where the possibility of repeat sales is greatest. As a result, Dr. Wagner was left with the prospect of either drop-

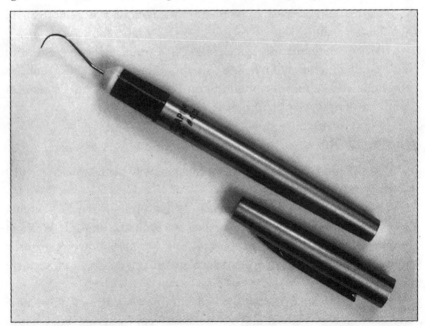

Figure 2-5. The dentist-inventor of "the $10 toothpick", Dr. Eugene Wagner, got the idea from his patients who asked to borrow and use his dental pick. Today, his ORAPIK® is sold in thousands of drug stores all over America.

ping the ORAPIK® project altogether, or venturing it himself, as a Stand-Alone Inventor. He decided to nurture the product with the help of a good friend, Peter Strauss, who joined him as partner.

Start-up costs for their company, more than $30,000, and the cost of the mold used for the prototype, were their early expenses. Dr. Wagner and his partner hired marketing specialists to design packaging as well as television advertising to coincide with the 1984 American Dental Association annual session. Later on, there were ORAPIK® ads running in newspapers in selected markets on the East coast. Their first big break came when the Marriott Hotel Corporation agreed to stock and sell the item in their hotel gift shops. Dr. Wagner said, "This is what actually forced us to go into retail." A second big break came when the American Dental Association gave its product recommendation to ORAPIK®.

Dr. Wagner didn't give up his dental practice, entirely, right away. Actually, he operated his company, Dental Concepts, Inc. as a sideline business for the first seven years!

Today, ORAPIK® is sold in more than 30,000 stores across the nation. "Women do most of the purchasing of dental goods like ours," said Dr. Wagner. "On the average, women are much more conscientious about their dental health."

By 1995 more than six million ORAPIK® units had been sold, both in the United States and overseas. Today, home for ORAPIK® and six other related products is a building in Elmsford, New York where 24 people are employed by a former dentist and his friend.

The Topsy Tail

Meet Tomima Edmark who makes millions with a simple invention that turned the beauty world topsy turvy!

What price vanity? Better to ask, "What profits vanity?" Tomima Edmark has proven that vanity can be very profitable indeed! Working from her home with only two assistants, the 36 year old inventor runs a multi-million dollar company that develops and markets her products for stylish hair-dos.

In 1989, like many other women, Tomima was attracted by a new trend in hair styles: the highly fashionable, very flattering, but complicated French braids and hair weaving styles adorning the rich and famous. One day while in a theater she noticed the unusually attractive hairdo of a woman seated in front of her. She knew that unless you had talented friends or lots of money for salons—not to mention the hours it took to create these wonderful new coifs—you were out of luck.

Tomima felt that if she could come up with a simple way to create the same look, without the cost or effort, there would be plenty of other women like herself who would love to look more stylish.

> ❝ Tomima felt that if she could come up with a simple way to create the same look, without the cost or effort, there would be plenty of other women like herself who would love to look more stylish. ❞

Tomima had reason to believe that she could invent such a device. After all, she had always been good at mechanical things, and her father had always encouraged her to be creative. It was her father, a doctor, who had invented the defibrillator, a medical device used to revive heart attack victims. So she set herself to the task, and in the same year came up with a plastic, loop device that resembled a whisk for beating eggs. But what you could do with the device in creating hair styles was amazing!

Calling her product 'The Topsy Tail,' she demonstrated it to her girl friends at IBM where she worked as a marketing representative. They were ecstatic and all wanted to buy one. Still "The Topsy Tail" might have been "just another good idea" if IBM hadn't decided that year to down-size. Tomima suddenly found herself with the opportunity, the time and a small nest egg of $25,000 separation pay to be what she always wanted to be: an inventor with her own company. She knew that her invention had a huge market demand, but Tomima also knew that unless women could see The Topsy Tail actually *demonstrated*, they wouldn't know what it was, or how easy it was to use. She decided that television was the only way to go. It was a big risk. With no job, and only a small bank account, she knew that she could not survive long if the expensive TV ads didn't work immediately.

She need not have worried, thanks to the TV home shopping craze that was sweeping the nation. Within the first six months, her two minute ads had sold over 3.6 million units. Next, QVC, one of most successful of the home shopping networks, picked up The Topsy Tail. They sold 5,000 units in eleven minutes! The product is now sold in such upscale stores as Bloomingdale's and Macy's.

Still running her company from her kitchen table, Tomima has developed related beauty accessories and even spin-off products, including a doll "My Pretty Topsy Tail" to be manufactured and distributed by Tyco Toys. More successful than the proverbial elf that could spin straw into

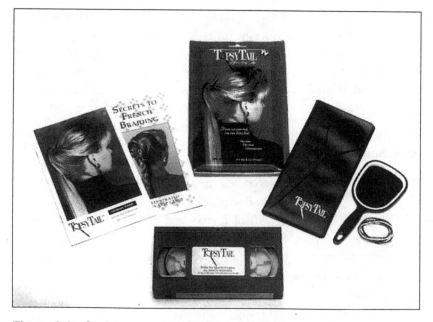

Figure 2-6. Stand-Alone Inventor Tomima Edmark's Topsy Tail is a very simple plastic loop device with a set of instructions that makes it useful in creating unique hair styles for the fashion-conscious female. She has sold her product in the millions.

gold, Tomima has discovered how to weave hair into a million dollar beauty empire!

The Topsy Tail's success follows several Stand-Alone Inventor Rules:

1. The Topsy Tail costs under $20, and so is affordable by *almost every woman* who wants to look a little more glamorous. It is an 'impulse buy' product. (Rule #2, Big Market)

2. Tomima keeps her *overhead very low* (she works out of her house!), and puts her dollars into advertising and promotion. (Rule #8, Investment Small)

3. The Topsy Tail is *easy to demonstrate*. High visual appeal. It actually can be shown to *do* something. Great for TV selling. (Rule #4 and 5, Simple and small)

4. The Topsy Tail is small, lightweight, and *inexpensive to manufacture*, but has a high value based on what it *does*. (Rule #7, Low Manufacturing Cost)

5. Tomima *subcontracts all manufacturing* and concentrates her efforts on sales and marketing and developing new products. (Rule #9, Outsource Manufacturing)

Professor Bob

I knew Bob Krolick before he became a Stand-Alone Inventor. I met him during the late 1970s when he was an assistant professor in the Design and Industry department at San Francisco State University. I had given a presentation to a class he was teaching in product design. I explained to the students how they could use my techniques to market their own inventions.

After my presentation, Bob Krolick showed me an invention he was involved in called a "Pasta Portioner." He was helping the inventor with manufacturing and sales. Although Bob and his partner did not have much success with this measuring product, Bob was getting his feet wet with a real product.

I learned that earlier he had been involved as co-inventor of a product called "The Travel Bureau." It was a set of suitcases with a pop-up feature for which they were awarded US Patent No. 3,974,898. Bob was not yet following the rules of a Stand-Alone Inventor. His luggage invention was far too big an undertaking for two individuals, and he was forced to go to one of the big manufacturers to see if he could license his patent and collect royalties.

❝ In the end, Samsonite turned down Bob's invention and also pointed out to him that "The Travel Bureau" was one of their registered trademarks, and to please stop using it! ❞

Bob submitted the idea to the Samsonite Luggage Company by contacting their new product research group. Later, when Bob analyzed his strategy, it occurred to him that he was trying to sell the very people inside that company who would pull the *least* for his product, because they are the ones charged with the responsibility of thinking up new products for their company.

In the end, Samsonite turned down Bob's invention and also pointed out to him that "The Travel Bureau" was one of their registered trademarks, and to please stop using it!

After this experience, Bob Krolick had a string of various products that he experimented with and considered as possible products that he could exploit, but nothing happened until...

Back in his undergraduate days in the early 1960s, Bob had recognized a problem in the plastics fabricating industry which bothered him. Clear plastic cases such as those used for displays, supermarket food bins, museum cases, etc., always used metal, usually brass, hinges for their doors and lids.

Metal hinges were not only unsightly, but labor intensive. Holes had to be drilled, bolts had to be fastened and the finished product looked hokey and was unreliable.

Bob always thought that someone should invent a clear plastic hinge for this application. It could save labor because acrylic plastic can be quickly welded to the same kind of plastic merely by wetting its surface with a common solvent. Bob had experimented with various ideas and some prototypes, but did not develop his idea further. About ten years later, while cleaning out his garage, he came across an old cardboard box that contained his early models and prototypes. He decided right then he was either going to throw them out and forget about the idea altogether, or do something with it.

Luckily, he chose to take the prototypes around to some plastics companies to see whether they thought it would have any use in fabrication. The reaction he got was very positive. So, after some doing, in 1984 Bob introduced the Acryl-Hinge™, and soon thereafter applied for and was awarded US Patent # 4,651,382.

By now he was a full professor at the university. He had tenure and was financially comfortable. Nevertheless, it was exciting for

❛The article in *The Wall Street Journal* lead to Bob appearing on the *Good Morning America* and *Evening Magazine* TV shows. All of this exposure adds up to a lot of valuable personal and product publicity.❜

him to contemplate the idea that his invention could lead to a viable business that might give him even greater personal fulfillment, and improve his standard of living at the same time.

With the help of his wife he began running a small company office, literally off his kitchen table at home. Bob worked with a local plastic injection mold maker and developed his idea into a commercial product. He started out with a one cavity mold, and later moved up to a multi-cavity mold designed to mass produce the increased quantities of hinges he was selling.

Bob found he could operate without any direct employees because not only did he subcontract the plastic molding operation, but he had his hinges shipped directly to a disabled employees rehabilitation workshop. Here people did the assembly and packaging, and even took care of drop shipments, or what is called the fulfillment of orders.

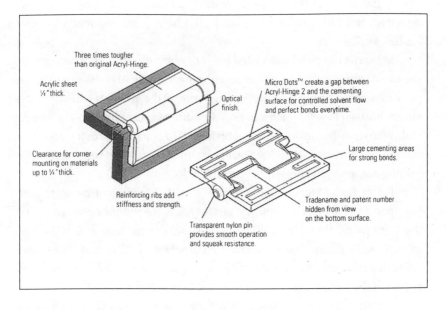

Three times tougher than original Acryl-Hinge.

Acrylic sheet ¼" thick.

Optical finish.

Micro Dots™ create a gap between Acryl-Hinge 2 and the cementing surface for controlled solvent flow and perfect bonds everytime.

Clearance for corner mounting on materials up to ¼" thick.

Large cementing areas for strong bonds.

Reinforcing ribs add stiffness and strength.

Tradename and patent number hidden from view on the bottom surface.

Transparent nylon pin provides smooth operation and squeak resistance.

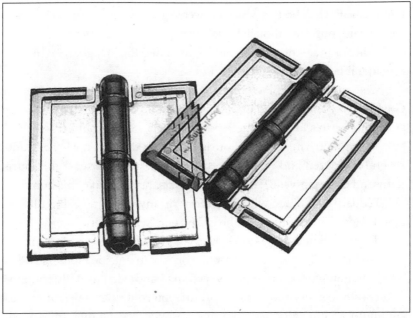

Figure 2-7. The Acryl-Hinge is the creation of Stand-Alone Inventor Bob Krolick, a former professor. The product is used in the fabrication of plastic boxes and display bins, such as those seen in supermarkets. This is a very simple invention, relatively easy to execute, with a market big enough to support its inventor very comfortably for many years.

In the first year Bob made more income from his side-line hinge business than from his professor's salary. But he was not yet ready to "quit his day job".

In his off hours he promoted his hinges by sending news releases to the trade press. Later on he began running a small advertisement in the principal magazine going to his segment of the plastics industry. He taught himself to sell by telephone, letter and fax machine. Today he sells mainly to distributors and to mail order catalogs in his industry, and does considerable export. He does not have an 800 number, but most of the catalog companies who sell his products do.

Before he quit teaching full time in 1990, he and his course were written up in *The Wall Street Journal*. The story was the number one feature on the front page, above the fold! The unusual course he was teaching required each student to learn about the invention process, and try to come up with a new invention. One of his students, Charles Hall, invented and patented the first waterbed as a result of Bob's teachings.

Another student, Remberto Carranza, invented a plastic handle for two-liter soft drink bottles which he licensed to my company. So far, we've sold several hundred thousand handles.

Still another student, Bill Seidel, invented the "Ungball" which has considerable sales through Toys ' R' Us.

The article in *The Wall Street Journal* lead to Bob appearing on the *Good Morning America* and *Evening Magazine* TV shows. All of this exposure adds up to a lot of valuable personal and product publicity.

Today, Bob's business is flourishing more than ever. He has added several improved and related products. His sales are several hundred thousand units per year. He's moved his operations out of his home into a 500 square-foot office which he rents. In my mind, he is the ultimate Stand-Alone Inventor because he has no employees. Zero.

Even his wife's duties have been taken over by an outside, part-time accountant. And, of course, Bob still works with outside molders and the rehabilitation workshop to get everything handled. His daily routine is to orchestrate everything so that production continues, sales promotion continues, and the products continue to flow in greater quantities.

A Puzzling Invention

One evening while working late, inventor Kent Zilliox was looking at a recent picture his wife had taken of their son asleep on a bookshelf. It was just one of many great pictures she had taken lately and pinned on a bulletin board. As he looked at it he thought, "What a terrific photo! But these other ones are great, too! I wish there was a way to frame them so I could just keep adding to them as we take more photos."

As Kent puzzled this over in his mind, it came to him that perhaps a puzzle was the solution to his quest. "What if each photo frame was like a piece of a jig-saw puzzle?" he thought. The pieces could be interlocked and the collection could grow through the years as each new photo was added. In time you might cover an entire wall!

Thus, the **Puz-L-Frame**™ was born! Kent made two plastic prototypes, one for small wallet size photos and the other for standard photos. He showed them to friends and the initial reactions were encouraging enough to prompt him to apply for and be awarded a patent on his frame design. Next he had a small quantity manufactured and bought equipment to do his own packaging.

Puz-L-Frame™ was launched in May of 1996 at INPEX (The Inventions and New Product Exposition) in Pittsburgh, PA. He received the gold medal award for Best Novelty/Gift invention.

Figure 2-8. Interlocking Puz-L-Frame™ units provide for an expanding display. Inventor Kent Zilliox has lined up reps in major markets.

Soon after, Kent went to the Gift Trade Show in San Francisco and made valuable contacts with manufacturers reps and distributors who wanted to add his product to their lines. "It didn't happen overnight though," muses Kent. "Many of the manufacturers rep firms were reluctant to handle a product from a manufacturer like myself who has only one item in their product line."

But through word of mouth referrals and by researching industry trade directories, Kent was able to continue to line up more territorial sales reps. Today, Kent's company, Iwanit, is shipping Puz-L-Frames to stores throughout the United States, and is even selling them via the Internet through his web page (http://www.iwanit.com). He recently developed a magnetic version of Puz-L-Frame designed for refrigerator doors. He is now sourcing overseas manufacturing to lower production costs, and is working on developing other products he intends to also manufacture and market as a Stand-Alone Inventor.

My Road to Self-employment

As Bob Krolick mentioned in the Introduction, the Pay-Rule military pay calculator was my first invention. There's an interesting story about how I happened to hit on this idea and get it going so I could quit my regular job.

It all began when I was fresh out of the Navy looking for a job. A friend told me that big things were happening in the electronics industry in Palo Alto. I went there and landed a managerial job in the marketing department of a young company called Fairchild Semiconductor Corporation, the first manufacturer of silicon transistors.

My Fairchild days proved to be an invaluable business experience. I was thrown into a 'den of lions' with outstanding entrepreneurial talent. These were young, energetic, highly-competitive businessmen with big ambition, many of whom would later start their own manufacturing companies, such as National Semiconductor, Advanced Micro Devices, Intel, and others. Today more than 100 companies trace their origins to Fairchild. Working in the exciting Fairchild environment, I had several public relations duties, including investor relations, that had me reporting directly to the founder, general manager, and inventor Dr. Robert Noyce. Before starting Fairchild, Noyce had worked with Dr. William Shockley, the Nobel Laureate and co-inventor of the first transistor.

I recall that one day Noyce (who was only five years older than me at age 32) called a meeting of his managers. He held in his hand a device that he had recently invented that looked like a miniature top hat about the size of the tip of your little finger. It had eight wires sticking out the bottom. This, Noyce announced, "is the "world's first production integrated circuit." (I.C. or chip. Later, Noyce's chip technology at Intel, which he and Dr. Gordon Moore founded, made possible the development of the microprocessor, the *brain* of the personal computer.)

That day, Noyce told the group very assuredly that this invention would literally "change the world we live in." He illustrated his point by predicting that this technology would spawn hand-held calculators, desktop computers the size of shoe boxes, and that someday when you "pass through the check stand at the grocery store, the clerk will wave a wand over your groceries causing them to be rung up on the cash register!" Many of my colleagues in the room looked at each other, rolling their eyes with skepticism about what they were hearing. All three predictions, of course, came true, and Noyce's groundbreaking invention did indeed change our world dramatically. It's a category of product that made many new industries possible.

> Fairchild's original start-up building was located at 844 East Charleston Road in Palo Alto. Today there is a State of California Historical Landmark monument in front of that building. Its bronze plaque marks it as the birthplace of Noyce's world class invention, the integrated circuit. Noyce died in 1990.

Try to name a product today that uses electronics but doesn't use a chip. Many believe that Noyce's integrated circuit is the most important and powerful invention of the twentieth century.

After six years in harness at Fairchild, I grew restless because I wanted to be my own boss, and do the marketing of my own inventions.

At Fairchild, I had seen first hand what could happen when (a.) you have a proprietary product, (b.) the time is right, and (c.) you put together the knowledge and skills to promote it and sell it.

In the course of doing marketing work at Fairchild, I created my first invention. It was a simple paperboard slide chart that displayed the performance characteristics of a group of Fairchild transistors. This slide chart was a structure that had been around since the 1940's. It was made of heavy paperboard, glued at the edges and had reinforcing rivets at the corners. On a movable slide, data was printed that was visible through cut-out "windows" in the outer case. This format was ideal for presenting transistor parameters (or any kind of tabular data) in a condensed and convenient way. I made arrangements for an outside supplier to manufacture several thousand units to be given away free to distributors and customers. Although I thought of this as my "first invention," it belonged to Fairchild.

Nevertheless, I was greatly impressed with the slide chart's *simplicity* and the low cost of its manufacture. "Why can't I dream up a special-purpose slide chart of my own for another market?" I wondered. "This kind of chart would make a fine product to help me launch a sideline business. What's more, because of its relative simplicity and economy I could ease into business safely on a part-time, low-risk basis."(This was important, because I was married, had one child, and a house payment.)

> ❝At Fairchild, I had seen first hand what could happen when (a.) you have a proprietary product, (b.) the time is right, and (c.) you put together the knowledge and skills to promote it and sell it.❞

But I knew I had to come up with a unique subject or category for the content of my slide chart that would make it appealing and salable. At first, I considered converting football, baseball, and other sports schedules to the slide chart format. I also considered foreign monetary conversion tables. But these applications proved neither unique nor very interesting.

Finally, the idea hit me—military pay! It was complicated and it needed organizing. I knew something about military pay because I was once a shipboard officer in the Navy. I recalled the monthly pay structure was very complex. This was because of the many types of military pay such as basic pay, flight pay, hazardous duty pay, subsistence pay, and housing allowance, many of which varied according to rank and years of service.

Each type of pay was authorized by separate legislation and administered by a separate government bureau. What I saw was minor chaos, and I thought some order was needed: Why not create a slide chart that would pull this data together? Such a chart would enable the user to quickly calculate the individual pay of every member of the armed services.

I felt certain this was a good idea to pursue. Before long, I had set up a sideline business at home to make and sell a 3" X 8" slide chart I called "Pay-Rule." The device could be used to compute the pay for any of the 3.5 million uniformed people on active duty at that time.

Pay-Rule created a new category of product, because never before had there been such a device. On one side of the slide chart appeared pay and allowance information for enlisted personnel; on the reverse side there was similar information for commissioned officers. I was advised by my patent attorney that my device, now in prototype form, was not patentable. Nevertheless, I elected to go with a registered trademark and copyright for protection. (See Chapter 5)

With the design complete, I was ready for production. I found that an initial order for 5,000 Pay-Rule® charts would cost $0.40 per piece, or around $2,000 total. (This represented more than two month's of my corporate pay at the time.) I talked over the expenses with Lee, my wife, and she agreed we should "roll the dice". We got a $1,200 loan from my life-insurance policy; and the remainder of $800 from our savings account, which nearly depleted it. The total covered the purchase, which put us in business.

Before long, a truck pulled up to our door, and we found ourselves the proud owners of a closet-full of unique military pay slide charts. A paid-up inventory!

The next hoop to jump through was sales. I figured that with 3.5 million people in uniform, I needed to sell my Pay-Rule to only a small percentage of them at $1. apiece to become a wealthy man. I needed to sell only 2000 Pay-Rules to break even!

> **❝ Before long, a truck pulled up to our door, and we found ourselves the proud owners of a closet-full of unique military pay slide charts. A paid-up inventory! ❞**

My first sales promotion was a publicity release that included a photograph of the new product. I sent this material to the *Army Times, Navy Times, Air Force Times,* and several other military magazines. The *Navy Times* printed the release with the photo, and many readers responded. But the volume of *orders* resulting (several hundred units) was not very encouraging. I reasoned that the amount of pay servicemen received at that time was so low they were unwilling to spend a dollar of it on a Pay-Rule just to be reminded of how little money they made!

It took over a year of part-time effort for me to fully launch Payrule. My wife took the job of shipping each order and keeping track of sales. (Today, she is corporate comptroller, which she says is just a fancy name for bookkeeper!)

Although the initial sales of Pay-Rule charts were slow, I figured that

I had plenty of time to sell my inventory. Wrong! Shortly after the introduction of my new product, the President of the United States announced an across-the-board pay increase for all members of the armed services, making my entire inventory of Pay-Rules out-of-date and obsolete!

Fortunately, I was able to salvage my inventory by printing new insert cards. I had my neighbors' kids sit around the TV, pulling out the old inserts, and putting in the new ones. This was the first of several "Pay-Rule pulling parties" because GI's got pay raises almost every year!

> ❝ The marketing lesson here is to analyze your inquiries and your sales, and direct your efforts to those categories of buyers that offer the greatest potential for sales. ❞

With my inventory now updated, I took time to analyze the meager Pay-Rule sales. I discovered that sales orders were coming from various companies that were near military installations and that did business with servicemen. For example, there were banks, finance companies, used car dealers, and real estate firms who bought. These various companies wanted the Pay-Rule for a quick check on the income of the servicemen to whom they were considering extending credit.

More importantly, I found that my Pay-Rule was looked upon as a valuable working tool by military recruiters and reenlistment specialists, called career counselors. Over the next few years this latter group would prove to be a gold mine for me.

The marketing lesson here is to analyze your inquiries and your sales, so you can direct your efforts to those categories of buyers that offer the greatest potential for sales.

My father suggested to me that Washington, DC, where the main purchasing office for each branch of the military was located, would be an ideal place for me to make sales calls.

The next year, my advertising agency work took me to the East Coast. I arranged a week's "vacation" while there so that I could visit Washington, DC. Arriving at the Pentagon, I made my way through the lobby and up to the huge reception desk. There I asked for and was given directions to the office of Army Personnel. After navigating the endless corridors of the Pentagon, I finally arrived at my destination. As I entered the office I saw that a major was on the telephone, apparently conversing with a career counselor in the field. The major motioned me to be seated by his desk.

The telephone conversation that I overheard had to do with the reluctance of a valuable Army specialist to re-enlist. Over the phone, the major asked the counselor if he had explained the recent pay raise as well as the pay bonuses available to this specialist should he decide to re-enlist. Satisfying himself that the counselor had done everything possible with the available tools at hand, the major concluded the conversation, hung up the phone, and gave his attention to me. "Now, young man, what can I do for you?"

I responded in my best Kennedyesque manner: "Major, it's not what *you* can do for *me*; I think *I* can do something for *you*.

I have a product that I believe will be of great help to you and to your career counselors." I demonstrated my Pay-Rule for the major.

The major studied the device for a moment and said, "Interesting... We've been looking for something like this for quite some time!"

I was heartened, to say the least. I immediately blurted out to the major that probably every career counselor in the service should receive a Pay-Rule for use as a sales tool when trying to persuade service people to re-enlist. (I estimated to myself that this would be an order for about 10,000 Pay-Rules.)

"No," the major responded, "I like *my* idea better. I think each year every member of the Army as he becomes eligible for re-enlistment should receive one of your Pay-Rules." (This would be an order for about 300,000 Pay-Rules per year!)

I quickly expressed my agreement. The major then asked me to submit a written proposal for a contract to supply several hundred thousand Pay-Rules.

Upon returning home, I sat down to prepare my proposal for the government contract. But I had to wonder, "How could I possibly come up with a convincing presentation when my business address is a post office box, and my office is literally the kitchen table?"

Luckily, my friend, Bob Legge, knew how to go about soliciting government contracts, and agreed to help me. In a formal proposal, I listed the names of some of my principal customers, which included commercial loan companies, banks, real estate firms, and the US Marine Corps. Bar charts were used, but I was careful not to assign actual dollar sales figures because they were so unimpressive.

Next, I showed a block diagram chart of my company's organization, indicating myself as the president, my wife as an administrative assistant, and Bob Legge, who had an MBA from Harvard University, as comptroller.

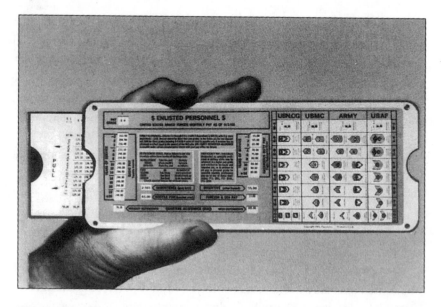

Figure 2-9. Pay-Rule™, a unique military pay calculator, was designed to figure the monthly pay for any of 3.5 million members of the Armed Forces. I thought buyers would be individual GI's, but the big market turned out to be recruiters and reenlistment counselors, who used them by the thousands as a give-away during interviews.

A final block contained the name of my sub-contractor vendor of the slide charts, which was a solid multi-million-dollar corporation. I also included resumes for all of my staff, along with a profile of the sub-contractor company that would do the manufacturing should my company receive the order. Finally, I proposed my price schedule, which was based on cost negotiations with the vendor.

By carefully preparing my formal proposal in this manner, I gave assurance to the contracting officer of my company's ability to perform on the contract that might be awarded.

❝ Next, I showed a block diagram chart of my company's organization, indicating myself as the president, my wife as an administrative assistant, and Bob Legge, who had an MBA from Harvard University, as comptroller. ❞

I submitted my proposal in November, and I began to wait. And wait. Finally, the next year on the first day of July a telephone call came into my home at seven o'clock in the morning.

The caller was the army major that I had met with on my visit to the Pentagon. The major said, "Mr. Merrick, I just want to tell you that this is the first day of our fiscal year, and we have your Pay-Rule in our budget. How soon can you get back here to discuss a possible contract?" I

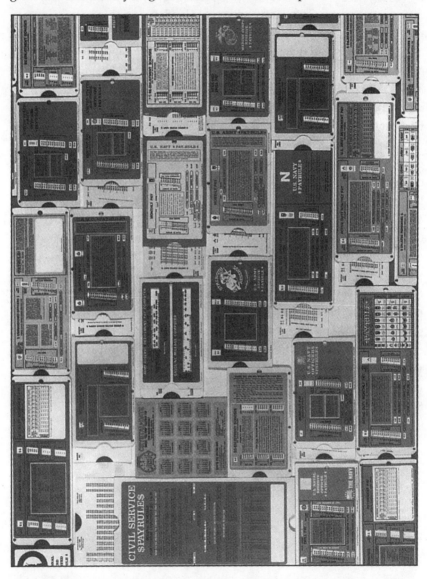

Figure 2-10. The Pay-Rule™ military pay calculator evolved into a "Career Guide" with many variations. During the course of twelve years I published a line of 21 editions, one for each branch of service, and its reserve component, with separate editions for officers and enlisted members.

gasped and joked, "Will tomorrow be too late?"

Some months following my second visit to Washington, I received a contract for 300,000 Army Pay-Rules! I should emphasize, however, that after having loaded our closet with Pay-Rules, it took me more than two years of concentrated persistence and patience to land that first big contract.

Initially I sub-contracted the manufacturing of all my Payrule charts to a company in Los Angeles that specialized in producing slide charts. Because they did mostly custom work, in a non-competitive atmosphere, I found their prices rather high, so I starting looking around. I found an ordinary paper box company that was experienced in folding and gluing paperboard. Because this company existed in a commodity market that was very price-competitive, they quoted prices much more to my liking. The paper box people proved they could do the job, and it was much more lucrative for me to sub-contract my larger-production orders to them. And larger orders I had.

By its third year I had expanded the Army Pay-Rule into a "Career Guide" with a two-panel informational wrap-around. Merrick Industries eventually offered eighteen different models of its Pay-Rule, including ones for officers, enlisted personnel, and reservists of the Army, Navy, Marine Corps, National Guard, and Air Force, plus models for Civil Service employees. I also produced a postal-rate calculator and a metric conversion slide chart. Manufacturing was done in Puerto Rico. The Pay-Rule thrived for seven years, but then declined and faded away by the twelfth year. During its product life, it produced several million dollars in revenue for Merrick Industries, Inc., and launched my career as a profitable Stand-Alone Inventor.

Note: The Resource Section begins on page 259 and is arranged by chapter to make it convenient for you to find related references.

CHAPTER 3

A World of Inventors

The greatest thing about the twentieth century is its tremendous number of inventions that make our lives so easy and enjoyable. Ninety percent of today's niceties didn't exist before 1950. Today, we treat most of these niceties as necessities. We know who many of the blockbuster inventors are, and some of the others. But few of us think much about the thousands of individuals who came up with the down-to-earth ideas that also streamline our lives in many ways. Many of these inventors are quiet individuals who hit on a good idea, and simply run with it until it pays. You could become one of them. This book is intended to help you along—if and when you hit on a manageable idea. But, I emphasize, *manageable*.

> ❛Someone once said that "million-dollar ideas are a dime a dozen"—and it wasn't Yogi Berra. ❜

Someone once said that "million-dollar ideas are a dime a dozen"—and it wasn't Yogi Berra.*

But even that oxymoronic idea has a certain amount of truth to it. A lot of inventing is really quite easy. It goes on all around us every day. Ideas for new products cross our minds all the time. I know you've seen a new product on a store shelf and kicked yourself because you had the same idea years before—but didn't pursue it. Hopefully, this book will convince you to act on your next brainstorm and convert it to cash.

Just about anybody would like to invent a hot product. It's one of the few ways left to get rich solely on your own effort. Other ways that come to mind are: making it in professional sports or entertainment.

Speaking of entertainment, it's interesting to note that one of Actress Jamie Lee Curtis' proudest possessions, besides her offspring, is US Patent 4,753,647 that she was awarded for a baby product she invented

---

*This was an unidentified quote in Leo Helzel's book, *A Goal is a Dream with a Deadline*. (See Resource Section)

in 1987. (Screen actors always want to be directors—or inventors!). Then there was the 1930's bandleader, Fred Waring, and his Waring blender (the 'miracle mixer' that predated the Cuisinart™ by 40 years!). And, let's not forget Paul Newman and his successful salad dressing product. (But, I don't know of a pro sports figure who ever patented anything. Do you?) It's also interesting that mega-mogul Bill Gates said in an interview that he almost envies the person who is an inventor. (The operative word here, of course, is 'almost'.)

> **❮ Speaking of entertainment, it's interesting to note that one of Actress Jamie Lee Curtis' proudest possessions, besides her offspring, is US Patent 4,753,647 that she was awarded for a baby product she invented in 1987. ❯**

The following is a look at some of the various approaches to inventing found in today's world:

The Stand-Alone Inventor

The Real Work

Inventing is the easy part of turning your ideas into dollars. But, after you think up a brand new product, there's a tough war you must fight for market acceptance and product distribution. Someone must dive into the trenches after the invention stage, and scramble his way through the development stage and try to reach the commercially-viable high ground.

The ideal person to do this is the Stand-Alone Inventor himself. No one else will be as motivated. No one else can do it for less money, and no one else has so much to gain by doing it.

Stand-Alone Inventors come up through the ranks of independent inventors. But, not all independent inventors are willing to promote themselves to Stand-Alone Inventor. Here's why: The Stand-Alone Inventor is an individual who not only does the inventing —the quick and fun part—but also starts a company and learns how to get the manufacturing and marketing done—the long-hours, not-so-much-fun part—but usually the part that makes the money.

In her book, *Atlas Shrugged*, Author Ayn Rand pointed out that Americans were the first to understand that wealth has to be created. Previously, in other cultures men had thought of wealth as something to be stolen, begged, inherited, shared, etc. Then we Americans created an expression that never before existed in any language, "to make money".

This book is intended to help *you* "make money" by yourself, through your own efforts and through your own ingenuity—as a Stand-Alone Inventor.

Self-Venturing Advantage

As you get into this book you will realize that it is written with a very strong slant towards persuading you to do most of the work yourself, and keeping control of your venture yourself. (Hence the title, *"Stand Alone, Inventor!*) Doing it my way, you set yourself up to be in charge of what happens to you, and you have a much better chance to make your invention a profitable reality. You may or may not "break the bank" in a big way, but along the way you'll get to keep most of the profits yourself.

When you choose to stay away from licensing, go it alone, and actually put a company together to commercialize your invention, I have good news for you: You won't have to sell very much product—maybe *less than one tenth* of what your licensee would have to sell—to produce extra income that will exceed the royalties he'd pay you.

To illustrate this, say you license your patent at a 3% royalty. (Also, let's assume that the total market for your patented product is 500,000 units per year, and you project a 20% per year maximum market penetration.) In the first year your licensee-manufacturer makes 20,000 of the patented product at a cost of $1.00 per unit, and sells them at wholesale for $5 per unit, for a total of $100,000. (A 4% market penetration.) He pays you 3% royalty, or $3000.

> ❢ The ideal person to do this is the Stand-Alone Inventor himself. No one else will be as motivated. No one else can do it for less money, and no one else has so much to gain by doing it. ❣

Conversely, say you decide to shun licensing, in favor of marketing the product yourself. You find the cost for you to make the same product (outsourced) is $2.50. A simple calculation shows you'll need sell only 6% of the quantity he sells, or 1200 units at $5, to produce the same $3,000 gross income for yourself!

More realistically, however, in the first year you would probably sell 10,000 units (only a 2% market penetration) and make $25,000 gross income!

And, if and when your annual sales reach 100,000 units, your annual income from the product will be a cool $250,000! In this example at a 3% royalty, there is little chance a licensee could pay you more than $15,000, because the maximum annual sales expected is 100,000 units for

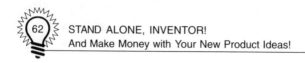

STAND ALONE, INVENTOR!
And Make Money with Your New Product Ideas!

a total of $500,000.

Therefore, a rule of thumb is: Unless projected annual sales for your new product exceed $1,000,000 for the first year, it is better to venture the product yourself, compared to pursuing a licensing agreement.

> **❝Therefore, a rule of thumb is: Unless projected annual sales for your new product exceed $1,000,000 for the first year, it is better to venture the product yourself, compared to pursuing a licensing agreement.❞**

Reasons: 1.) Because licensee payments on a 3% royalty would give you an annual income of only $30,000 on sales of $1,000,000. But, most likely it would be several years, if ever, before this level of sales would be reached. 2.) You could go it alone and in the first year exceed this level of gross income, by selling, instead of $1,000,000, only $60,000 worth of product! 3.) If your product projects annual sales of less than $1,000,000, it would be quite unusual to find a company interested in licensing it.

Your decision to commercialize and to control your invention yourself ultimately will define you as a Stand-Alone Inventor. It could make you a financially independent person right away, and perhaps later, an independently wealthy person. Rarely will licensing do this for you.

Your decision to become a Stand-Alone Inventor doesn't mean you should "quit your day job." During my first four years in business I was running it as a sideline venture in my spare time at home. I could have continued to operate it on a part-time basis indefinitely. But, eventually, the sideline venture produced several times the income I was earning from my day job. Obviously, at this point, it was a very easy decision for me to resign and commit to a new life as a full-time entrepreneur. Something like this could happen to you, if you act on the information in this book.

Look into the income tax advantages of having your own business. Medical and dental plans, other insurance, company cars, travel and expense accounts and retirement plans are some of the valuable tax-saving perks available to company owners. As a passive licensor without his or her own company, one would not qualify for these pre-income tax benefits.

The Licensing Inventor

Who invented the automobile? If you think it was Daimler, Duryea or Ford—it wasn't. It was George B. Seldon who filed in 1879, and in 1895 was issued US Patent number 549,160. His invention was a "road loco-motive" powered by an internal combustion engine that he developed.

If George B. Seldon invented the automobile, why have so few of us ever heard of him? The answer is that *he sold his patent rights and had little to do with manufacturing cars.*

Seldon got an up-front payment of $10,000, and a royalty on every car sold under his patent. But the buyer of his patent sub-licensed it to a group of car makers who agreed to pay a royalty of only 1.25%, of which Seldon was supposed to get 10%. Henry Ford's company was not in-cluded in the sub-licensing group, and Ford refused to pay any royalties. Ford was sued for infringing, but he fought back taking the position that the Seldon patent was invalid. After a costly legal battle lasting eight years, the court ruled that Seldon's patent was indeed valid, but that Ford and the others had not infringed it, because of a legal interpretation that could have gone either way, but went against Seldon.

The moral of this story is that companies hate to pay royalties so much, they will fight tooth and nail to avoid it—often using shrewd legal maneuvers. As a result, in this case Seldon, the true inventor of the auto-mobile, never achieved fortune or even fame for his work on this important invention.

❝ If George B. Seldon in-vented the automobile, why have so few of us ever heard of him? The answer is that *he sold his patent rights and had little to do with manufac-turing cars.* ❞

There are relatively few licensing success sto-ries that involve independent inventors. The chances are slim that you will be the next indi-vidual to get rich licensing. This is one of the rea-sons licensing is not the primary recommendation of this author. The licensing inventor is not a Stand-Alone Inventor. He limits his participation (and his rewards) to selling or licensing his inventions to others. The "others" are the ones who do the work—the manufacturing and the marketing—and therefore most of the money making. This is the main reason I do not suggest licensing, unless you find you must.

If your invention is not simple, licensing may be the only way you, as an individual, can cash in. For example, if you have a complex or elabo-rate invention, beyond your personal capabilities, it will cost a bundle to have it developed. It's probably out of the question for you to finance this on your own, unless you are very wealthy, you can obtain a grant, or you can get your hands on someone else's risk capital.

Individuals who set out to invent just so they can license for royalties are not being very realistic. Why? Because it's hard to find a company willing to put money in a new product idea from a rookie inventor. The odds are at least a thousand to one against you finding any company interested in rolling the dice on your invention. Licensing is not practical because even if you find a licensee, your product will have to be a blockbuster before it will produce royalty money that will pay you more than your patent and legal expenses.

> ❝ Why? Because of what I call the Stand-Alone Inventor's theory of relativity: "A relatively small, uninteresting market to a large company can be a large, interesting market to an individual inventor. ❞

As mentioned earlier, even if your invention is a good one, but it has only a relatively small market, probably no large company will be interested in licensing it. But ironically, this is exactly the type of invention that can make an individual rich, if he or she pursues it as a Stand-Alone Inventor.

Why? because of what I call the Stand-Alone Inventor's theory of relativity: "A relatively small, uninteresting market to a large company can be a large, interesting market to an individual inventor."

This theory tells you that it's a good idea to pursue those bright ideas that have only relatively small dollar markets. Many inventors have multiplied their income by doing just this.

In my seminar work I meet many first-time inventors who tell me their goal is to find someone who will just "take their ideas and run with them." These naive, would-be inventors expect someone else to pay them for a raw idea, and as the "inventor", they won't have to do any of the work. As diplomatically as possible, I explain to them that they need to be more realistic. First, they must reduce their idea to practice by making drawings and/or prototypes, or they must file for a patent, to have their idea qualify as an invention that could be sold.

Before any company will discuss licensing with them, they will need some market research, and maybe even a track record of producing and selling some of the product. Many times if they take their invention this far, they find they want to keep it and run with it themselves. Usually, they realize they are having fun, especially if they start making a profit.

Trying to license has one obstacle that many inexperienced inventors are unaware of: Unless your invention is patented, you will usually have a hard time finding any company that will even talk to you about licensing it. Companies working on their own inventions have been sued by inventors who make a presentation and later claim that their unprotected idea was stolen. Also, companies are unwilling to invest money in an unprotected product for fear of possible competition later on, should the product take off. However, as an independent inventor who has applied for a patent, you may be able to find a company that is willing to license or buy your patent *application*. The company usually assumes the responsibility for getting the patent issued. But, in the real world this is a rarity. You should not count on selling or licensing your unpatented inventions, unless you can establish yourself as an accomplished inventor.

If you must have a licensee, look for a manufacturer dealing in products similar to yours. Hopefully, one with a big budget for research and development. Your job: find that company and convince its management to license your invention and pay you a decent royalty. Oh, and one more thing, Good luck!

The High-Tech Inventor

Here in Silicon Valley, called the epicenter of the technology and information age, we find many inventors of the first magnitude. These geniuses need lots of direct help getting their companies started and expanded. This is because they are involved in high technology inventions that have great potential, but that require huge amounts of cash. These technological wizards must round up tens of millions of dollars in venture captital, and serious numbers of talented people, to put together the kind of growth companies they envision. We admire these inventors because their powerful innovations can start and grow tremendously profitable organizations, the kind that create tens of thousands of jobs for people all over the world. These extraordinary inventors, rightly so, usually become extremely wealthy.

In addition to these super starters, each year thousands of other entrepreneurial inventors—high-tech and non-tech—go for lots of outside help because the start-up they are trying to launch simply cannot be done with the meager bank account of one person.

The Low and Non-Tech Inventor

In contrast, there are many more inventors whose companies, because they deal in simple low- or non-technology innovation, don't require a lot of money to start. Every year thousands of these inventors figure out how to launch new companies with their own money—essentially by themselves. Many of these ventures never need to grow very big to satisfy the founder and to survive for many years. Instead of becoming bizillionaires like their high-tech counterparts, many successful everyday inventor/entrepreneurs earn doctor-or lawyer-type incomes, while a few do indeed become millionaires and multi-millionaires.

Theirs and the non-invention-based mini-ventures make up the overwhelming majority of businesses in this country—some 15 million of them. As a group, small businesses, be they product or service companies, provide work for millions of people. Collectively, this category of business can create more new jobs in one year than all the biggies combined, making them crucial to the health of our nation's economy.

> **❛This is why it's to everyone's advantage to support and nurture Stand-Alone Inventors and small business entrepreneurs in every way possible.❜**

This is why it's to everyone's advantage to support and nurture Stand-Alone Inventors and small business entrepreneurs in every way possible.

The Corporate Inventor

Many inventors work for corporations that pay them to invent. They are called employed inventors, or corporate inventors. This is an okay arrangement as long as these inventors understand and accept their situation. Unfortunately, many of these inventors have learned the hard way that the corporate environment is not a place where you cash in big on inventions.

As a condition of employment, many corporations make you sign over your rights to all your innovations, especially if they hire you into a position where they expect you to do some inventing.

Usually, corporations make an exception for any inventions you come up with on your own time, providing these inventions are not in the same field as the company's. But, you should clarify this point with your employer before you sign on.

> **❛As a condition of employment, many corporations make you sign over your rights to all your innovations, especially if they hire you into a position where they expect you to do some inventing.❜**

If and when a corporate inventor's idea strikes gold for his company, he could begin to feel that the company owes him a lot more than just his salary. The following are a few of the many examples of unrewarded genius:

A research scientist named Barry Green was the employee at National Cash Register (later NCR) who invented NCR paper in the early 1950's. NCR paper is the paper that displaced messy carbon paper. Many call it, coincidentally, "No Carbon Required" paper. It was not an easy invention, because it embodies layers of dissimilar materials combined into a system that works well to produce clean copies. So well that even today NCR paper is produced by the billions of sheets for banking and business forms that are used all over the globe. However, this ingenious inventor never achieved fortune or fame. His employer, it is said, did acknowledge him with a nominal bonus, but that's all.

Art Fry, the father of those wonderful Post-it Notes at 3M, achieved a certain measure of fame for himself, but not much more. His employer gave him a dinner and praised him for his contribution and made him a spokesman for the product.

I knew an inventor named Bob Widlar when he was a young technician fresh out of the Air Force. We were both working at Fairchild Semiconductor Corp. Soon after he was hired he designed the first analog circuits that could be built into silicon chips. Widlar's analog chip inventions represented a startling technological breakthrough.

❝ Widlar's name went on many patents, but their ownership was automatically 'assigned' to Fairchild under a standard employment agreement. ❞

Widlar's name went on many patents, but their ownership was automatically 'assigned' to Fairchild under a standard employment agreement.

Often, companies pay their inventors $1.00 to legalize the transfer of a patent. The inventor's name goes on the patent, but it is assigned (legally transferred) to the corporation.

Fairchild began raking in literally tens of millions of dollars by selling these powerful circuits and by licensing the Widlar patents. One day Widlar went to the front office and asked that his salary be raised from $14,000 per year to $500,000 per year, because of his value to the company. (This was the same year pitchers Sandy Kofax and Don Drysdale were holding out to the LA Dodgers for the then unheard-of annual salaries of $500,000.) Fairchild management, which was not into stock options, could think of nothing else to do but ask him which competitor had made him an offer.

The next day Widlar took a job with National Semiconductor Corp. They gave him a nice salary (but not the half mil), along with a hefty stock option that would make him a millionaire before he turned thirty. The next week I saw him driving a brand new roadster.

There has been a lot of lobbying by inventors' groups on behalf of the "employed inventor" and his rights to greater rewards. As a result we've seen some special legislation in some states that benefit the employed inventor. In his book, *Millions From the Mind*, Alan R. Tripp wrote that some employers, such as duPont Company, "reward their inventors richly." But, although this author inquired at duPont, I was not able to learn from the company just how richly.

On the other side of the coin, the issue of fairness to the employed inventor has convinced a good number of corporations to voluntarily recognize their employed inventors and to pay them something more than just a token reward for their innovative contributions. Some have set up corporate programs providing for "substantial" financial awards. Still, even the most generous of these awards is said to be only a very small fraction of the actual dollar value of the invention.

> ❝He told *The Wall Street Journal*, "They took away my good name"... [and]... "five most productive years of my life." He sued both companies and was awarded more than $5 million in actual damages, and an undisclosed amount from Exxon in a settlement for punitive damages. ❞

Don't think that when an inventor quits a company he is free from that company. A huge oil company claimed rights to a former employee's inventions years after he had left, while he was working for a competing firm. The inventions—involving metallocene plastics—were called "ground-breaking" with a potential dollar value in the *billions*. The inventor's first employer, Exxon, sued him and his new employer, Fina, Inc., claiming certain inventions patented by Fina had been *conceived* at Exxon. In the ensuing legal battles the inventor, a brilliant scientist named Dr. John Ewen, claimed he had been defamed by both employers.

He told *The Wall Street Journal*, "They took away my good name"... [and]... "five most productive years of my life." He sued both companies and was awarded more than $5 million in actual damages, and an undisclosed amount from Exxon in a settlement for punitive damages.

It would appear that one or both of these oil companies will wind up with technology worth billions in exchange for a few million paid to the inventor and to lawyers.

In commenting on the saga of Exxon and Fina, *The Wall Street Jour-*

nal said in a front page article on March 1, 1996, "Patent battles are often heated affairs, for at stake is something at the core of the mythology, and sometimes the reality, of American capitalism: a good idea."

The Toy Inventor

Many toys and games are created by individual inventors who license to big-name manufacturers. This is a specialized field of inventing that is the subject of several very good books. (See Resource Section)

The Care-Less Inventor

I think we should take responsibility for what we invent. We should all think about the consequences of our inventions. We shouldn't allow an invention to solve one problem, while creating another. Let me give you an example:

Have you ever noticed how annoying it is to be unpacking in a hotel room only to find there are too few or no hangers in the closet? It seems the hangers have a way of exiting the hotel in the luggage of guests. Hoteliers, a hospitable bunch always out to please, rewarded one inventor who addressed this problem. His solution is at the top of my list of thoughtless inventions (even though it appears to be commercially successful). It's an invention that has rankled guests for decades in hotels and motels all over the country. It's the theft-proof hotel *hanger*.

> **❝ Using this ill-conceived invention the hotel is endorsing it and sending a message to its guests, "We want our hangers to stay put, and we don't care how inconvenient it is for you." ❞**

You've dealt with it—it's a two-piece metal job with a bracket that permanently encircles the closet rod, which is also metal and *undersized* in diameter. You can detach the lower part of the hanger from its bracket *only* if you lift it and pull it carefully toward you through a slot. (Do this only if you don't mind looking and feeling stupid, standing there holding half a hanger.) The annoying part comes when you go to hang your coat on this thing, and try to feed the little ball back *into* its slot in the bracket. It usually takes two or three hands and a cool temper. Apparently, the inventor "couldn't care *less!*"

Using this ill-conceived invention, the hotel is endorsing it and sending a message to its guests, "We want our hangers to stay put, and we don't care how inconvenient it is for you."

The Thoughtful Inventor

In recent years someone like you brought out an improved theft-proof hanger that's a much more thoughtful solution than the miserable two-piece hanger. It is very easy for guests to use. The idea is simply a set of special hangers that have hanger hooks of *undersized* diameter. The hooks fit the existing small metal rod found in hotels, but won't fit the larger diameter wooden rods in our closets at home.

Using this invention the hotel is saying to its guests, "We think most people are smart enough to see that these hangers won't work at home. And, we want our hangers to be *convenient* for you to use!" I love the simplicity and convenience of this inventor's idea. Still, not very many hotels have made the switch. (I suggest that if you agree with me, you photocopy these pages from, *Stand Alone, Inventor!* and fax them to your favorite hotel.)

The Focused Inventor

A popular question that fledgling inventors ask me at seminars and workshops is, "What's the most important thing I need to do to capitalize on my invention?" I tell them to try to take their best product as far as possible into the development stages by themselves. I emphasize *best* product because once they discover they can create, new inventors are notorious for thinking up many other ideas, causing them to lose focus on their best one. The further you develop your idea into a viable product having satisfied users, the more value it gains, and the greater financial rewards you will realize, regardless of whether you end up licensing it or self-venturing it. The lesson here is to stay focused on your best invention and advance it as far as you can.

The Trained Inventor

It doesn't take a lot of formal schooling to be a Stand-Alone Inventor. Only a willingness to keep learning new things. For example, although I have been operating as a Stand-Alone Inventor for more than 25 years, I never took a course in engineering, entrepreneurship, marketing or business. Over the years—by reading the right books, finding the right people and staying focused—I learned the necessary skills that enabled me to accomplish the work that I will explain to you in this book.

The lessons you will read in this book are not business school case studies involving blue chip companies. They are simple guidelines that

I believe can steer individuals to a reasonably profitable outcome.

In the following chapters, I will cover topics I think are important for you to concern yourself with as an inventor/entrepreneur. When I touch on a topic, I will try to include some personal anecdote, hopefully making a point that you can translate and apply to your own invention and/ or to your own circumstances. But be careful. If you follow the advice given in this book too closely, you may end up with problems like—how to invest all the money you're making!

Note: The Resource Section begins on page 259 and is arranged by chapter to make it convenient for you to find related references.

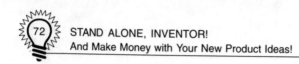

CHAPTER 4

Marketing is Everything

Marketing is Everywhere.

As you read this book, you will find that marketing considerations permeate the content of nearly every chapter. That's because marketing needs to be part of everything you do in creating, developing and selling your invention. For example:

> **❝Marketing has been defined by one writer (Michael Porter) as, "...anything you do to get or keep a customer," which is a good way to think about it. ❞**

Which product you patent (Ch 5) must be decided on its marketability (Ch 1, Rule 2).

How and where you manufacture your product and what it looks like (Ch 7) are components of your overall marketing strategy.

How you publicize, merchandise, advertise and distribute your product (Ch 8, 9, 10, 11, 12 and 13) are your marketing tactics.

In these chapters I will endeavor to cover all the marketing you'll need to know for the various tasks required in starting your small business.

What is Marketing?

Marketing has been defined by one writer (Michael Porter) as, "...anything you do to get or keep a customer," which is a good way to think about it.

Marketing is producing what customers will want. It's also the related sales promotion, advertising, merchandising and public relations in support of distributing what you produce. It could be a good employee attitude that filters down from top management.

Marketing is comprised of a great number of technical disciplines that can be applied in hundreds of ways, depending on circumstances. For example, suppose you are asked how you intend to "position" your product in the marketplace. In your response you'll need to talk not about location on a store shelf, but how you want your customer to *think* about your product. How your product is positioned compared to alternatives in the *mind* of the consumer is what is meant by product positioning.

The insurance industry pulled off the greatest marketing coup of all time when it positioned *death insurance* in all of our minds as *life insurance*, and it stuck.

Other marketing considerations: What about a new product feasibility study, before you go ahead with its development? Or, you may contemplate market size and how big a share of a market to go after, or whether your new product will create its *own* market. What about promotion, distribution and merchandising? These are the kinds of issues companies address—all under the catch-all heading of marketing. However, marketing considerations will differ widely depending on whether you are a Procter & Gamble, a lone start-up entrepreneur, or something in between. Read the rest of this book to learn what you'll need to know to successfully launch your invention.

Be Your Own VP Marketing

Just how much you need to know about marketing as a Stand-Alone Inventor is problematic. One person would never be able to find, let alone read, all the books written on the subject. Marketing is a discipline so vast that it's a major field of study at most post-graduate business schools, including Berkeley, Harvard, Stanford and Wharton.

A fresh MBA degree in marketing today will put you in immediate demand by many big, well-financed corporations. Take your MBA to work at a big company, and chances are they'll make you responsible for the profitability of one of their products or product categories. You'll have to dig in and learn how the company manufactures, advertises and distributes its products, and go to work to find better ways. Perhaps your title would be Product Manager in a large company, or Vice President, Marketing in a smaller one. But one thing is for sure: Because you understand and work in the marketing function, you'll have an inside track to the top, and one day you could head the company.

> **❛The insurance industry pulled off the greatest marketing coup of all time when it positioned *death insurance* in all of our minds as *life insurance*, and it stuck.❜**

The reason I discuss the marketing career is to point out that on a much smaller scale, you, as a Stand-Alone Inventor, must learn to be your own Vice President, Marketing.

One of your duties in marketing is to make sure your company is concerned with products that your customers want to buy, and are able to buy. A dynamic endeavor, effective marketing also requires you to identify what products your customer will need *next*, and decide whether to position your company to fill that need.

In the 1970's a business management scholar devised the creative designation, "intrapreneur", spelled with an "i". This is what they dubbed a person inside a big company who was expected to think and act—as much as he could—like an honest-to-goodness entrepreneur. Much was written about the concept, and it was ballyhooed a lot in the media. I believe the idea was pushed in an effort to motivate marketing executives—who were in fact employees—by giving them a chance at a greater sense of self-fulfillment. It probably helped at the time to slow the increasing exodus to individual entrepreneurship. Later, though, downsizing came into vogue, and it no longer mattered as much if someone left.

> **❝ The fact is, that once you set yourself up as a Stand-Alone Inventor, you will be a real Entrepreneur, and you will shoulder sole responsibility for every function of your business, including marketing. ❞**

People involved in business today are more sophisticated, and you don't hear the intrapreneur term much anymore. But you do hear a lot more about entrepreneurship today than you ever did. More people are wanting to do their own thing. Today many think of themselves as "ideapreneurs." They want to be CEO of their life.

The fact is, that once you set yourself up as a Stand-Alone Inventor, you will be a real Entrepreneur, and you will shoulder the sole responsibility for every function of your business, including marketing.

Everything is Marketing

Today, because of evolving technology and communications, marketing has been defined much more broadly, at least by one expert, as "a way of doing business".

The expert is Regis McKenna, one of America's top marketing consultants. He says in his 1991 book, *Relationship Marketing*, that "Marketing is everything and everything is marketing." He explains that "Marketing has to be all-pervasive, part of everyone's job description, from the receptionist to the board of directors. Its job is neither to fool the customer nor to falsify the company's image. It is to integrate the customer into the design of the product and to design a systematic process for interaction that will create substance in the relationship." As an entrepreneur, you will do well to take this idea to heart.

Market Research

One marketer suggests that before you proceed with your new product, you should make sure it will pass the "snicker test." Show or tell your idea for a new product and ask for a reaction. If people don't snicker, your idea has passed the test. I don't think you should rely a lot on this test, because good ideas are often greeted with ridicule, which might include a snicker. Or, a snicker might mean the concept of the invention is misunderstood. Or, a snicker might be just a nervous response by the evaluator. Or, it could mean that the idea is seen as so clever, it elicits a relaxed snicker that means cool. If you get no snicker, this could signify apathy by someone. Your job is to sort through the various reactions to your new invention, consider the source, and draw conclusions as objectively as possible. (Refer to Ch 11 for test marketing in stores.)

In general, market research is used to provide information to you for purposes of decision making. Think of it as a tool used for risk reduction, because it keeps you from making an investment in a new idea until you have some positive indicators. Some products will require a lot more research than others, depending on how complex or straightforward the marketing problem. If you're dealing with a commodity type item that has lots of historical data for it on file, your research job will be quite simple compared to dealing with a unique invention that could create a new product category.

Invention Evaluation

As soon as you decide to get serious about an idea for a new product, the first thing to do is to get it evaluated. No sense spending time and money on something that doesn't offer good potential. There are several research tools that are used with new products that you should be aware of.

Focus groups, interviews, surveys, and mall interventions are popular research tools used mostly by big consumer product companies. But you can learn some valuable techniques by knowing about them. Let's take a look at some of these tools so you can think about how you might test your new product.

The object of using these tools is to help marketers evaluate a new product, package, program, etc., in advance of its launch. The focus groups provide qualitative data, while surveys and mall interventions provide quantitative data. This data is used as the basis for modification or cancellation of whatever is being evaluated.

> ❝ Twenty-five percent of the population, composed of maturing and mature consumers (50 and over) hold 50 percent of the country's discretionary spending power and 75 percent of personal net worth. ❞

A **focus group**, for example, is typically eight to twelve paid people meeting over a subject for up to two hours guided by a trained moderator. Focus groups for test marketing began in the 1950's. They grew out of psychiatry's group sessions that are today's support groups for coping with personal problems. The meetings usually take place in a special room with a one-way mirror that allows the client to be unobserved while witnessing the discussion.

Often there is audio taping, video taping and a written analysis of what is learned from such groups. For example, results can help answer questions about preferences regarding different aspects of a product. Focus groups are good for national brand testing, but are generally too expensive for the start-up inventor. But, just knowing about how various surveys work should be helpful to you. If you can understand what goes on in a focus group you might be able to translate it to the evaluation of your product by your friends and associates. There are also other less expensive tools to consider.

A **mall intervention** is putting interviewers in busy pedestrian areas of malls to survey individuals in the passing traffic. It might involve asking a couple of questions to passersby, or it might involve asking volunteers to a conference room in the center. The cost of this type testing is much less than focus groups, but it may still be more than the lone inventor can justify paying. But now that you know that this type of testing goes on, why not do your own "mini-intervention" at the mall? Just say, "Excuse me, but would you mind giving me your opinion of this new product?" If you ask ten people, perhaps two or three will stop and cooperate. After such a survey you should have a much better feel about what people think of your idea, and whether you should pursue it. And, if you do pursue it, to what economic group, age group, etc., which is called demographics.

Don't ignore older folks when you evaluate your market or you'll be guilty of practicing ageism, which could prove costly. Informed marketing takes into account the "25-50-75 Rule", which goes like this:

Twenty-five percent of the population, composed of maturing and mature consumers (50 and over) hold 50 percent of the country's discretionary spending power and 75 percent of personal net worth.

Marketing consultant Dick Lee of St. Paul points out that these figures are from 1991, before the maturing of early baby boomers began in earnest. By the year 2000 the rule might be 35-60-80.

Run it by Wal-Mart's WIN Program

You can submit your new product idea to the Wal-Mart Innovation Network (WIN) by paying a nominal fee to the Innovation Institute to cover the expenses of providing you with a detailed report. It doesn't matter if your product idea is just words and sketches on paper, or a finished product in a package. Don't worry about a patent application, because you submit to WIN under a confidential disclosure agreement, (described in CH 5). Take advantage of this little-known opportunity and you not only get your idea ex-

> ❝ He says the purpose of the WIN invention evaluation is not to predict commercial successes, but rather to identify serious technical or commercial flaws in the idea submitted. ❞

pertly evaluated, but actually submitted directly to Wal-Mart buyers, and indirectly to other store buyers, if it scores high enough. This kind of formal pre-evaluation can save you a lot of time and money, and that's why I recommend it. There are also many other universities with programs that offer evaluation services. (See Resource Section)

But, let's take a closer look at WIN, arguably the leader in the evaluation field. Say you come up with what you think is a terrific idea, and you think you want to pursue it. If you're like most inventors, you don't have the know-how to determine the commercial potential of a product idea. This is why the Wal-Mart Innovation Network focuses on invention evaluation. Wal-Mart management feels it can serve America's inventors, who constantly approach them, by helping them avoid making costly mistakes by providing them with an honest, competent, and objective third-party pre-analysis of their ideas and inventions.

WIN is believed to be the largest systematic inventor assistance service in the country. It has established a formal resource referral network to assist you. Wal-Mart's top management feels that America's inventors are important to the national interest of our country. WIN has teamed up with the Center for Business and Economic Development of the College of Business Administration at Southwest Missouri State University and the Innovation Institute. The Innovation Institute uses the Preliminary Innovation Evaluation System (PIES) format. This is a comprehensive, structured evaluation system consisting of 41 criteria to evaluate the commercial potential of an idea or invention. When completed, it provides you with a risk profile of your project.

The founder of the Innovation Institute and director of the WIN program is Dr. Gerald G. Udell who has more than 20 years experience in invention evaluation. He is generally regarded as the dean of invention evaluation in the United States. He is the author of the National Science Foundation's PIES format which is the most widely used evaluation format in this country.

He says the purpose of the WIN invention evaluation is not to predict commercial successes, but rather to identify serious technical or commercial flaws in the idea submitted.

When WIN has completed the evaluation of your idea/invention, you will receive a 13-page feedback report and a 4-6 page letter that frequently contains specific comments from your chief evaluator. All of this information will increase your insight into the commercial strengths and weaknesses of your product. You will also receive WIN's 277-page manual, *Evaluating Potential New Products,* which contains a wealth of information and resources.

Your report will conclude with a final recommendation by your chief evaluator about further investment in your project. Let's take a look at a run-down of how past submissions have fared.

WIN Recommendation Summary

Further Investment...   *Percent So Rated*

is not recommended 15

should be very limited and cautious 30

should be limited and cautious 30

is recommended,

but you need to resolve unknowns 11

for other channels of distribution 07

and referred to Wal-Mart 07

If your product is referred to Wal-Mart, it will be reviewed by an appropriate buyer. If it is approved for market testing in their stores, you will be responsible for the final development and commercialization of the product. Note that a positive recommendation by the buyer is not a guarantee of a purchase order. Your finished product will still need to meet Wal-Mart's standards and fit into its merchandising plan at that time.

As of this writing the cost to have your idea/invention evaluated by WIN, including the report and manual, is only $175, about what you'd pay for a patent search.

In my opinion, the first thing you should do with your new idea or invention is invest in an evaluation of this kind. Do this before you spend any money on it for a patent search or patent application.

In my opinion, the first thing you should do with your new idea or invention is invest in an evaluation of this kind. Do this before you spend any money on it for a patent search or patent application.

For more information, contact the WIN Innovation Institute in Everton, MO. (See Resource Section.) The Institute will send you a confidential disclosure agreement/ registration document for your consideration.

Another leading source of evaluation is the Wisconsin Innovation Service Center in Whitewater, WI. (See Resource Section)

The newly-formed California Invention Center at California State University in Hayward, CA will soon have a program similar to WIN. CIC will be leading twenty-two other Cal State campuses in setting up evaluation programs similar to WIN. (Please see Resource Section).

Independent inventors like you account for about 20,000 of the 110,000 U.S. Patents issued every year. (About 12,000 of you file your patent without an attorney.) And, although it is said that only about 2 per cent of *all* patents ever make money for the owner, I believe the instruction found in this book will help you increase your chances of success.

By screening your invention using evaluation you can increase your chances of making money on your patented invention from 2% to about 50% to 60%!

Don't file for a patent until you have evaluated your invention and have satisfied yourself about its feasibility and its marketability using one or more of the methods outlined above.

By screening your invention using evaluation you can increase your chances of making money on your patented invention from 2% to about 50% to 60%!

Export Marketing

Realize that globally there are 6 billion consumers. If your product would be in demand in various foreign countries, contact the US Department of Commerce and ask for information about listing your product in bulletins that go to our foreign embassies. (See Resource Section.)

Invention Marketing Scams

Answer an ad for inventors on your radio or TV and it could be a scam that eventually costs you a bundle! *"Do you invent? Or, do you know anyone who invents?"* goes a typical pitch. *"We will patent your idea and submit it to industry, etc., etc."*

Ads by marketing promoters like the one above often cost unwary inventors five or ten thousand dollars, and usually deliver nothing! When the inventors complain, they find there are few laws protecting them. There are hundreds of these unscrupulous operators out there looking for creative (but perhaps naive) people like you.

> *Last year alone these "unconvicted felons" scammed more than 25,000 aspiring inventors out of approximately $200 million! Fortunately, as I write this in 1996, the US Congress is at long last acting to stop these fraudulent invention marketing companies.*

Last year alone these "unconvicted felons" scammed more than 25,000 aspiring inventors out of approximately $200 million! Fortunately, as I write this in 1996, the US Congress is at long last acting to stop these fraudulent invention marketing companies.

The bills now before congress require so-called invention marketing operators to register into a data base with the federal government, and to disclose several key things, including ownership, past legal actions against them, as well as their *success rate* (the number of inventors who made more money from their inventions than they paid to the marketing company). Seldom can a scam company claim more than a handful of "successes." Some claim one or even none!

Much of the pending legislation is the result of work done by Robert G. Lougher and his all-volunteer non-profit Inventors Awareness Group, the driving force to stop the fraud. In the *Congressional Record*,

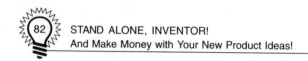

82 STAND ALONE, INVENTOR!
And Make Money with Your New Product Ideas!

Lougher explained to the congressmen:

"These frauds all operate in the same manner. They all offer a free evaluation and then accept almost every idea sent to them. After the free evaluation, they offer the unsuspecting inventor a more comprehensive evaluation and patent search for hundreds of dollars. This supposed evaluation is nothing more than computer-generated generic garbage that can fit any number of thousands of ideas. ...The patent search is cursory at best and almost always says the idea is patentable, when in fact most are not. This so-called comprehensive evaluation is prepared for one reason and one reason only, to get the inventor to go to the next stage and pay several thousand dollars for their worthless services. What makes most inventors an easy target for any con-artist is that they are naive about the processes involved and rightfully enthusiastic about their ideas.

> **❝ Only fraudulent operators who are scamming big bucks out of unsuspecting inventors have the wherewithal to buy mass media advertising. ❞**

We do not want anyone, especially our nation's aspiring inventors to get the impression that everyone connected with invention development is a fraud. In fact, quite the opposite is true. There is a growing number of non-profit inventor support groups throughout the U.S. Once fragmented, over the past few years these groups are now becoming more organized and effective thanks to national organizations like the United Inventors Association of the USA (a non-profit umbrella group for numerous inventor support groups and legitimate inventor service providers), the Washington-based Alliance for American Innovation and the Intellectual Property Creators."

To protect yourself, do not deal with any invention marketing companies who advertise on radio or TV, which is relatively expensive.

Only fraudulent operators who are scamming big bucks out of unsuspecting inventors have the wherewithal to buy mass media advertising.

Even when they tell you the big bucks will get you a registered patent, it's usually a cheap *design* patent, lasting only 14 years, which is easy to get and is usually of little value.

If you believe that you have already been bilked by one of these scams, you may be able to participate in a class action law suit. Contact: AIC Victims Advocate, Attn: Linda J. Inman, 644 South Trafton Street, Tacoma, WA 98405-3050.

If you want to find legitimate providers of help to independent inventors, contact the United Inventors Association of the USA at Box 23447, Rochester, NY 14692 (716) 359-9310. Or, send for the Federal Trade Commission brochure, "Invention Promotion Firms" that offers tips for consumers who are considering trying to patent and commercialize their inventions. A copy is available for 50 cents from the Consumer Information Center, Pueblo, CO 81009. FTC news releases, consumer brochures, and other materials also are available on the Internet at the FTC's web site: *http://www.ftc.gov*

Inventor Organizations

Have you ever attended a meeting of your local inventors club? If so, you may have heard a speaker on the topic of "making prototypes" or "generating publicity," because club formats usually include a presentation from a visiting expert. Networking at these meetings with successful inventors, and others in fields relating to inventing, is almost always enlightening. Also, you can compare notes and get moral support from fellow novices. Often there are investors attending these meetings looking for an exciting new idea to put money into.

Larger regional and national organizations offer tradeshows, workshops, seminars, educational materials, newsletters and more. For a listing of hundreds of inventor organizations, please refer to the Resource Section in the back of this book.

Business Plan

Once you decide to start a business, you will need a business plan—for two important reasons. First, it's your "charter," your carefully-thought-out map of where you want to go with this business and how you plan to get there. Second, you can use it to convince prospective lenders, vendors and employees that your venture is worthy of their participation.

A business plan should include a description of your initial product, a statement of your marketing strategy, plus estimates of startup costs, costs of sales and sales projections. The projections should look ahead three to five years. (See Resource Section for books.)

Note: The Resource Section begins on page 259 and is arranged by chapter to make it convenient for you to find related references.

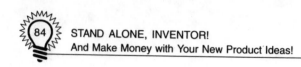

84 STAND ALONE, INVENTOR!
And Make Money with Your New Product Ideas!

CHAPTER 5	**Intellectual Property:**
	Paid Protection

It's Like Real Estate

Will Rogers told people to buy land "cuz they ain't makin' any more of it!" He was talking about *real estate* property, which is of finite supply. I'm going to be discussing *intellectual* property, which is of infinite supply, at least wherever there are people with access to a patent office. Our US Patent and Trademark Office (USPTO) awards about 2,200 patents each week! Most go to corporations, but many go to individuals like you and me. (To get an idea of the scope and variety of inventions we humans dream up, just flip through a copy of the USPTO's *Official Gazette* that lists the week's new patents every Tuesday.)

❝ Instead, I will relate to you some of my own experiences with intellectual property that illustrate its value. Also, I will point out some problems you might encounter when others transgress your intellectual property. ❞

The term "intellectual property" has a nice ring to it, don't you think? It's what you own if you obtain patents, trademarks or copyrights on your work. Just think up something unique, get it legally protected, and you've created a piece of property! When you own a piece of intellectual property, it is possible for you to borrow against it, rent it, sell it, or develop it—just like you can with a piece of land! The patent is your deed to your intellectual property. Think about this the next time someone tells you patents are worthless.

There are many books available to you that explain the numerous details and technicalities of patents, trademarks, copyrights, and trade secrets. You can find such books at your library, and even copies of patent documents on file, if you go to one of the more than 80 US Patent and Trademark Depository Libraries (PTDL's) located in or near major cities throughout the country. In this chapter I am not going to try to educate you on the technicalities of each form of intellectual property. (See Resource Section for books and Patent Libraries.)

Instead, I will relate to you some of my own experiences with intellectual property that illustrate its value. Also, I will point out some problems you might encounter when others do not respect your intellectual property rights.

Patents

When I came up with my idea for a transparent calendar for attachment to a watch crystal, I felt that some sort of patent protection was needed. The invention was so simple I thought it would be quite easy for others to copy. I didn't want to pursue this idea unless there was a way I could use a patent to keep competition out. But I knew very little about getting a patent. So, I talked to a friend of mine who was the patent attorney at the corporation where I had worked.

> *My attorney went on to explain that although I did not invent watches, calendars, or pressure-sensitive labels, I had fashioned a transparent pressure-sensitive *label* with a monthly *calendar* printed on it, which is removably attachable to the crystal of a *watch*.*

When I asked him about patenting my calendar idea, the first thing he said was "You can't patent a calendar." He said that patent laws prevent you from patenting things that are already in use and that are needed in our everyday lives, such as tables, formulas, printed matter, calendars, tape measures, rulers and the like. Nuts!

Patent Pending

Not to be discouraged, I asked him what would it take to be able to put "Patent Pending" on my product so that I could "scare people away." And he replied, "That won't scare people away! But, if you still want to put 'Patent Pending' on your product, the law says you must first file a patent application at the U.S. Patent and Trademark Office in Washington, DC. Some people put Patent Pending on their product because they are *thinking* about filing. This is not recommended, because it is illegal and punishable, so don't do it until you actually file."

He told me that the description in the application should clearly articulate the invention. I asked him how much the application would cost. Of course, this was so many years ago that we were able to work out a total budget of about $600 for an issued patent, including his attorney's fee and the filing and issuance fees. But, this was nearly one month's salary for me at the time! (This attorney's hourly fee back then was $25, whereas today he charges $375!) I felt I needed the "Patent Pending," so I told him, let's file for a patent. We decided to go ahead and file *without* conducting the usual pre-filing patent search. Reason: I would save time and money, and I felt reasonably sure no "prior art" would be found, because I had never before heard of anything going on the crystal of a watch. Besides, the attorney's fee for the initial filing is about equal to the cost of a patent search. So with a very simple patent, go ahead and file and let the USPTO do your search for you. As long as the examiner doesn't find an invention identical to or very close to yours, you are money and time ahead. (When you file at the USPTO, be sure to include their form to specify that you're a "small entity", and not a big business (500 or more employees) so you can qualify for the 50% discount off regular filing fees.)

After my attorney got into the nitty-gritty of my application, he told me that contrary to what he had said earlier, he now thought that it was possible for me to get a patent if he wrote up the application as a "combination patent."

The Combination Patent

He explained that a combination patent is possible when the inventor combines two or more existing things in an unobvious way to produce an unexpected result, a novel creation. He continued, "Your invention is analogous to an early combination patent, that is, the removable eraser for the top of a pencil. In that invention the creator, Eberhard, was not inventing pencils, rubber, or erasers, which had already been invented. However, he fashioned a *rubber eraser* so that it was removably attachable to a *pencil* and was awarded the landmark, or first, combination patent. It was called "Pencil With Removable Eraser."

My attorney went on to explain that although I did not invent watches, calendars, or pressure-sensitive labels, I had fashioned a transparent pressure-sensitive *label* with a monthly *calendar* printed on it, which is removably attachable to the crystal of a *watch*.

My attorney called it, a "Watch with removable calendar," which we filed as a combination patent. The application was examined in the section of the Patent Office responsible for timekeeping technology, which at that time was not very busy. (This was before the advent of the digital watch that was later to make this section one of the busiest.) So my appli-

88

STAND ALONE, INVENTOR!
And Make Money with Your New Product Ideas!

cation was processed very quickly. It's a bit ironic to note that Eberhard's patent was later challenged in court, and declared invalid, because the resulting structure it produced was not novel: There had already existed pencils with erasers on them! Lucky for me, no watches had previously existed with monthly calendars on the crystals.

Within six months I was awarded US Patent #3,464,200, "Watch With Transparent Calendar." This patent had three claims, and because it was a utility patent, it had a term of 17 years. This meant that for the next 17 years, I could exclude anyone from making, using or selling my invention anywhere in America, which I did.

(Design patents, in contrast, which protect the ornamental shape or *look* of an item, but not its function, have a term of fourteen years.) Incidentally, the 17-year term for utility patents has since been changed. I'll explain more about this later in this chapter.)

Lesson: Do not assume, regardless of what you are told, that some-

Figure 5-1. This is the transparent calendar for the watch, called Crystal-Date®, which was awarded a 17-year utility patent. During its product life, this invention produced tremendous sales for my company, and paid the salaries of 5 to 10 workers for many years.

thing cannot be patented. Incidentally, my patent attorney told me recently that he uses my watch calendar case history (complete with the "you-can't-patent-a-calendar" part) as course material in a class he teaches at Stanford University Law School.

The USPTO's Disclosure Document Program

Years ago, word went around that if you wanted to establish a record of exactly *when* you invented something, you could simply write a description of it on a piece of paper, seal it up in an envelope and send it to yourself via registered mail. When it arrived, you would not open it, but you would keep it to be opened whenever you needed to prove you were the originator of the idea. Whether or not this method would hold up in court is arguable, since seals on envelopes are subject to tampering.

The folks at the Patent Office suggested that a more credible form of evidence was needed. Thus today, the USPTO provides a special service called the Disclosure Document Program. Here's how it works: Write a clear description of your invention including how the invention is made and used. Include drawings and /or photographs of the invention. Sheets should be 8-1/2" X 13" maximum and they should be numbered.

Mail your material with a letter stating that you are the inventor of the disclosed invention and that you want it to be accepted under the Disclosure Document Program. Tell the USPTO that you want it to be preserved in confidence for a period of two years. Sign and date your letter and enclose a duplicate set of your disclosure documents, your check for $10.00, and a self-addressed envelope. Mail to: Box DD, Asst. Commissioner for Patents, USPTO, Washington, DC 20231.

After a time, you will receive in your self-addressed envelope duplicates of your documents stamped by the USPTO with an identifying number and date of receipt. The USPTO always warns: *The Disclosure Document may be relied upon only as evidence, and a patent application should be diligently filed if patent protection is desired.* The USPTO will destroy your document after two years unless it is specifically referred to in a separate letter in a related patent application filed by you within the two year period.

I believe this is a very useful program for the independent inventor. Even though it's not a patent, it's a quick and inexpensive way for you to establish proof of conception while you are working to improve and develop your invention in anticipation of *possibly* filing a patent application.

The USPTO, in effect stands as your witness to the conception date as represented by the Disclosure Document filing.

The New Provisional Patent Application

In June 1995 the USPTO began accepting what it calls a provisional application. Available only for utility patents, it's a simpler, cheaper way for an inventor to get his foot in the door of the patenting process, albeit only temporarily.

This new application, which can result in an earlier filing date, proved popular and resulted in more than 20,000 filings in the first year.

A provisional application quickly gives your invention valuable "patent-pending" status for up to one year, permitting you to disclose your idea in safety while you shop for vendors, potential backers and licensees. If you decide to drop the invention, just don't file a follow-on regular application within one year.

This new application, which can result in an earlier filing date, proved popular, and resulted in more than 20,000 filings in the first year.

Important: For purposes of *priority*, the filing date of your provisional application will be used as the filing date of a follow-on regular, non-provisional patent application that you file within one year. Meanwhile, the USPTO does not "examine" your provisional application, and it keeps it in confidence. The provisional application automatically goes abandoned at the end of one year. A complete, non-provisional application must be filed prior to the end of that year in order to gain the benefit of the provisional filing date.

Specifications in the provisional and the follow-on non-provisional application must be complete and consistent, because the only way you can change them is with another filing. The 20-year term of your follow-on patent, should it issue, will be measured from the actual date of *its* filing.

Your current fee as an individual (small entity) to file a provisional application is only $75, while your fee for a follow-on non-provisional application is $385, plus attorney's or agent's fees, should you hire help.

Your current fee as an individual (small entity) to file a provisional application is only $75, while your fee for a follow-on non-provisional application is $385, plus attorney's or agent's fees, should you hire help.

You can probably file the provisional application by yourself because it does not require writing formal claims for your invention. Also, an oath or declaration is not required. Just contact the USPTO at 703/305-

PTO/SB/16 (11-95)
Approved for use through 01/31/98. OMB 0651-0037
Patent and Trademark Office; U.S. DEPARTMENT OF COMMERCE

PROVISIONAL APPLICATION FOR PATENT COVER SHEET

This is a request for filing a PROVISIONAL APPLICATION FOR PATENT under 37 CFR 1.53 (b)(2).

Docket Number			Type a plus sign (+) inside this box -->

INVENTOR(s)/APPLICANT(s)

LAST NAME	FIRST NAME	MIDDLE INITIAL	RESIDENCE (CITY AND EITHER STATE OR FOREIGN COUNTRY)

TITLE OF THE INVENTION (280 characters max)

CORRESPONDENCE ADDRESS

STATE		ZIP CODE		COUNTRY	

ENCLOSED APPLICATION PARTS *(check all that apply)*

☐ Specification *Number of Pages* [   ]   ☐ Small Entity Statement

☐ Drawing(s) *Number of Sheets* [   ]   ☐ Other (specify)

METHOD OF PAYMENT OF FILING FEES FOR THIS PROVISIONAL APPLICATION FOR PATENT *(check one)*

☐ A check or money order is enclosed to cover the filing fees

☐ The Commissioner is hereby authorized to charge filing fees and credit Deposit Account Number: _____

FILING FEE AMOUNT ($)

The invention was made by an agency of the United States Government or under a contract with an agency of the United States Government.
☐ No.
☐ Yes, the name of the U.S. Government agency and the Government contract number are: _____

Respectfully submitted,

SIGNATURE _____   Date [/ /]

TYPED or PRINTED NAME _____   REGISTRATION NO. [-] *(if appropriate)*

☐ Additional inventors are being named on separately numbered sheets attached hereto

USE ONLY FOR FILING A PROVISIONAL APPLICATION FOR PATENT

Burden Hour Statement: This form is estimated to take .2 hours to complete. Time will vary depending upon the needs of the individual case. Any comments on the amount of time you are required to complete this form should be sent to the Chief Information Officer, Patent and Trademark Office, Washington, DC 20231. DO NOT SEND FEES OR COMPLETED FORMS TO THIS ADDRESS. SEND TO: Box Provisional Application, Assistant Commissioner for Patents, Washington, DC 20231.

Figure 5-2. This is form PTO/SB/16 (11-95) to be used when filing a Provisional Application for a patent.

9300, request a Provisional Application Cover Sheet, Form PTO/SB/16 (11-95), and a Small Entity Form. Fill out these two forms, include a detailed description of your invention along with drawings, if they are needed to explain your invention, and send these papers to the USPTO with your check for $75. Soon thereafter you will receive an acknowledgment that you have reduced your idea to practice, which is what is required to give your invention official patent pending status. You must be diligent in pursuing your invention from the date you file a provisional application to the date you file the non-provisional application.

> ❝ Congress needs to enact an "Invention Encouragement Act" that would mandate lower fees for the little guy. Write your congressperson and send him or her a photocopy of this page from *Stand Alone, Inventor!* ❞

Equal Opportunity

Permit me to editorialize for a moment. I think our Patent Office should recognize and single out independent inventors—because they are potential starters of new businesses—and make it financially easier for them to get and keep a patent. For example, under the present fee schedule, the individual inventor is thrown into the same category as "small business entities," which can have up to 499 employees. This means that lone inventors have to pay the same fees to file and maintain a patent as bio-tech and other capital-rich companies pay for years, until they grow past 500 employees!

This small entity category pays 50% less than the full filing and maintenance fees paid by big companies like IBM*. However, these reduced fees are still beyond the means of most new inventors working off their kitchen table. Take the simplest utility patent for instance: Current Patent Office fees for filing, issuing and maintaining, discounted 50%, will amount to more than $4000.00 over its life! I believe that in an effort to give equal opportunity to the unincorporated inventor in the US, with, say, ten or fewer employees, the Patent Office should set lower fees—perhaps only 10 to 25% of the fees for a company like IBM or H-P. Incidentally, the Patent Office could afford this if the Congress would let them keep and utilize all the fees they collect.

The Congress takes money from the Patent Office's planned appropriations that were based on its fee income. In the past few years, nearly $100 million has been taken in this manner. And, the money has been distributed to fund other agency programs. The Congress does this in an ef-

*IBM was awarded 1,383 US patents in 1995—more than any other company in the world.

fort to balance the National Budget under the Omnibus Budget Reduction Act (or "OBRA").

The Patent Office puts up a valiant fight each year, because they are often forced to curtail plans. For example, already they have deleted certain quality control programs, and eliminated projects that improve the patent classification system. In my opinion, and I am not standing alone on this one, this capturing and redistribution of Patent Office fee moneys represents a taxation on our country's inventors. I say, GIVE IT BACK TO THE INDEPENDENT INVENTORS!

Congress needs to enact an "Invention Encouragement Act" that would mandate lower fees for the little guy. Write your congressperson and send him or her a photocopy of this page from *Stand Alone, Inventor!*

Patent It Yourself

In 1994 the USPTO received 190,000 patent applications, 12,000 of which were self-filed directly by the inventor, not through a patent attorney. (You might say that the purist Stand-Alone Inventor even files his or her own patent application!)

If your invention is very simple, you have the option to prepare and file a patent application by yourself. If you decide to do this, your only out-of-pocket expenses are the Patent Office fees and possibly the cost of drawings. You will be dealing directly with a patent examiner whose job it is to help you obtain a patent if he or she sees you have allowable claims. But, if you want to make sure you are filing your application correctly, I recommend you buy (or read at the library) Attorney David Pressman's book, *Patent It Yourself!* If you can read only one other book on inventing besides mine, make sure it's David's.

His is a very comprehensive and professional treatment of protecting intellectual property, yet he makes it all very easy to understand. More than 150,000 copies have been sold.

Even if you intend to hire the services of a patent attorney, it's a good idea to read Pressman's book. Use it to do some homework before you see the attorney, which should speed things up so you pay for less of the attorney's time. Once I used information in David's book to help convince a patent examiner (through my attorney) to "allow" an important claim in one of my applications.

> ❝ His is a very comprehensive and professional treatment of protecting intellectual property, yet he makes it all very easy to understand. More than 150,000 copies have been sold. ❞

The publisher, NOLO Press, also offers this valuable publication as a computer software program. It advertises the software as a "fully-searchable version of the *Patent It Yourself* book, complete with all the forms you need with step-by-step instructions and on-line legal and program help." (See Resource Section.)

Foreign-Country Patents

Since nearly 80 countries have patent offices that will accept your application, you may be thinking where do I start? You start by determining where the markets are for your invention. If your product is strictly American, you need not bother with patents in other countries. Take my business card punch, for example. It is an accessory for a rotary card file, which is a product of our American culture. With a little research I learned that this type of card file is relatively rare in most other countries. And, since the American market consists of 270 million folks with English as their main language, I figured I'd have a sufficient market in the 50 states, and didn't need to worry about patenting and selling overseas.

My watch calendar was a different story, however. Almost every citizen of the globe owns a wrist watch. I decided my main markets after the U.S. would be Europe and Asia, and that I would look into getting some patent protection in those areas.

Europe is easy, because you have the European Patent Convention (EPC) made up of 13 countries that accept applications from anywhere. The EPC has offices in Munich and The Hague that perform the search and examination functions on your submitted application. When yours is successfully completed, you are granted a European patent. Next, unless you have selected all 13 countries, you must submit this patent to your shorter list of European countries' patent offices. Upon filing translations where needed, and payment of fees, each country will issue you its own national patent. The beauty of the EPC is that there is only one examination of your application—upon the initial filing. And, since English is one of their three official languages, this means that you can conduct all your needed correspondence regarding your application in English. I obtained patents

> **Without a patent in a foreign country, you cannot prevent your product from being copied there. But, your US Patent can help you prevent foreign-made products covered by it from being imported into this country. If you suspect unauthorized copies are coming in, ask your attorney about alerting US Customs, who, armed with the proper paperwork, will seize such goods at US ports of entry.**

in the United Kingdom and Spain. I withdrew my application in Japan after a long and expensive pending period.

If you decide you need patent coverage in other areas besides Europe, you may want to use the Patent Cooperation Treaty or PCT. Under this system, within 12 months after you file your US patent application, you file the same application for a PCT international patent at the USPTO Receiving Office, indicating which of the 74 member countries are of interest to you.

Once filed, your PCT application is subjected to an international novelty search at the International Searching Office in Washington. You can buy time by filing your PCT within the 12 months (and obtaining your effective filing date), and waiting to see if you want to proceed later with the translation and filing expenses of each country.

If you decide to file in only one or two foreign countries, it's quicker and cheaper to skip the above, and file directly in those countries Ask your patent attorney or agent for an estimate of costs for foreign patents.

Trademarks

Picking a name for your product is important. The "right" name will "catch on," if it associates with the product, and it's easy to spell and pronounce. I gave my watch calendar the brand name, "Crystal-Date," which my attorney advised me to protect as a *trademark*. He explained that people would not be able to sell watch calendars under this particular brand name if I established ownership of it. This turned out to be a simple matter (and a good idea). A brief search was done, it was "published for opposition", and within a few months I had a registered trademark. You can register your trademark yourself, and do it correctly with the help of the book, *Trademark,* by NOLO Press. You can register your trademark in your state, or federally at the USPTO. The cost for this registration is nominal. (See Resource Section.)

Until the registration notice came through, I printed a small superscript following the name like this: Crystal-Date™. This put others on notice that I was using and reserving the word "Crystal Date" as a *common law* trademark. After the registration came through from the USPTO it was now legal for me to replace the TM with a circle R (that we see identifying all registered trademarks) like this: Crystal Date®. A trademark can be contested until the fifth year of registration at which time it can be made incontestable, making it even more valuable to the owner. You may also print the footnote, "Reg. U.S. Pat. & TM. Off." as a notice of registration. (I make it a point to do this with my unpatented products, because some knock-off artists, who do not read carefully, will believe (erroneously) that the product has a registered US Patent.)

Copyrights

With my Crystal Date® watch calendar I was in the somewhat unusual position of being able to add a *third* protection to the product itself through a copyright. I produced my watch calendars on a sheet of paper 3"x 4" that contained twelve little monthly calendar labels. There was a header label at the top with space for a sponsoring company's advertising, and some extra space along the bottom where I printed a list of four instructions on how to peel off and apply the calendars to one's watch.

> You can't register certain words as a trademark if they are purely descriptive of a product, because others need to use these words in ordinary speech. For example, "Car Battery" cannot be registered, but DieHard®, which is a brand of car battery, can.

My attorney advised me to immediately put a © symbol, which is the international copyright notice, or "Copyright," or "Copr." in a footnote to the printed instructions. (This procedure is now optional, but highly recommended. If you use the ©, no one can claim "innocent infringement"—that is that he or she did not realize that the work is protected.) Following the © goes the year, followed by your name or the name of your company. Example: © 1999 John Doe. This would put people on notice worldwide that I was claiming and protecting the particular *wording* I used in the instructions. (If you publish without this notice, the right to the work can be lost.) Later, I could *perfect* the copyright by getting it registered. This is done by filling out a simple application and sending two copies of the printed piece with a $20 fee to the Copyright Office at the Library of Congress. (See Resource Section for address.) Incidentally, by registering a copyright of your work, one copy automatically goes on file at the Library of Congress and can be accessed and reviewed by anyone.

> ❝I took my attorney's advice and always got registered copyrights.❞

I took my attorney's advice and always got registered copyrights.

Later, I will give you an example of how my registered trademark and registered copyright enabled me to collect a surprise cash settlement from a major corporation who used them without my permission. And, how a registered copyright of another invention enabled me to collect a cash settlement from the *U.S. Government* for an infringement by the Department of Defense. Certainly, it was not my preference to collect settlements; actually, it would have been better for me had there been no infringements. But, the point is, using these protections, you have recourse if someone rides roughshod over your intellectual property. And hopefully this recourse acts as a deterrent to others.

Figure 5-3. The Crystal-Date® watch calendar was covered by patent, trademark and copyright, all three of which proved useful in protecting it from infringers.

Patent Infringement

Just because you have claimed legal *protection* for your creation does not mean that the printed notices will be heeded by all who see them. As I began racking up bigger and bigger sales of my watch calendar, I discovered that I had an imitator . . . and I wasn't flattered, as they say you should be. I was actually pretty angry, and I wanted to stop him.

The way I discovered this encroacher was through a buyer at one of the General Electric units in the Eastern United States. The buyer had inquired to my company by phone about a large quantity of Crystal-Date watch calendars to be used as a mailing insert, imprinted with the GE logo and some advertising. In response I had sent samples and prices for the buyer's review. Later, when I telephoned him to see if he wanted to place an order, he said no, and that my "prices were too high." "Compared to *whose*?" I asked. He said he had found a local label maker to whom he had given a purchase order for the manufacture of 10,000 copies of such calendars at a cost considerably lower than my published price.

I explained to the buyer that I had patent protection on my invention to see if that would make any difference to him. He told me that my patent might be a problem for his vendor to deal with, but that he was not concerned with it. I didn't agree.

The next telephone call I made was to my patent attorney. After he had heard my GE story he said, "I think I'll have a little chat with the patent counsel at General Electric headquarters."

My attorney called me back later. He told me that he had called the patent attorney at General Electric and cautioned him that his purchasing department was on the brink of committing a probable infringement, and that the Merrick company intended to enforce its patent rights to the fullest. The GE patent counsel assured my attorney not to worry about it, because he would "take care" of the matter.

He must have had a heart-to-heart talk with that particular buyer in the purchasing department, because the next thing I knew I got a purchase order in the mail from General Electric for 10,000 watch calendars at my price. (At the time, I remember reflecting that the profit on this one order exceeded the cost of obtaining the patent that made it possible!)

My patent attorney explained to me that General Electric owns very valuable patents themselves, and that it would not be good business for them to ride roughshod on patents belonging to someone else, especially little guys like me.

This is not to say that you will find this kind of mutual respect for patents in general—because it just doesn't work that way. The big corporations will fight each other tooth and nail to win patent litigation whenever it involves their primary products and business. But, in a relatively minor purchase of an advertising item such as a calendar, it wouldn't make any sense to irritate an independent inventor who in a lawsuit would be favored as the underdog by the public (in the media) and by a jury over a 'big, heartless, multi-national corporation'.

> ❝ The lesson here is that just because you are inventing ultra-simple objects that are relatively insignificant in the big scheme of things, don't think you can't enforce your patents against giant corporations. ❞

On the other hand if it came down to taking the infringer to court, your costs could be astronomical. Then you'd have to try to find a lawyer who would take your case on contingency. Or, if you had it you could fall back on your infringement insurance. (More about this later.)

The lesson here is that just because you are inventing ultra-simple objects that are relatively insignificant in the big scheme of things, don't think you can't enforce your patents against giant corporations.

Often, just the opposite is true because of the "David and Goliath" syndrome. It's alive and well in the world of public opinion, and you can take advantage of it.

During the first ten years of the watch calendar patent, my little company sold huge quantities of Crystal Date® watch calendars. We custom made them in fifteen languages and shipped them all over the world. My best estimate is that more than fifty million sheets of twelve-calendar labels were manufactured and sold during the life of this patented product.

There were many other instances of Crystal Date® patent infringements and subsequent enforcements—all without ever resorting to a lawsuit. The rewarding part was that no one got away with much. If we discovered that someone had made up 5,000 or 10,000 and sold them, we just put them on notice and got them to say that they wouldn't do it anymore. My patent effectively eliminated any significant competition against my product. Talk about a monopoly!

About ten years into my patent, the marketplace changed. The digital watch was introduced. It was an invention that had been conceived by some of my old Fairchild buddies right here in Silicon Valley. Although the digital watch invention did not display the entire month at a glance like mine did, because of its dark dial it was not suitable for my calendar. As a result, sales for my watch calendar—which worked best on analog watches—began slipping. And, in a few years—just about the time the patent ran out—my calendar sales were down to almost zero. In recent years, however, the digital watch popularity has peaked, and there has been a strong resurgence of analog watch sales that leaves the way open for a renewed market for my stick-on calendars. Stay tuned.

Licensing Your Patent

Let's say you get lucky and you find a company to take a license under your patent. You'll be signing an agreement that gives the licensee company the right to make, use and sell product(s) covered by your patent as long as it continues to pay you agreed fees and royalty amounts. You will want the agreement to call for a minimum annual royalty payment.

This is intended to provide an incentive for the company to put forth at least enough effort to make sales that will cover this payment.

There are various provisions that you can put into your license agreement. You can make it non-exclusive, which leaves you free to license others. Or, you can make it exclusive, which says you permit only one licensee to use your patent. You can also fine tune it to be exclusive to a certain market, and/or exclude certain areas or markets, and so on.

In an exclusive license agreement you can include a requirement that the licensee pay all the periodic maintenance fees charged by the US Patent Office. These fees can amount to several thousand dollars over the life of a patent. It's best to have an attorney with experience in licensing prepare your agreement, so you cover all the bases.

> ❢ Over the years I've entered into four patent licensing agreements. None of these opportunities to license arose until after I had made a commercial success of the invention. ❟

Over the years I've entered into four patent licensing agreements. None of these opportunities to license arose until after I had made a commercial success of the invention.

Two were entered into as settlements over possible infringements. I needed the other two as a way to expand into markets I could not otherwise cover.

You might want to check out a young company in Dallas called Venture Initiatives, headed by Geoffrey F. Walsh. According to a recent *Wall Street Journal* article, Walsh's company uses licensing arrangements to manufacture, market and distribute "gadgets created by amateur inventors."

Walsh told *The Wall Street Journal*, " We offer inventors the ability to take an item and run with it more effectively than they can."

Several inventor-licensors told the *Journal* that they were pleased with their arrangement with Venture Initiatives, because they did not have to give up their regular job. Walsh either buys the invention, or pays inventors a royalty with a possible up-front fee. Some inventors in dealing with Walsh retain their right to continue selling to certain market segments. This is a good way for the inventor to continue his cash flow, while waiting to see how his royalty arrangement pays off. Walsh told me that inventors should con-

> ❢ Walsh told *The Wall Street Journal*, " We offer inventors the ability to take an item and run with it more effectively than they can." ❟

tact his company and request information about his programs. (See Resource Section, pg 283).

Royalties

Once you decide to license your invention for a royalty, you must settle for a relatively meager monetary reward. Royalties range typically from 3% to 7% of wholesale sales, depending on margins and markets, and your ability to negotiate a deal. It's important in the agreement to precisely define "net sales," if that is what royalties are to be based on.

Certainly it is true that royalties can make you rich, but only if your invention turns out to be a big long-term seller, and you've got a good agreement. For example, if you've agreed to a 3% royalty, and annual sales build up to $2 million, this is $60,000 per year for you while sales hold up. Royalties are nice while they keep growing. But, later on, if they decline, or stop, you might regret that you haven't built a company, and you haven't kept enough control over your inventions and your potential income from them.

❛ Because of this you can probably negotiate a bigger up-front payment upon signing the agreement, a higher minimum annual royalty, and a percentage point or two higher on the royalty figure itself. ❜

If the invention you are trying to license is a simple one, I suggest you move it into the manufacturing stage, and actually start making and marketing the product yourself. Having advanced your invention to this stage, if you now decide to negotiate a license to a manufacturer, you can command higher royalties because you have reduced your invention to a product that is certifiably salable. By delivering proof of actual sales, you've taken a lot of risk out of the deal for the potential licensee.

Because of this you can probably negotiate a bigger up-front payment upon signing the agreement, a higher minimum annual royalty, and a percentage point or two higher on the royalty figure itself.

If licensing is your main interest, look into *Marketing Your Invention* by Thomas E. Mosley, Jr., or *Licensing—A Strategy for Profits* by Edward P. White. (See Resource Section)

Enforcement

It's interesting to note that about five years after my watch calendar patent *expired*, I got a call from an advertising specialty distributor in Maryland. His company was one of the many distributors that had been selling my watch calendar during its heyday. The reason he called was to say that he was glad to learn that we were still making the watch calendar. I told him he must be mistaken, because we had stopped. He said, "Well, then, why is it just today I received in the mail 'your' current calendar that advertises a fund raising organization? It has your patent, trademark and copyright notices on it." He said he would send it to me so I could look into it, which I did.

I discovered that the big label making concern in Southern California, who had been my licensee and main subcontractor for the manufacture of the Crystal Date® watch calendar, had continued to sell the watch calendar after my patent had run out. Some of the sales were very large. I had my patent attorney write them a letter pointing out that there was still a license agreement in force that permitted them to manufacture the calendars so long as a 5% royalty on the sales was paid to me. (It is important to note here that even though the *patent* had expired, the license agreement, which had not been terminated, also encompassed the use of my *trademark and copyright*, both of which were still in force!)

Consequently, the infringing corporation was quite agreeable to a negotiated cash settlement for past trademark and copyright infringement, and coughed up several thousand dollars. The settlement included their terminating the licensing agreement, because the patent had expired and they chose no longer to use my copyright and trademark. But my company added a tidy little sum to its bottom line that year.

> **❝ It is impossible for you to predict how the intellectual property protection will pay off. If you have a properly-written license agreement, however, you are in a very strong position to enforce your rights. ❞**

My experience with intellectual property as it relates to this example illustrates the value of protecting your invention in as many ways as possible.

It is impossible for you to predict how the intellectual property protection will pay off. If you have a properly-written license agreement, however, you are in a very strong position to enforce your rights.

Government Infringement

The most surprising infringement that happened to me was when the US Government itself ignored the very patent it had issued me for my transparent calendar for the watch.

The Department of Defense had become a big buyer of my calendars for recruiting, until one day they decided to put it out for bid. Since they inquired directly to label makers, they found lower prices. After I lost the first of several big contracts to companies who simply copied my work verbatim, I spoke to my attorney to have him stop this "injustice." My attorney looked into the matter and informed me that the Department of Defense was invoking a little-known law (that was really intended for wartime) that permitted it to infringe any patent or copyright in the procurement of whatever it needed for the armed services. The same law provided for the patent holder to seek compensation after the fact through a claim, which I did. Uncle Sam paid me a cash settlement (that more than covered my legal fees) and took a license at 3% for future use. I decided to take the experience philosophically, and have a little fun getting some publicity out of the episode. You never know what a newspaper writer will do with your press release. (See clipping from *The Miami Herald*.)

Infringement Insurance

Few owners of intellectual property are aware that insurance is available to them that can protect them against infringement. It's called Infringement Abatement Insurance and it works like this. It reimburses you for your legal expenses when you have to enforce your patents, trademarks or copyrights against infringers, as well as for financial loss due to the defendant's insolvency. Usually, when you sue for infringement, the defendant countersues claiming invalidity of your patent, trademark or copyright. However, this type of insurance also pays your legal costs when your patent, trademark or copyright is challenged by such a countersuit. It covers US and foreign patents, trademarks and/or copyrights, as well as patent applications. I could find only one carrier that offers this type of insurance, but you can ask your independent insurance agent about it. You could have him contact the Intellectual Property Insurance Services Corporation located in Kentucky, or you can go directly to them. For one of my patents they recently quoted me annual premiums of $1300 for $100,000 coverage, and about $3000 for $500,000. (See Resource Section)

Trade Secrets

Stand-Alone Inventors usually do not get involved with trade secrets. A trade secret is a piece of intellectual property that can be licensed or sold in much the same way as a patent, although this would be very unusual. Trade secrets often relate to proprietary processes, formulas,

MINORITY RETORT

Stick It to 'Em, Bob

Peel off and press on firmly.

YOU'VE got to hand it to Robert G. Merrick. Well, not exactly, because the U.S. Government has to hand it to R.G. But since it will be handing him some of your money you could say you have to hand it to him.

Dance

And probably with no hard feelings. After all, when an ordinary citizen can catch the mighty U.S. Government, which has its own Patent Office, infringing on his own patent and collect damages and an agreement to pay him future royalties, it warms the cockles of all us little guys.

Robert did not have one of your tentative U.S. Pat. Pend. type patents, he had a full blown, flat-out Patent, No. 3,464,200, issued in 1969 and good until 1986. His patent is on a little transparent stick-on calendar which can be placed on the crystal of a watch to reveal to one, vis-a-vis the day of the week and the month, and the year, just where he is, timewise. There are 12 of these to a set, and Bob says it is simplicity itself to change months.

How did the U.S. Government wind up bootlegging Inventor Merrick's invention? Well it bought some from him as an advertising giveaway so that every time somebody looked at a watch he would see a little "Join The Navy" or Re-Up In The Marines" or "The Air Force Could Use Several Good Men — Or Women, Of Course," there being a little plug for this or that on each month's transparent calendar.

Having apparently met with some success with this see-through come-on, the U.S. Government then decided to buy $100,000 more worth of sets of calendars but contracted with other companies rather than Original Bob's, although these other people did not have a patent or a license from Crystal-Date Watch Calendar Co. of Sunnyvale, Calif., 94807.

The U.S. Government is supposed to know better than this, because it made the very laws that says nobody can do like that, including the aforementioned Government. Especially put out was Mr. Merrick, President of Merrick Industries, Inc., for not only was he losing business that he had had but he was losing it to a bunch of counterfeiters lured into swiping the fruits of his creative genius by Invitations To Bid issued willy-nilly by Governmental purchasing agents.

Mr. Merrick is pleased with the outcome because it is not just the principle of the thing, it's the money, too. And he is doing very well in that department with private enterprise, a more trustworthy bunch, and says more than half the "*Fortune* Top 500" are buying his stick-on calendars with various slogans and logos on them.

Reprinted from the Aug. 29, 1978 issue of

The Miami Herald
A KNIGHT NEWSPAPER

JIM DANCE

Figure 5-4. Even though my patent was infringed, I decided to have some fun publicizing the settlement. The news release I sent out was "straight," but this is what one writer did with it. My product got some extra promotional mileage because I circulated copies of this clipping to my distributors. "Any ink is good ink!"

techniques or inventions that are not subject to patents, or that the inventor chooses not to patent. After all, when you patent something, it gets published for all the world to see, and you may not want this. Secrecy may be more protective than a patent.

It is believed by many that the most famous trade secret is the formula for Coca Cola, said to be known only by three people. But others say that after many years, it was finally compromised.

The Inventor's Notebook

If you're going to think and operate like an inventor, you must start an inventor's notebook, sometimes called a workbook or journal. The one I use now goes back nearly 20 years. It had been my practice to record ideas in this book as they came to me and to continually develop ideas toward marketable products. Each entry marked my progress toward an invention

My patent attorney had advised me that some day I may find it very important to be able to prove the exact date I invented something, and the dates I made improvements to that invention. For example in the case of another inventor filing for a patent on an invention essentially the same as yours, the patent office calls this an interference. Usually the inventor to prove he is the first to invent will get the patent. I used a notebook because I thought it was mainly a good way to keep track of my ideas for products, and be able to go back and build on them as part of a creative process.

❝ It is believed by many that the most famous trade secret is the formula for Coca Cola, said to be known only by three people. But others say that after many years, it was finally compromised. ❞

One day, I realized my company needed a new product to boost sales. So I flipped through my inventor's notebook and stopped at a page where I had sketched a punch for business cards. This particular entry had been made about two years earlier, and I had made subsequent notes of several modifications and refinements. I recalled that my opinion at the time was that very probably it was not unique, and that someone had tried something similar before (unsuccessfully). But now was a good time to scope it out, which I did.

Looking back today, I realize how valuable my notebook is as a source of "ideas in progress." From this resource, I am able to select a viable idea for patenting and marketing. Had I not recorded that fleeting thought back then, and continued to develop that idea, my life might be quite different today.

Making an entry: First give your idea a title and record the date. Next, sketch it and do "call-outs" to label its parts. Make all entries in ink. Then beneath the sketch, write a clear description of your invention and its merits.

If you think this particular brainchild deserves it, have a non-related person witness your invention by signing after "Read and understood" and dating the page. The witness must understand the concept described. Be sure to date all your inventions, even if you do not have them witnessed. Finally, keep your treasured notebook in a nice safe place.

The book: Find a sturdy note book at the stationery store that has *stitched* pages and a stiff cover. Sit down and number all the pages if they aren't already numbered. Title it, "Inventor's Notebook" on the front cover. Be sure to put your name, address and phone number inside the cover. Get into the habit of recording your ideas regardless of what you first think of them. Later on, be more discriminating. But invent and record; invent and record.

> ❛ Making an entry: First give your idea a title and record the date. Next, sketch it and do "call-outs" to label its parts. Make all entries in ink. Then beneath the sketch, write a clear description of your invention and its merits. ❜

Competition and Knockoffs

After I introduced my Business Card Punch, I began hearing about other business card punches coming on the market. How can this be? Don't they know I have a patent? The first competitive unit I discovered was a product from Texas, and naturally it was bigger. Although, it was mainly plastic, it had many moving parts, including two metal springs, and it therefore cost much more to make. I don't believe I could have proved the Texan had infringed my patent, but I didn't need to. His punch bit the dust all by itself because of its higher price, and mainly—in my opinion—because it just didn't work very well. It didn't cut complete notches in the cards.

The next competitive unit I found was the creation of an engineer in Los Angeles. His punch was all metal. It consisted of several forged parts, two springs and some pot metal. It was very elaborate, had a retail box, and must have cost many thousand of dollars to develop. It had a nice visual design, and it worked well. I don't believe it infringed my patent.

His price was even higher than the Texan's, and maybe that's why his sales were nil. He ended up trying to sell his whole punch project to my company, suggesting I "could then offer both a Chevrolet and a Cadillac". I declined his offer and continued with the punch that was selling.

The most recent competition I spotted was in 1995 and it really made me mad. Though not an exact copy of mine, I thought it was similar in enough ways to be a knockoff. I discovered it hanging on a hook right next to mine in a retail store! The store was one of a very large chain. Rather than going ballistic, I sat down and calmly wrote a carefully-worded letter to top management. I mentioned my disappointment, and also my patent. Once I called their attention to what was going on, they reversed the situation, quit selling the knockoff, and continued with the real thing.

Before I wrote the letter, I had contacted my patent attorney. I asked him how big a lawsuit he thought we could file because of what had happened. He countered by asking me one simple question I'll never forget: "Do you want to *sue* your customer, or *keep* your customer?" After a moment's thought I replied, "Why don't I just write them a letter?" The lesson here is that it's not always necessary, or advisable, to resort to litigation—or even bring in lawyers—to get something like this straightened out.

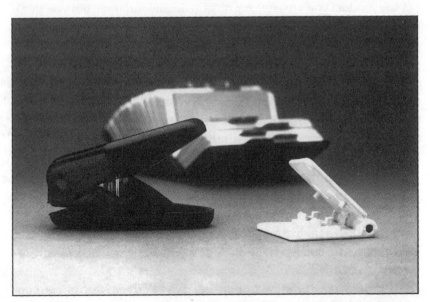

Figure 5-5. Punch Wars. Was it a knock-off or just honest competition? As it turned out, it didn't matter, because this Texas-sized business card punch (left) bit the dust at retail before it could make any trouble for me.

The Confidential Disclosure Agreement

As an inventor, you may need to disclose a product idea to someone before it is patented, or before you have applied for one. For example, you may want to show your idea to a vendor, potential investor, licensee, etc. But it could be risky to disclose an idea to anyone without complete assurance from that person that your idea will not be disclosed, because you consider it your property. A commonly-used device is the confidentiality or non-disclosure agreement. This is usually a simple, single-page document presented by the inventor to a company owner or other individual for signature before any information is disclosed. Read the one I use (see illustration), and you'll see how brief one can be. Be sure to write out a description of your disclosure and attach it to the agreement. Feel free to copy my form and use it. If someone won't sign it, don't disclose your idea to that person. This document could prove useful in a lawsuit in the event someone uses or discloses your idea in violation of its terms.

The Patents of Others

Sometimes in a search, you will discover an existing patent that looks like it might get in the way of a new invention you are working on. Say the product you are working on is generally different, but you think it could be judged to infringe one or more of the claims of the existing patent. You don't want to go ahead, because you would risk an infringement suit. What you should do is call the USPTO maintenance fee records office (703/308-5069). This office can tell you immediately if the inventor has paid the required maintenance fees to keep this patent in force.

> **Patent Maintenance Fees as of October 1, 1996: For individuals to keep an issued patent in force they must pay periodic fees as follows: $510 at 3-1/2 years, $1025 at 7-1/2 years and $1540 at 11-1/2 years.**

You must provide the records office with the patent number and the inventor's name. If you find the most recent maintenance fee has not been paid, and the 6-month grace period and the two-year restoration refiling periods have run out, then you are dealing with a patent that has irrevocably lapsed into the public domain, and you can ignore it.

If the fees have been paid, or are still payable, there is an opportunity for you to contact the inventor and find out if he or she has commercialized the invention. If not, you might be able to negotiate a license to use it. Such a license will enable you to market your invention as a product

CONFIDENTIAL
DISCLOSURE AGREEMENT

This agreement entered into between _____, (hereinafter known as **Inventor**) and _____, (hereinafter know as **Recipient**) confirms the terms under which **Inventor** will provide to **Recipient** proprietary information or material relating to the invention of the _____ for the assessment by **Recipient** for patenting, developing, manufacturing, and/or distributing the said invention, on terms to be established, leading towards the commercial utilization of such information or material. The disclosed information is summarized on Attachment A, and is made part of this agreement.

Recipient agrees that any such information or material submitted to it by **Inventor** shall be held in confidence, and will not be disclosed by **Recipient** or its affiliates directly or indirectly for a period of three years. **Recipient** shall use all reasonable diligence to prevent commercial use or disclosure by it, except to its necessary personnel from the day of signing of this agreement.

No obligation of confidentiality shall exist between either party in this agreement as to information or material that:

1. is public domain or becomes public knowledge through no fault of the party receiving said information or material; or
2. is previously known to and properly obtained by **Recipient** from other sources.

Any and all proprietary written material or other information in tangible form transferred to **Recipient** from **Inventor** shall, upon request, be immediately returned.

Nothing in this agreement shall be construed as granting either party any license or rights for any purpose under any patent or other intellectual property laws of the United States.

Signed:_____   Signed:_____

Print Name:_____   Print Name:_____

Inventor   **Recipient of Confidential Data**

Firm:_____   Invention:_____

Date:_____   Date:_____

Figure 5-6. A typical Confidential Disclosure Agreement (shown above) needs to include a written description of what you disclose. (You may copy this form for your own use if you wish.)

"manufactured under US Patent No. such and such". This approach could be effective and cheaper than going for your own patent.

NAFTA and Harmonization

Permit me to editorialize again for a moment: As an independent inventor I am troubled by a trend in Congress (seen in proposed and enacted legislation) to make our patent laws "harmonize" with those of other countries. On the part of the US, this has been a voluntary follow-on to the ratification of the NAFTA and GATT treaties. If this trend continues, it could seriously affect all independent inventors in the US, because of changes to our traditional policies.

For example, if enacted, some recent legislation would throw out our 200-year old " first to invent" patent priority policy, and adopt a "first to file" policy. This would mean that unless you file patent applications on all your ideas immediately, you stand to lose any rights to them.

> Recent patent laws enacted have changed the length of a patent's term, or period of enforceability. Any patent granted before June 8, 1995, and still in force, expires either 17 years from the patent grant date, or 20 years from the original filing date, whichever is longer. Applications pending on June 8, 1995, and later granted, would result in the same 17- or 20-year alternative terms. Patents granted on applications filed after June 8, 1995, carry only a term of 20 years from the date of first filing.

In its wisdom, and in direct opposition to the trend, the 1995 White House Conference on Small Business (made up of 2000 entrepreneurial delegates from 50 states) adopted Recommendation #115, which reads in part, "...that Congress protect international patent rights in a way that takes into account the needs of small business, including retaining the patent term to run for twenty years from the date of application or seventeen years from date of issue, whichever is longer, that a patent application remains unpublished until the patent is granted and that the patent remains with the first to invent rather than the first to file." If this resolution is enacted into law by Congress, it would help retain the integrity of our traditional patent system.

Congress needs to be convinced that independent inventors need to keep our old US patent policy to survive. The US built the most successful patent system in the world—so what's the rationale for changing our system to harmonize with other countries? I'm sure there are two sides to this debate, but in my opinion as an inventor, other countries would be better off if they were to conform to our system. If you agree with the White House Conference's recommendation, please consider this:

I suggest you photocopy this section of *Stand Alone, Inventor!* and send it to your congressman and ask for an explanation. Do this even if by the time you read this the "wrong" legislation has been enacted.

Note: The Resource Section begins on page 259 and is arranged by chapter to make it convenient for you to find related references.

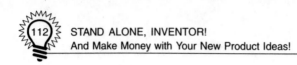

STAND ALONE, INVENTOR!
And Make Money with Your New Product Ideas!

CHAPTER 6

Financing Your Product

Use Your Own Money

This is going to be a short chapter. Not because there are so few ways to raise money, because there are really very many. But, because using your *own* money to self-finance your venture is the only option I recommend. My way might mean that you have to build up your savings account before you can start, but it is the best way. Remember, my Rule #8 in Chapter 1 says to keep your initial cash investment small. If you follow this rule—and it is very important—you should be able to pull together all the money you need by yourself, because it won't be very much. In addition, if you follow my Rules #5 and #7, you will be dealing with a simple product that has a low manufacturing cost—and it won't take very much money to make it.

If you limit yourself to your own money, you will avoid a lot of headaches that plague borrowers. Do your best to finance your first invention yourself. Why? Because in the event you fail, you can put it all behind you as soon as possible—usually with no outside debts to pay off. This will leave the way clear for you to begin saving for your next creation.

How to Self-Finance

Ways to self-finance are: dip into your savings account, borrow from your pension or profit-sharing plan, borrow from your life insurance policy, use your credit cards for business purchases, or persuade vendors to give you extra dating, or extended terms on their invoices. If you have a regular job and a lot of taxes are being withheld from each paycheck, you can re-submit your W-4 to reduce the tax withheld to zero, in anticipation of writing off your new business expenses. This will greatly reduce your tax liability. (But you must keep good records of your expenses to reduce your tax payment at the end of the year.) Once you are full-time self-employed, you lose this advantage, because the IRS will make you pay estimated taxes each quarter. All of these methods listed above are really borrowing from yourself—and the soundest way to go.

Other People's Money

Other people's money is also called "O.P.M." because, like opium, it's expensive and addictive. You may choose to ignore me and try to get some outside financing. But, you're going to find it's hard to raise outside money for new inventions. Most banks won't discuss it with you.

Our kind of deals are usually too small for venture capital firms to look at. And, new inventions are often too risky for you to want to involve your relatives and friends.

Royalty Financing

If you decide you must get an outside loan, consider royalty financing. This is where an investor (usually a private party) lends you a sum of money for the launch of your product, in return for a royalty on every unit of your product that you sell. This can be a good deal for you, because you don't have to re-pay *any* of the loan until you receive money from your sales. If your product fails, he's out the money, not you. Naturally, the lender is betting that over time you will pay him back much more money in royalties than he has loaned you. The longer you keep paying him after his break even point, the greater his return on the investment, but the greater your cost for the money. Depending on the royalty percentage in your agreement, you may want to put a "cap" on the total amount of money you are obligated to pay him. If the lender wants you to pay a 15% royalty, or more, put a cap on the payback of, say, two times the amount of the loan, or whatever both of you agree to. However, if it's only a 5% royalty, you may be willing to pay this amount indefinitely, with no cap, if that's what it takes to get the money in the first place. But, be sure to run the numbers, and make the necessary projections that show you can afford a certain level of royalty payments over a fixed time period. Then use a professionally-written agreement to protect yourself.

> **❝Our kind of deals are usually too small for venture capital firms to look at. And, new inventions are often too risky for you to want to involve your relatives and friends.❞**

Partnership Money

A lot of inventors and others who need money for a venture look for a silent partner, or even an active one. They find a person willing to put money into the venture, and enter into a partnership agreement. This agreement spells out the duties of each partner and the rewards that go to each partner. Partnerships have been likened to marriages—mainly because they have about the same failure rate. It's hard to find two people so compatible that they can get along through thick and thin, while fairly dividing the responsibilities and the profits. A lot of your time and energy is likely to be spent in meetings with your partner, instead of getting your product made and sold. If you end up going through a partnership breakup, the cost could be catastrophic.

> **❝ Try this method of financing if you must, but I do not recommend it because of its low success rate, and because it is in conflict to the concept of the Stand-Alone Inventor. ❞**

Try this method of financing if you must, but I do not recommend it because of its low success rate, and because it is in conflict to the concept of the Stand-Alone Inventor.

Sell Stock

You can do this if you want, but I thought one of the reasons we start our own business is to be our own boss. Guess what? Once you have stockholders, you have others to answer to besides your customers. I think it's tough enough to be an entrepreneur and build a business without having others breathing down your neck looking for a dividend or an IPO. Because of the expense, you should not try to finance the start-up stage by forming a corporation and selling stock. But, later on it may make sense for you to use this method to finance expansion that you cannot fund yourself. It may take 40% to 85% of your equity in your business to get the money you need, so be prepared to pay the piper. But be sure to look into other ways before you give away the store.

> **❝ But if your requirements for start-up cash are really big—say, several million dollars—you may have to abandon the idea of being a Stand-Alone Inventor, and go for venture capital financing. ❞**

If your requirements for start-up cash are really big—say, several million dollars—you may have to abandon the idea of being a Stand-Alone Inventor, and go for venture capital financing.

In this case I suggest you refer to a 1995 book called, *Starting Your Own BIG Business with Venture Capital,* written by William A. Gilmartin, who is a friend of mine. Bill has been a principal in two startups that used

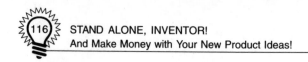

116 STAND ALONE, INVENTOR!
And Make Money with Your New Product Ideas!

venture capital financing, and his book contains some valuable insights. (See Resource Section)

Get Advice

To get ideas and suggestions, talk to other entrepreneurs who have bootstrapped their startup, and find out how they did it. In my own case, I borrowed from my life insurance policy and used our bank savings. Later on, I used my company's internal profits to finance expansion and subsequent new product launchings.

> **❝ I honestly never needed an outside business loan. My banker told me that this is a nice way to live. I figure he ought to know. ❞**

I honestly never needed an outside business loan. My banker told me that this is a nice way to live. I figure he ought to know.

Note: The Resource Section begins on page 259 and is arranged by chapter to make it convenient for you to find related references.

CHAPTER 7

How to Get It Manufactured

Making a Prototype

I t's important to realize that you need not be a tinkerer to be an inventor. Not all of us have the skills or equipment needed to make our ideas take shape. This is where industrial designers, machinists and model makers come in. For a fee, you can hire their skills to get anything from a rough design model, to a pre-production prototype.

It's easier to discuss the cost of manufacturing something when it's embodied in some form. For the inventor this usually means building a crude model or prototype that shows how the object looks and works. This is what is called a "concept prototype". If your idea is for a very simple product, you can probably create a prototype yourself.

> **Be prepared to pay several hundred dollars, or more, for a relatively simple prototype. If your product is big and complicated, a prototype will cost considerably more.**

If you have sketches and you are fairly clear how your product should look and work, you can probably go directly to a machine shop, cabinet shop, sheet metal shop, etc., and find a master craftsman who will create a scale prototype for you. Ask upfront for a dollar estimate to produce what you want.

Be prepared to pay several hundred dollars, or more, for a relatively simple prototype. If your product is big and complicated, a prototype will cost considerably more.

A rough prototype is useful in conducting an informal feasibility study. Talk to consumers, or to others in the field of the invention to get their evaluations. Don't be discouraged if someone is not impressed with what you show them. Often people lack imagination and cannot fully appreciate what you are proposing. You must carefully consider the source of all comments. It will be a very enlightening process. When it's over you must face all the reactions honestly, and recognize whether you are now *more* excited about your idea, *equally* excited or *less* excited. Press on only if you are left with at least the same level of excitement about your idea as before.

Next, you will want to show your prototype to potential manufacturers to get a rough idea of production costs.

Later, you will need to specify more exactly how all the cogs and wheels are supposed to come together, you may need to hire an industrial designer, mechanical engineer, or other expert to create a more finished prototype. A good designer can provide dimensioned drawings and build a working prototype. Typically, he will be able to suggest retail packaging, and even build a pre-production model suitable for showing buyers and/or using for photography. Often he can direct you to manufacturers you can see about producing the product.

The cost of "pre-production" design work depends on how complicated your product is, but figure $1,000 to $3,000 for a moderately simple object. With the drawings and model, you can do a more comprehensive test market to see what buyers say now. With luck, you can write some advance orders. Before working with any professional, make certain that he is experienced in your type of product. Have him show you examples of his work. Make sure he has good references and that he spells out exactly what he will do and what his price will be before he begins.

> ❛ All vendors should be willing to sign a confidentiality or non-disclosure agreement, which forbids him to divulge or use your idea for a certain period. (See Chapter 5) ❜

All vendors should be willing to sign a confidentiality or non-disclosure agreement, which forbids him to divulge or use your idea for a certain period. (See Chapter 5)

If you live near a university or college that has a design program, you can often hire senior design students to help you do much of this work, such as model-making, etc. (Senior or graduate marketing students can help you test market your idea, as well) While the cost will be less, the trade-off is that you forfeit the valuable experience and contacts of a professional designer. To locate a designer, call your local university or college, or look in the Yellow Pages under "Industrial Design." Or, you may want to contact the Industrial Designers Society of America (See Resource Section)

Stereolithography is the most advanced method for making proto-types. It's a computer-based process that works like this: First, you have someone generate a three-dimensional drawing (image) of your invention on a computer screen and save it as an electronic file. Next, a company like 3D Systems of Valencia. CA, takes your file and uses it to drive a stereolithographic machine.

> **❛ This machine passes pre-cision-guided laser beams through a polymer gel, and before long your invention exists as a solid three-dimensional object! The advantage of this method is speed and precision in the creation of prototypes. ❜**

This machine passes precision-guided laser beams through a polymer gel, and before long your invention exists as a solid three-dimensional object! The advantage of this method is speed and precision in the creation of prototypes.

Depending on the size and shape of your product, it may lend itself to this new process. There are about seventy companies in the US that offer this service. For the one nearest you, phone 3D Systems at 805-295-5600, Ext.2249 or visit their web site at www.3dsystems.com. (See Resource Section)

Here's Something *NOT* to Do Yourself: Manufacturing

Frequently inventors see me for advice about their first invention. Many tell me of their plans to purchase machinery so that they can set up to manufacture their new product themselves.

These inventors seem to think that once their machinery is delivered they can just sit back and watch it produce products. This is not a realistic expectation.

Typically, the machines that people have in mind are very costly. A manufacturing machine usually requires a trained operator and suitable space where it can be safely operated. All these requirements cost money, diverting bottom-line dollars to overhead expenses such as rent, lease payments and extra employee wages. Yet the inventor would probably need to run these machines only a small fraction of the time. Still, the operator of the idle machine must be paid. Dollars down the drain! My advice to the independent inventor is: if you want to stay in business and make money off your invention, don't get involved with manufacturing it yourself. A good rule is don't buy any machine that you can't already operate yourself. Things like copy machines and fax machines are okay, but things like milling machines and injection molding presses are not okay.

Sub-contracting Your Manufacturing

So, what is the best solution to the problem of getting your invention manufactured? Simply subcontract your manufacturing! This used to be called "jobbing it out," or "farming it out." Today, it is called "outsourcing." If you choose to do this, you will still be seen as "the manufacturer," which could be important to your businessman's ego and to your company's image in the marketplace. This is nothing to be embarrassed about. Say you invent a new specialty beer. Don't go setting up your own micro-brewery. Do like the originators of Samuel Adams Boston Lager and Pete's Wicked Ale do—they sub-contract with the big guys like Heilman or Stroh and use these breweries to actually make their product. This strategy enables the inventor to avoid big capital investments and to stick to his or her marketing. Many successful large companies avoid a lot of manufacturing by using sub-contractors. Even automobile factories are really assembly plants, with nearly everything outsourced.

> ❛Most manufacturers do not mind taking on outside projects because it means additional business that will help keep their machines busy and help cover their overhead. ❜

In the United States, we are very fortunate to have manufacturing facilities of every description located all over the country. Once you put your mind to it and spend a little time researching, it's easy to find a manufacturing subcontractor who will make your product for you.

Your Factory is Just a Purchase Order Away

What you need to do is identify and locate a factory that makes the kind of product that you have invented. For example, if you have invented a new kind of wire coat hanger, find out who is in the business of making wire coat hangers and where they are located. (In the next section, I'll show you how to locate potential subcontracting manufacturers for your product)

Once you have found several coat hanger factories, you simply write, fax or E-mail each of them to determine if they will give you a quotation to manufacture various quantities of your special coat hanger design.

Most manufacturers do not mind taking on outside projects because it means additional business that will help keep their machines busy and help cover their overhead.

In fact, many advertise to solicit custom or job business. By adver-

MERRICK INDUSTRIES INCORPORATED   BOX 2277, SUNNYVALE, CA 94087
(408) 738-2200 FAX/739-4351

REQUEST FOR QUOTATION

DATE	11/1

VENDOR

ABC COMPANY
555 MAIN STREET
ANYWHERE, CA

I.D. NO.		
PHONE	212/555-1212
FAX	212/555-1213

PACKED	WEIGHT	FOB POINT	PRODUCTION TIME	TERMS
ADVISE	ADVISE	FACTORY	ASAP	TBD

QUANTITIES	DESCRIPTION	QUOTE
1,000 5,000 10,000 25,000	WIRE HANGERS PER CUSTOMER DRAWING	

REMARKS	SHIP TO
PLEASE QUOTE COST OF ANY TOOLING REQUIRED	SAI ENTERPRISES 123 FIRST STREET CANTON, OH

AUTHORIZED SIGNATURE OF QUOTER _____

QUOTE EXPIRES	

ACCEPTED: _____

P.O.# _____   DATE: _____

ASI 70660
aSi
LISTED SINCE 1982

Figure 7-1. The Request for Quotation (RFQ) form provides a convenient way to get "apples-to-apples" price quotes for your requirements from various manufacturers. I usually Fax my requests on this form to several companies to get as many quotes as I can. (You may copy this form if you wish.)

tising, they are hoping for purchase orders from companies, even like yours.

Once you have your idea protected in some way, give your drawings and specifications to several manufacturers and request prices on various quantities. Remember that what you are doing up to this point is provisional. That is, until you find out what the minimum manufacturing quantities might be from various sources, and what the cost per unit turns out to be, you are merely exploring the feasibility of your new product idea. So don't worry about having to make commitments, because it's not yet necessary. Relax, gather and record as much information about manufacturing your product as possible. Your next step is to analyze the data you have obtained.

> **❝If you have enough information (and courage), and you go ahead and write a purchase order, for a grand total of $1,400, you have now begun your own business!❞**

You may find, to your pleasant surprise, that a relatively small quantity of your coat hanger product can be manufactured by one of the factories for a very reasonable sum of money. For example, you might find that the tooling, which in this case would be a custom modification of the machine to be used to shape your product, will cost, say, $1,000. And, after that, the manufacturing cost of, say, the first 5,000 units would be 8 cents per hanger. Ten thousand might cost 7 cents, 25,000, 6.5 cents, and so on. Adding a profit mark-up to this cost data will enable you to create a quantity price list, which you should send out with samples to prospective buyers. But, first you will need some samples!

What would it cost to lay in a minimum inventory of 5,000 hangers so you will have sales samples available. Let's see: $1,000 for the tooling, and 5,000 x 8 cents for the manufactured pieces, comes to $1,400. This is certainly a relatively modest figure for putting together a salable test inventory and actually being able to launch a business! And, it is obviously far less than what it would cost you to buy machinery, set it up and do the manufacturing yourself! And, even a lot less than you might hand over to one of those invention marketing scams!

If you have enough information (and courage), and you go ahead and write a purchase order, for a grand total of $1,400, you have now begun your own business!

The important lesson is that *you are only a purchase order away* from thousands of factories all over the country. So why set up your own fac-

MERRICK
INDUSTRIES INCORPORATED

BOX 2277, SUNNYVALE, CA 94087
(408) 738-2200 FAX/739-4351

PURCHASE ORDER

D-U-N-S 04-922-9164
RESALE# SRGH 26-624630

Job Number:

Vendor Contact:

Phone:

FAX:

268580
asi
LISTED SINCE 1968

PURCHASE ORDER #

5678

VENDOR Code:

ABC COMPANY

555 MAIN STREET
ANYWHERE , CA

SHIP TO

SAI ENTERPRISES
123 FIRST STREET
CANTON , OH

DATE	CONTACT	DATE WANTED	SHIP VIA
01/02/97		ASAP	TRUCK

QUANTITY	ITEM NO.	DESCRIPTION	UNIT PRICE
5000	1-A	WIRE HANGERS PER CUSTOMER DRAWING	$0.08
1	EA	TOOLING FOR ABOVE	$1,000.00

Please make every effort to ship quantity ordered
The maximum acceptable overrun or underrun is 10%, to be billed pro-rata, unless specified on this order.

SPECIAL INSTRUCTIONS

1. FIRST ARTICLE APPROVAL REQUIRED BY CUSTOMER.

COST	CONDITIONS
$1,400.00	1. Ship this order only. 2. Do not correspond with our customer under any circumstances without our permission. Return all cuts, artwork, photos, etc. to us. 3. Acknowledge and advise shipping date. Refer to our order number on all correspondence. 4. Your firm name must not appear on or in this shipment. 5. We reserve the right to reject any goods not delivered on time or not in accord with the specifications and conditions of this order

John Smith

AUTHORIZED SIGNATURE

Figure 7-2. You will need your own purchase order (P.O.) form once you are open for business. Make sure you put all of your requirements for your order on this kind of form, and make sure your vendor acknowledges. (You may copy this form if you wish.)

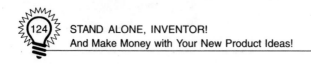

124 STAND ALONE, INVENTOR!
And Make Money with Your New Product Ideas!

tory when somebody else's factory is standing at the ready, available for you to use?

Locating Potential Manufacturers

You may be thinking, "Exactly how do I go about finding these manufacturers or factories?" You could start by checking the AT&T 800 Directory (hard copy or Internet), which is organized by industry, and lets you call around toll free. The next place I usually check is the good old *Thomas Register*, which is the most comprehensive listing of manufacturers and their products in the United States. There are usually about 25 huge green hard-bound books in the *Thomas Register* set, which large libraries are likely to have. These books list products and services from "Abacuses" to "Zoo equipment." (It is

> ❝No doubt your nearest library has the *Thomas Register* or other directory of U.S. manufacturers. Once you become familiar with such resources, you'll find them invaluable. ❞

also published in a computerized, CD-ROM format.) Just for fun, let's look in the 1996 Thomas Register Vol. 8, which is from "Handles" through "Lacquers." Turning to page 14,448, we find the beginning of the listings for "Hangers."

Once we get past "Aircraft Hangars" and "Hardware hangers," we find "Advertising hangers" of which there are 16 manufacturers. Farther on down the listings we find a huge category of "Hangers, garment," of which there are more than 25 manufacturers listed!

Many of the manufacturers have paid *Thomas Register* to include their advertisement and/or catalog sheet in addition to their free listing. Check these out to see what more you can learn about each factory and what it can offer. Try to find a factory that is located nearby, if possible, so you can visit there in person (and later keep your freight costs down). I usually begin by telephoning a selected list and chatting with whoever the switchboard operator or voice mail computer puts me through to. This is always an interesting learning experience, to be sure! My goal is to qualify each source, and to find the person to whom I should send my Request For Quotation, or RFQ, if they will entertain one. I'm not worried, because there are so many to try.

No doubt your nearest library has the *Thomas Register* or other directory of U.S. manufacturers. Once you become familiar with such resources, you'll find them invaluable.

Another way to search is to go to the library and ask for *Bacon's Magazine Directory* or *Standard Rate & Data* and look up the trade magazines, for example, of the dry-cleaning and laundering industry. (Section 17 in *Bacon's* - Cleaning, Dyeing & Laundry). You will find there are over a dozen magazines published in this field, including *Dry-Cleaners' News*, *Laundry News* and *the American Laundry Digest*. If you contact the publishers of these magazines and get copies of the issues, you will find advertisements placed by manufacturers of products for this industry, including the advertisements of *hanger manufacturers*. I've found the best way to get a copy of one of these magazines is to call the magazine's advertising department. Tell them you have a new product and that you may want to place an ad some day. The advertising department will be more than happy to send you a recent copy of their magazine along with an advertising rate card, etc.

Later, contact the advertising sales rep in your area who sells for this magazine. You will find that this person will be a storehouse of information about the dry-cleaning and laundry industry. He or she may even know people at some of the coat hanger factories (advertisers) and help you find the person who will quote on manufacturing your new invention. Caution: Do not unintentionally disclose information about your invention to ad sales reps, as many are notorious gossips! (Later you may want to intentionally feed them some of your hype!)

If you don't have a patent, or a patent application on file, before you disclose your new idea to any manufacturer, you will want to take steps to make sure that the manufacturer will treat your product idea as your property, and agree not to make your product or a similar product for anyone else. Figure 7-3 is the kind of letter agreement I used to tie up my Lint Mitt vendor for many years, although my idea was never patented.

Plastic Injection Molding

If your invention can be made of plastic, it may lend itself to production using *injection molding*. This is a very efficient way to mass produce plastic parts with a high degree of uniformity. There are thousands of different plastic materials to choose from. There are plastics of all colors that are hard, soft, clear, unbreakable, elastic or heat sensitive, etc. With the help of your molder, you can find a plastic with the exact properties you need for your new product. You can have him mold test samples using different varieties until you find the right material.

MERRICK
INDUSTRIES   INCORPORATED

Littlefield Packaging Corp.
Attn: Mr. Jack Martin, Pres.
6823 Watcher Street
Commerce, CA 90040

Subject: Exclusive Sales Agreement

Gentlemen:

When signed by both parties, this letter will constitute the entire agreement between Merrick Industries, Inc. (MERRICK) and Littlefield Packaging Corp. (LPC) with regard to sales and purchases of a specialty envelope promoted as a disposable lint remover (PRODUCT).

Inasmuch as MERRICK designed the PRODUCT, is in the process of obtaining trademark and copyright protection for same, and desires to have LPC manufacture the PRODUCT exclusively for MERRICK, it is necessary to have the following agreement:

1. In consideration of MERRICK'S promotional investments and other efforts to create a market for this new product, LPC agrees to sell the PRODUCT, i.e., all envelopes intended for use as disposable lint removers, exclusively to MERRICK.
2. LPC further agrees to keep confidential the product details outlined above until after the first orders have been produced.
3. LPC further agrees to notify MERRICK at least 30 days in advance of any price increase relative to the quotation dated 10/12/78.
4. MERRICK agrees to purchase the PRODUCT exclusively from LPC.
5. LPC agrees to refer all inquires received at LPC directly to MERRICK at P.O. Box 2277, Sunnyvale, CA 94087, Area Code 408/ 738-2200 for processing by MERRICK

If all of the above is acceptable, please execute the original of this letter and retain a copy for your files.

Submitted: Accepted:

_____   _____
Robert G. Merrick, President   Jack Martin, President
Merrick Industries, Inc.   Littlefield Packaging Corp.

Date:_____   Date:_____

BOX 2277 • SUNNYVALE, CALIFORNIA 94087 • (408) 738-2200 FAX (408) 739-4351

Figure 7-3. Use this kind of two-way exclusive letter agreement to tie up a manufacturer when you don't have a patent. If he wants your business, he'll sign it, but he may require you to purchase at certain minimum levels to keep it in force.

Plastic injection molding requires the precise machining of solid blocks of steel into a two-piece mold. Sometimes molds are referred to as "tooling."

> **❝ Plastic injection molding requires the precise machining of solid blocks of steel into a two-piece mold. Sometimes molds are referred to as "tooling." ❞**

The mold is mounted on a molding machine, or press, which opens and closes the mold. With the mold closed, under very high pressure the machine injects or shoots plastic material, which has been heated to its melting point, filling the mold. In the next few seconds the plastic material cools a bit and solidifies, the machine opens the mold, and the finished part is ejected and drops into a bin. The same cycle is repeated. Usually, a molding machine can produce your parts automatically without an operator, if the mold is designed to provide for this.

The advantage of injection molding is that the cost of the parts produced by such a process is quite inexpensive compared to any other way of making them. The exact cost is determined by four variables:

1. **The number of cavities** in your mold (Multiple-cavity molds cost more, but because they multiply the part production rate, they reduce your cost per part.)

2. **The volume, and or weight** of the plastic material required for each part, and its cost, relative to alternate materials.

3. **The cycle time,** which is the elapsed time to close the mold, to inject the plastic, and to open it and eject the part. The faster the cycle time, the greater the rate of production.

4. **The size of the machine used,** because the larger the molding machine used, the higher the hourly cost to operate that machine. The size of the machine required is determined by the size and weight of your mold, which is a function of its number of cavities and the size of the part to be molded.

Rate of Production

Cycle times vary, but let's say you use a two-cavity mold and your cycle time is 20 seconds. You'll produce two parts every 20 seconds, which is 6 parts per minute, 360 parts per hour, or 2880 parts per 8 hour shift. Run three shifts and you'll produce 8,640 parts per day. So, if you land an order for a million pieces, you must allow at least 116 working days, round-the-clock production, barring any delays! If you expect to land orders of this size, you may want to build a four-cavity or eight cavity mold, if practical.

In the United States there are literally thousands of injection mold makers. Most of them are "job shops." This means their business is fabricating custom molds for companies and individuals. Usually, they will also have machines to mold the parts for you.

I find it imperative to have the *same* company that builds the mold—run the parts. If you use *different* companies and the molded parts are unsatisfactory, one will blame the other, leaving you in the middle.

I have found that the company that makes the mold and runs the parts usually will guarantee the maintenance of that tool indefinitely, so long as you leave the tool at that location. If you accept this kind of arrangement, and later decide to move the mold, you may incur a mold removal charge. So read your agreement carefully.

> ❝I find it imperative to have the *same* company that builds the mold— run the parts. If you use *different* companies and the molded parts are unsatisfactory, one will blame the other, leaving you in the middle.❞

Made-in-USA vs. Off-shore

It is possible for you to save money by having plastic parts or other products made in China, Taiwan, or other Pacific Rim countries, typically called "off-shore." You could also consider Mexico, South Africa and many other countries.

How do you decide whether to have your plastic parts made in the USA, or go with foreign production? As a general rule, if your plastic part is somewhat complex, having moving parts and/or close dimensional tolerances, it is best to do the *development* work close to home. Have your molder build you a single-cavity mold made of a "soft" steel or aluminum. This is called a development mold. It is quicker to build and less expensive than a production mold of hardened steel, though it won't last as long.

The "soft" development mold permits you to run experimental parts, make modifications to the mold, and fine tune it to get the parts shaped exactly as you want them.

My advice is to do your development work in the U.S., but do your mass production off-shore, depending on the quotations and proposals you receive. You should be able to save 30-50% with off-shore production.

The reason I like to do my development close to home is that the process requires a lot of going back and forth to your vendor—molding parts, testing them, making adjustments, molding more parts, evaluating, etc. It is best to do all of this nearby in your own language to save time and to keep careful control of details. Keep molding here if your runs are only 5,000 or 10,000 pieces. Off-shore economies are for long runs that let you amortize the transportation costs, duty and agent's fee over a greater number.

A development mold is a temporary mold that is not expected to last very long. It should be suitable for running your initial production of 5,000 to 10,000 parts. Sometimes a development mold will hold up and run 40,000 to 50,000 parts, perhaps even more, before it gives out.

Meanwhile, you can be having a multi-cavity hardened-steel production mold built, if your sales indicate it will be needed. A hardened steel mold can run many parts before wearing down and needing repair or replacement: 400,000 to 1,000,000 "shots" or cycles is not uncommon. Since hardened-steel molds are more costly and take longer to build than development molds, do not invest in them until you feel certain you can sell the kinds of quantities they will produce.

❬ The "soft" development mold permits you to run experimental parts, make modifications to the mold, and fine tune it to get the parts shaped exactly as you want them. ❭

At the point when your development mold is producing acceptable parts, I recommend that you send samples of them with a mold drawing to a mold maker off-shore. Request quotations on: a) The fabrication of single-cavity and various multi-cavity molds of hardened steel, and b) the cost to run parts from each of those molds, say in quantities of 25,000, 50,000, 100,000, 250,000-up. Again, with off-shore molders, make the same company responsible for fabricating the tooling *and* doing the molding, so you won't be caught in the middle.

If your part does not require close tolerances and is not complex at all, you can send your prototype off-shore for production quotes immediately. Always require that a "first article" proof be sent to you for evaluation and approval before production begins. If the first article proof is not acceptable to you, specify your changes and require additional pre-production samples be sent until they get it right. Once you receive acceptable parts, mark one indelibly as "approved", and return it as the first article approved. Your purchase order should spell out that, "all parts

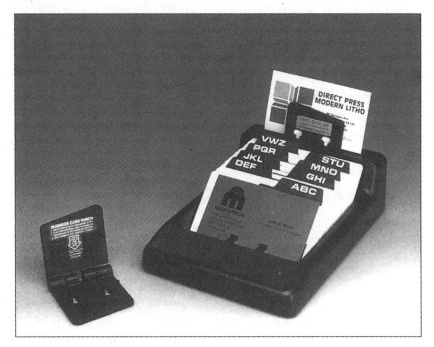

Figure 7-4. The business card punch (left) is an example of a small plastic injection-molded object that is made off-shore. The file tray shown is an example of a larger object that happens to be molded in the USA.

must conform to the approved first article sample." Should you receive parts that do not conform, you can reject them.

Your purchase order for off-shore production should also require that additional production *run* samples be sent to you by Federal Express for your approval from the *middle* and *end* of the run before you authorize shipment.

Through your sourcing agent, have the off-shore factory guarantee that the parts they produce and deliver shall be identical to the original "first-article" samples you approved.

Off-Shore Agents

If you go off-shore, it's recommended that you work through a sourcing agent. The sourcing agent will assist you in getting quotations from reliable factories in other countries, and will have the multi-lingual capability needed to translate your order into production in Hong Kong, Taiwan, or wherever. More important, the sourcing agent will have the leverage needed to have the vendor take care of quality or delivery problems. This is because the agent has on-going relationships with certain vendors that also serve his other clients.

The sourcing agent will advise you with regard to payments to the vendor. Sometimes a bank letter of credit, or "L.C." is necessary. If so, you must establish a relationship with a commercial bank that will issue a letter of credit. This is a safe way for buyers to pay for imported goods. It holds up any payment until certain stipulations have been certified. With an L.C. you must put the total payment amount in an account at the bank. Also, you must work with the bank and help them draft the terms of the L.C. You will want to require that your goods be inspected and certified to be of a specified color, quantity and quality, that they are packed as you specify, and that they are ready for shipment by a certain date. These types of stipulations go into the letter of credit, plus there may be other items relating to transportation methods and costs, payment of import duty at US Customs and other freight forwarding responsibilities.

> **‘ Typical fees charged by a sourcing agent for services are 15% for plastic injection molds, or other tooling, and 5% to 10% on production parts, depending on the product complexity, and the size of your orders. ’**

I suggest that you talk to a "freight forwarder" (See Resource Section) and have him/her give you a five-minute course covering importing products, letters of credit, customs clearance, duties, costs of transportation and the like. Freight forwarders will be very willing to spend time with you, because later they will want you to hire their services to handle your imports.

The sourcing agent is the person you will communicate with about all your orders. He or she can help negotiate lower prices, handle various questions, and arrange for production schedules and shipping dates. Some agents can arrange terms for you, such as 50% down with balance paid when goods are received.

Typical fees charged by a sourcing agent for services are 15% for plastic injection molds, or other tooling, and 5% to 10% on production parts, depending on the product complexity, and the size of your orders.

One sourcing agent I have used is Feeco Limited with offices in New Hampshire and Hong Kong. Another is International Procurement Sourcing of Taipei. (See Resource Section)

Note: The Resource Section begins on page 259 and is arranged by chapter to make it convenient for you to find related references.

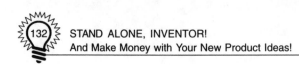

132 STAND ALONE, INVENTOR!
And Make Money with Your New Product Ideas!

CHAPTER 8

How to Get Free Hype

How to get your inventions noticed, talked about,
and sold — all over the country — without
spending much of your hard-earned cash.

"Good mousetrap builders so they say
can scarcely keep the world away!"

—Olive Tardiff

Wouldn't it be wonderful if Ms. Tardiff's sentiments were *true*? ...You put your time and money into an invention, create something truly new and useful, somehow word leaks out about it, and before long people start breaking down your door wanting to buy your invention. People in your market just seem to *know* about your product—and you never have to mess around with public relations, marketing or distribution.

Unfortunately, in the real world *"it just don't work that way!"*

Smart marketing and advertising are essential to the success of any commercial venture. That's why companies spend billions of dollars every year on print and broadcast ads for new products ranging from pump-up basketball shoes to cars with airbags. According to news stories, a pharmaceutical company recently coughed up $120 million just to announce a new pain remedy called Aleve™. Also, if Windows 95™ is so sensational, why did Microsoft plunk down $200 million to launch it? The fact is, *your* wonderful new invention isn't going to sell itself either. You're going to learn quickly that you have to market it and promote it if you want to succeed as a Stand-Alone Inventor.

But, before you reach for your checkbook and begin throwing your hard-earned cash at advertising agencies and marketing consultants, let's take a look at some of the many ways you can get newspapers, magazines, radio, and even television to spread the word about your invention, free. It's called public relations (PR), or hype.

Media Hype: What it is, Why you need it

You've been working on your invention for months now — maybe years. You've revised it, refined it, de-bugged it, and forged it into a finished product. You've found the right materials, fine tuned your manufacturing process, and mapped out your distribution channels. Now, at last, you're ready to launch it—your baby—into the marketplace.

But now you face a typical problem: Nobody knows about it — not even those who need it, and might actually buy it. So your next logical step is to do something to get the word out.

Exactly how do you go about getting the word out? The first answer that probably jumps to mind is, "With advertising." But as an inventor, you know the first answer isn't always the best one.

Advertising is very important. But it's usually very expensive. Unless you've got a bank roll that would choke a llama, you will want to consider some alternatives to paid advertising, especially when you first set out to market your invention. But even if you have sufficient funds to launch a major advertising and marketing campaign, remember two things: (a) paid advertising in the media cannot buy the same *quality* of exposure you get when the media themselves write and talk about you, and (b) you should go for all the free publicity you can get *before* you run any paid ads.

Publicity, or "media hype," is really a llama of a different color. Surveys show that readers consider editorial matter—newspaper stories, magazine articles, broadcast news reports—much more believable than paid advertising. It is true that you should be "talking" about your invention, all the time, everywhere, to everyone. But when someone else talks about it, there is much more weight and credibility in the communication. This is geometrically true when the "talker" is the media, especially the mass media.

> ❝As a Stand-Alone Inventor, you must learn how to promote your invention yourself. I'm betting you'll even enjoy the process. ❞

There's a good reason to hold back initial advertising until you've fully exploited the news value of your announcement through publicity: Editors may not be very enthusiastic about your news story if they've previously seen your ads trumpeting the same news.

My dictionary defines "hype" as "excessive publicity and the ensuing commotion." At times hype carries the connotation of deception. But I'm using the term here as it relates to stimulation or excitation in the marketplace. Never try to mislead anyone, when you go after media hype. Your objective is to stir up the market, get people excited about your invention, and stimulate them to go out and buy it for its true benefits and features.

It's not that difficult or costly to generate media hype at the level needed to announce your new invention. But, you will have to invest a little time and creativity.

As a Stand-Alone Inventor, you must learn how to promote your invention yourself. I'm betting you'll even enjoy the process.

Many inventors I talk to are reluctant to try publicizing their inventions themselves. They say, "Look, I've done my work. I invented the thing. Let the professionals handle the hype." But self-promotion is a necessary part of the process of succeeding on your own. My advice is, don't fight it. Jump in with the same fervor and determination you used to give form to your ideas in the first place. Inventing is a creative endeavor. So is promoting. You will be rewarded many times over for your efforts.

The Fine Art of the Press Release

A press release is a carefully prepared news story, which you hope an editor may reprint in whole or in part. A reporter may use it as background to begin work on a longer article. A brief release may be the announcement of your new product. Articles may be about you and your invention; or you may be just part of the story. You don't have much control over what's written once you send out your press release. But, if you get mentioned in print or on radio or TV, the release has served its purpose. Figure 8-1 is a release I used to introduce my business card punch.

The release shown was done in the customary format that you should follow when you put together your press releases. Don't worry about fancy letterheads; editors aren't impressed by them. Do your best to keep your release to a single page, though sending out a two-pager is no crime. Always double space. Put your name, address, and phone number at the top of the release, to give editors and reporters someone to call for more information. If you have one, include your E-mail address and/or the URL for your web page. Maybe you never thought about get-

FROM: Merrick Industries, Inc.   CONTACT: Judi Harper
      Box 2277   Phone: (408) 738-2200
      Sunnyvale, CA 94087   Fax: (408) 739-4351

FOR IMMEDIATE RELEASE: August 1, 1986

(New Punch Helps Organize Business Cards)

A California company has introduced a new punch that makes business cards work like Rolodex® cards. Merrick Industries, Inc. of Sunnyvale, CA, reports that its new hand held punch puts twin notches in business cards with a single squeeze. The custom-punched cards fit the twin rails of ordinary 2-1/4" X 4" rotary card files or 'flip-file' trays, such as those made by Rolodex, Bates, Eldon and others. The new punch will be sold in stationery and office products stores at a suggested retail price of $8.95.

A two-piece assembly, molded entirely of glass-reinforced Nylon, the punch has no metal parts. The cutting prongs themselves are shaped like human teeth. "It was the only design that would work in plastic," CEO Bob Merrick says. "They are surprisingly sharp and durable. In tests, the device has punched 5,000 cards without wearing much, or failing," Merrick says.

Merrick says, "Secretaries and others can use the punch to avoid transcribing voluminous data onto blank cards. Salesmen can punch their own cards when they see their prospect uses a Rolodex® file. Homemakers can use the punch with their Rolodex® file to keep track of the many business cards they receive from contractors and service companies."

For more information, contact Merrick Industries, Inc., Box 2277 Sunnyvale, CA 94087. Phone (408) 738-2200; Fax (408) 739-4351.

Figure 8-1. This is the new product announcement press release I used when I launched my business card punch. It was mailed to dozens of trade magazines with a 4x5 glossy photo.

ting calls from nosy reporters, but keep in mind: you *want* them to call you.

An editor may run your press release as is, shorten it, reword it, or

Figure 8-1a. This is the 4"x5" glossy photo I included with the press release. Its caption read: "New punch from Merrick Industries makes business cards work like Rolodex® file cards. The user simply inserts card and squeezes the punch. The punch will be marketed through office products stores."

give it to a reporter to use as background. In order for an editor to be able to run your release unchanged, it has to read like the news stories he would normally print. This means the first few paragraphs must answer the obligatory *"who, what, when, where, why, and how"* questions of your product or story. All of the "answers" to these are best included in the first three or four sentences, and can be in various sequences. Expanded and less important information follows in descending order with the least important data last. The reason you want to follow this inverted pyramid format is that editors often cut stories arbitrarily from the bottom-up to fit them into their pages or broadcast scripts—you don't want any of your important stuff lopped off!

> **❛ If all this sounds like a lot of writing, don't worry. Nobody is expecting you to become a professional writer. ❜**

If all this sounds like a lot of writing, don't worry. Nobody is expecting you to become a professional writer.

There are plenty of free lance writers out there you can turn to for help if you feel you need it. But, for now, take a stab at this challenge yourself. Read a few trade magazine and newspaper new product stories, and try to copy their language and format. Keep it simple and straightforward. Get help from friends and family. Read some books on publicity (see Resource Section). And above all, remember: editors are more interested in *what* you have to say than *how* you say it.

Before you go to all this trouble, you're probably wondering, do press releases really work? The answer is, without a doubt, *yes*. A survey conducted a few years ago by *The Columbia Journalism Review* shows just how well they work. This survey revealed that 111 stories published on the inside pages of one issue of *The Wall Street Journal* were generated from press releases submitted by organizations and individuals. According to the survey the releases ran mainly word for word in many cases; additional facts were added in only about a third of the stories.

Of the hundreds of releases I have personally sent out over the years to various newspapers, newsletters, trade publications, and magazines, almost every one was run verbatim by at least one publication. Others were run virtually unchanged, paraphrased, or led to a related story.

In the beginning of your promotional campaign you will want to monitor your efforts fairly closely; you will want to keep track of who is publishing your materials, when, and where. Some inventors I know include a self- addressed, stamped post card with their press kits for this purpose. On the back is a pre-printed statement, which reads something like, "We will be publishing the news of your invention in our (blank) issue."

I recommend using this approach only in the beginning, until you get a sense of how certain editors are responding to what you submit. You should call the editors who do not return your post card to keep after them. (Note: Many editors hate to be bothered like this, especially while trying to meet their deadlines, so you'll need to be very brief and businesslike when calling.)

Your Press Kit

Eventually you will want to approach the various media organizations that might give you the kind of story or article you're looking for. You will want to be armed with your most basic marketing tool: a press kit.

A press kit is nothing more than an envelope or folder containing a press release, a photograph, and possibly an assortment of public relations materials. These can include your personal biography, or "bio," a catalog sheet on your product, a brochure, ad reprints, and photocopies of press clippings. This package becomes a ready-made file for use by media editors and writers.

Your first press kit can be very simple. For example: the original press kit for my Personal Punch™ consisted of a one-page press release, a black and white glossy photograph of the punch, and a sample of the punch itself.

Reporters and editors use press kits as starting points for articles they write; in some situations, editors will select a certain release and its photo and print them both, as is. This could happen with your press kit announcing your invention.

The press kit is a tool you will use continually to promote your invention. As time goes on, you will modify it and add to it. Any changes or improvements to your invention should be reflected in your kit: new colors, additional applications, peripheral products. The current press kit for my Personal Punch™ now includes a two-page press release, a catalog sheet and a selection of press clippings that didn't exist when I first put it together. Now, I also include references to some of my other inventions I'd like to promote, though each of those has its own kit as well.

Put time and care into preparing your press kit, and always have several on hand. You never know when an opportunity to get some free hype will present itself. I always keep a stack of press kits in my office, in envelopes, ready to mail out at a moment's notice. And, whenever I travel on business, I take several press kits along in my briefcase.

What's Wrong With This Picture? *A word about photos*

Every inventor's press kit should be sent out with a good "glossy" product photo. The photo should be black-and-white, with a one- or two-sentence descriptive caption typed on a strip of paper that is taped to the back. (This is always expected by editors who want to ensure your photo will be matched up with your release if they get separated.)

Your product photo is very important, so this is not the place to pinch pennies! If you want it to be published, your photo must tell a story, and be of reproducible quality. Snapshots taken by you or a friend, unless you are professional photographers, are not likely to be good enough to be

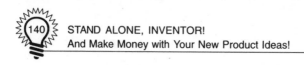

140 STAND ALONE, INVENTOR!
And Make Money with Your New Product Ideas!

used by editors.

I urge all inventors to go to a professional studio for their product photos. Avoid shopping mall portrait shops. Check the *Yellow Pages* under "Photographers-Commercial" and locate a pro with the experience and special studio set up for doing product shots. Take a careful look at his or her sample album; if there are not a lot of good product shots in it, go somewhere else. Always get cost estimates and negotiate prices before you choose a studio. Once you locate the professional you want to work with, explain that you want the photo to be suitable for newspaper and magazine publicity; he will know that you need optimum-contrast prints that will reproduce well when printed.

> **❛Some people will tell you that editors want big 8"x10" glossy photographs. I have not found this to be true.❜**

Also, be sure to get black and white shots taken along with your color transparencies. This is easy for the photographer, because once he's finished your color shots, he need only insert a cartridge with black and white film and shoot some exposures. But don't be talked into accepting so-called "color conversions," unless they are done by computer. Insist that the photographer shoot both black-and-white, and color film. You will be spending only a few dollars more on your product shots, and the extra expense will result in usable photos—what editors are looking for.

Some people will tell you that editors want big 8"x10" glossy photographs. I have not found this to be true.

I always send prints that are 4"X5"; they are cheaper to buy and they fit nicely into a #10 (letter-size) envelope. This makes photos more convenient for you to handle and cheaper to mail. And no editor has complained to me yet.

It is important to get the best price you can find on your photo print reproductions. Multiple prints bought at the photo studio can be very expensive, especially when you consider how many of them you will be sending out. One way to cut down your photo costs is to utilize a photo duplicating house. I found a company in Hollywood, California, that mainly reproduces publicity photos for movie stars. You can work it with this company so your cost is about $0.25 to $0.50 apiece (See Resource Section). I usually have them print 100 eight-by-ten sheets with four 4"X 5" photos on them. Then I simply cut them up myself, so that one 8"X10" print yields four 4"X5"'s. I get four hundred press kit photos for about a fraction of the price. So can you.

Using Your Press Kit

Now that you've put together your basic press kit, you must decide how you are going to use it. You could employ a shotgun approach and send out hundreds of kits to editors all over the country. Many people do this with varying degrees of success. But this approach is not very cost effective, and I don't recommend it. Why waste your time with editors whose readers are unlikely to have any interest in the area of your invention? My advice is to use a targeted or rifle approach.

Your First Consultant

Avoid fancy public relations firms that get big bucks for helping clients target their audience or markets. You can handle this yourself with the help of a consultant whose fee you've already paid with your taxes: your librarian.

Your local librarian is an invaluable resource during this stage of your promotional program. Behind his or her desk are reference books that are essential to your efforts. They list not just the titles of publications that are appropriate for your invention, but also the names of editors who will be making the decisions about whether to run your release.

A good place to start your library research is with the *Encyclopedia of Associations*. This two-volume set lists hundreds of organizations around the country, many of which publish magazines and newsletters for their members. Also included in most of the listings are phone numbers and addresses, which you can use to secure a copy of association publications—an essential step.

Standard Rate and Data, a telephone book-sized volume, which is used by advertising agencies to research magazine advertising space rates, lists every magazine that takes advertising, both consumer and trade, published in this country. A new issue is published every few weeks, so it's a simple matter to acquire a copy of your own if you try. Just ask a local advertising agency if they will give you one of their recent older copies before they toss it.

Bacon's Magazine Directory lists every trade magazine published in North America. Each periodical is listed by market under headings, such as electronics, computers, clothing, machinery, etc. The entries also include some details about each publication, such as names of editors and whether the magazine accepts new products stories, photographs, etc. *Bacon's Newspaper Directory* lists every daily and weekly newspaper, news service, and news syndicate in North America, along with additional data.

Every two or three years I buy a copy of both *Bacon's* directories. Since the volumes are priced at around $270 per set, I can't really justify the expense of buying new editions every year, but I've found them to be quite useful for at least two years at a stretch. You may find that your library has Bacons.

> **❝ Some magazines have what is called "controlled" circulations that require readers to be in a certain specialty or hold a particular title before they qualify to receive the magazine, which is free. ❞**

The *Oxbridge Directory of Magazines and Newsletters* is another important resource. (See Resource Section)

The most important question to ask yourself as you compile your list of likely publications is, who are the readers of these magazines? If your efforts are successful and you manage to elicit a printed story about your invention, these are the people who will be reading it. Are they the ones who will *need* and possibly want to *buy* your invention?

While you conduct your research — which really shouldn't take more than an afternoon or two — talk with your librarian about what you are doing. He or she will probably have some great ideas that haven't occurred to you to help you with your research. This person is a valuable resource; be sure to get acquainted!

Selecting Your Target

As you look over your list of potential media targets, keep in mind your objective: to build consumer awareness of your invention in the marketplace. (Some inventors will target distributors, only, which is a mistake.) Publications with big circulations can be important, but don't overlook the little magazines, local weeklies, and industry newsletters — especially the ones with readerships that include potential users of your invention.

Publications in and around your hometown present perfect targets on which to sharpen your aim. They're close, they're friendly, they generally have the kinds of local news sections that are perfect for your story, and you are local, too—that makes your achievements automatically of interest to local editors.

I took this approach when I sent out my early press releases announcing my business card punch. I selected three local newspapers, and every one of them picked up my story and ran it. I photocopied the clippings on a sheet to show what the media were writing about my new product. This sheet went into my press kit and was also included in mailings to wholesalers, dealers and others.

"Niche" publications present very important opportunities for targeted exposure. *Home Office Computing, Bicycling, Dog Fancier, Car and Driver,* and *Popular Mechanics*; readers of these types of narrow-focus consumer publications have already been culled from the general population by virtue of their interest in the topics covered by the magazines.

But, few publications are more bulls-eye-targeted than what are called trade publications. They are written by and for specialists and professionals in a particular field, and they are almost never found on the racks of newsstands.

Some magazines have what is called "controlled" circulations that require readers to be in a certain specialty or hold a particular title before they qualify to receive the magazine, which is free.

Other trade magazines have "paid" subscribers whose special interest in the magazine's subject is strong enough to motivate them to pay for their subscription. Talk about targeted marketing—half your work is done for you—a direct shot at people certifiably interested in your type of product!

> 6 Most trade magazines contain about 50 percent *advertising* pages, with the other half *editorial* pages written mainly from news releases submitted by companies promoting products. 9

For example: Say your invention is an outside thermometer for an automobile. You will certainly want to contact the automotive editors of general circulation newspapers. Also, niche consumer magazines, such as *Car and Driver, Popular Mechanics* and dozens of others. But, I recommend starting with the automotive trade publications. In addition to spreading the word to potential buyers, the trades will elicit inquiries from those wanting to help you distribute your thermometer. Of the 400-plus publications in the automotive field, there are about 100 magazines specifically for industry segments, such as brand of car, etc. If you want to communicate with "car people," I can't think of a more direct pipeline to them.

Most trade magazines contain about 50 percent *advertising* pages, with the other half *editorial* pages written mainly from news releases submitted by companies promoting products.

Because the trades usually have few or no reporters on staff, they rely heavily on their mailbox. So, the appropriate trades will be the most receptive publications to the type of releases you will be submitting.

Once you've selected a publication, get your hands on a recent issue. This is very important. Only by seeing a copy of the publication and reviewing its editorial content will you know for certain whether it's a good one for you.

When you have a copy of the publication in your hand, thumb through it. Look for departments that might lend themselves to your needs, such as new product sections, special news briefs, gift idea sections, and even people profiles. Then direct your release to the department(s) of your choice.

Tailoring your press release to the style of writing in the publication you have targeted is often a good idea, but not essential. You can create a single version of your release and just send it out. This is what most people do, even professionals.

But remember, the closer you come to giving the editors exactly what they want, the more likely they are to publish your release, usually in the exact words you wrote it.

If you're not sure whether it's a good idea to send your press kit to a particular publication, I say, go for it. *When in doubt, send it out.*

Always err on the side of over-exposure. You might be wasting some time and postage, but you never know where a contact might lead. It reminds me of the story about the publicist who said, "I know only half the magazines I mail to will print my release; If I knew which half, I wouldn't have to send it to the other!"

Alert the Media

Now that you've targeted a few publications, I recommend one more step before sending out your press kit. Place telephone calls to the editors. Keep the calls short; editors are usually very busy. Tell them who you are and that you are announcing a new product you have invented. Ask if they would be interested in receiving your press kit, and who is the appropriate person to send it to. You want your kit to reach a person by name, a person with whom you can follow up. Be sure to include a cover letter to that person — your contact — in which you mention your earlier phone conversation, and say thanks.

Always remember: Editors usually need you as much as you need them. You saw in *The Columbia Journalism Review* study how many stories were the result of press releases. Editors are under great pressure to

Card Punch

Merrick Industries, Inc., Box 2277, Sunnyvale, Calif. 94087, has developed a punch which cuts two slots in a business card to make it attach directly to

Rolodex* files. The Exec-U-Punch punches "T-slots" in a business card, which enables the card to be attached directly to an existing file tray or wheel. Punch is made of glass-reinforced plastic for lightweight durability. It contains no metal parts. Rolodex* is a registered trademark of Rolodex Corp. **For More Information Circle No. 525.**

The Office, August 1985

Showcase USA September/October 1985

BUSINESS CARD PUNCH

Business Card Punch

The new Exec-U-Punch cuts the correct pair of slots in a business card to make it attach to ROLODEX® or other files instantly.

According to the manufacturer, Merrick Industries punch is made of glass reinforced plastic for sharp and light weight durability. There are eight special dividers included. For information contact: 1 Shannon, Merrick Indust 690 W. Fremont Ave., 2277, Sunnyvale, CA 9- Circle No. 161 on Action

MEDIA SUPPORT

▶ **They Beat Us to the Punch** and come up with one of the most ingenious solutions ever to a familiar problem. Exec-U-Punch™ lets you punch two T-slots at the bottom of every business card you collect, so you can slip it right into your Rolodex® tray or wheel for easy future reference. So much simpler than stapling or pasting, or retyping the information; it's handy at work or at home, for filing away needed services or new acquaintances. (File under B for Brilliant!) 2¼"x2," (#J941328), $8.95.

ADAM YORK

Business Card PUNCH & CARD FILE Punch two slots in every calling card you get for a simple, quick-access address, phone and business reference file, or punch cards you give customers for their own snap-in files. Slots fit standard 1" centered, two-rail files. Our file holds 500 cards (500 blanks included to supplement information to business cards you file). Executive-style pen fits base for ready access. A-Z index.
N-9558-5 Card Punch $9.95
N-8796-5 Card File $14.95

THE BUSINESS BOOK

Business card notcher from Merrick Industries, Inc., punches business cards with correct pair of notches to attach to Rolodex, similar trays, wheels having 1" rails. Punch made of glass-reinforced plastic; available plain, with custom imprint. Pg 100

Reader Info 206

Merchandisers...

Countertop display holds blister-

DEPARTMENTS

6 **LETTERS**

12 **ENTREPRENEWS**

18 **MAKING IT HAPPEN** Julius Erving teams up with the real thing; Quality software at softer prices; A hubby or your money back; A two-time winner's grand finale

24 **VENTURE SURVEY** Creating an image

PERSONAL PORTFOLIOS
28 A lousy judge of character backs winners
32 Some rules of the

Merrick: A fad fanatic   P. 46

New!
$8.95 ea

ROLODEX®-COMPATIBLE!
BUSINESS CARD PUNCH
Use our new hand held punch to cut two T-slots in a business card. We guarantee card will now attach to 1" ROLODEX® and all similar files, or your money back. No more taping or stapling business cards to pre-punched blanks! A unique timesaver for office or home. Made of glass-reinforced ceramic-like nylon. Ask for it at a stationery store, or send check* to factory for immediate shipment. Ask your ad specialty man (or factory) about logo imprints and quantity discounts. Patent pending.
MERRICK Box 2277, 690 W. Fremont Ave. Sunnyvale, CA 94087-0277.
*Send $8.95 plus $1.00 for postage and handling to

2 THE WALL STREET JOURNAL
THURSDAY, OCTOBER 3, 1985

Figure 8-2. This is a montage of pasted-up press clippings and small-space ads from trade magazines. I reproduced this as a media support sheet and sent it out to my wholesalers, dealers and sales reps. Do this with your clippings to document your promotions and to keep people thinking about your product.

fill up their publications with useful, newsy stories, and they have to face those blank pages month after month, week after week — even day after day. Sometimes they may sound annoyed because they are often stressed out, but they usually don't mind getting your calls — especially if you don't waste their time and you lead them to stories they can use.

The knowledge that most editors are going to be pleased to get anything you send them should make it easier for you to pick up the phone and make your first contacts. Don't be shy. Your announcement may seem trivial when compared to the current news of crime in the streets and political scandals, but releases like yours are the life blood of certain editors. Your job: Find them.

After you send out your press kit, wait a week or so, and then call back. Follow-up is very important. Just because they haven't published your story yet, doesn't mean they aren't interested. You want to make sure your "material was received." It might be in a file somewhere, or lost, or under the many piles of paper that burden every editor's desk. Ask if they got your press kit. Ask if there are any questions. Ask if they think they will be running your story. Offer to be interviewed. Be courteous, but persistent.

> ❝When you are starting out as a Stand-Alone Inventor, you have the advantage of putting all your PR effort into just one product. However, the PR efforts of big companies are diluted, because they are spread over dozens of products that need attention. So don't be afraid to overkill with PR on your first product. ❞

Be prepared to hear that no one knows what you're talking about. Your press kit is either at the bottom of a pile, lost, or in the trash. So, also be ready to send out another kit. Address it to the person who told you to send it, and then follow up with that person.

Remember, the important thing is to get editors to just look at your story, to simply get their attention. To do that, you may have to be persevering — not annoying, just determined. Once you get their attention, and schmooze with them a bit, there's not much more you can do. Editors will either run your story, or they won't. Don't get so attached to the outcome that you lose your perspective. Play the odds.

When you are starting out as a Stand-Alone Inventor, you have the advantage of putting all your PR effort into just one product. However, the PR efforts of big companies are diluted, because they are spread over dozens of products that need attention. So don't be afraid to overkill with

PR on your first product.

Since you can stay focused on one product for a long time until you get results, your job is easier. In general you can be more effective.

One has little or no direct control over the press. But, that hasn't stopped me from getting lots and lots of free hype, and it won't stop you.

Persistence Pays Off: The Road to *The Wall Street Journal*

From the beginning I had a goal to get something about my Personal Punch printed in the pages of *The Wall Street Journal*. Hands down, the *Journal* is the most prestigious business publication in the world. But after all, my new Punch was proving to be a very useful *business* product. I believed that somehow, some way my punch deserved some ink in the *Journal*. At this stage in my marketing efforts any decent mention of my punch in a publication of this magnitude would almost assure its success.

Yet, how does one go about getting a relatively insignificant little "Stand-Alone" product mentioned in a big, imposing, national publication like *The Wall Street Journal*?

I thought my big break had come when I met a *Journal* reporter at a convention. We struck up an acquaintance, and I learned that his beat was small business. Since I was, of course, a small business, when I returned to my office I wrote my new buddy a letter and enclosed my press kit. I never got a reply, and I never got any ink! So much for the power of inside connections!

About two years later, I noticed that the *Journal* had a column appearing every Thursday called "Form and Function." I noticed it talked about innovative designs in anything from architecture to various commercial products. So, I tracked down the writer and called him at his office at home in upstate New York. I told him about my Personal Punch™ and he said he would be interested in receiving a press kit. I gave him time to receive it, and then I called him to follow up. He said he got my kit along with sample punch, and he liked it. But, unfortunately he said my story was a straight product puff, and he didn't see a way he could justify mentioning the punch in his column. He said he needed a "peg" to hang this kind of story on, and he just couldn't think of one.

While we were talking, an angle for his story just popped into my head. I said, "Do you know that more than 30 million business cards are exchanged every business day in the US, and this punch is designed to help business people organize all those cards?" (Notice how many times the word "business" is used.)

He decided to use my quote as his "peg" and he wrote about my punch in his column. The story, about one column by six inches, appeared on the front page of Section II above the fold of the paper.

Talk about the value of free hype! I checked the *Journal's* advertising rate card and did a little figuring. If I had to pay for a display ad the same size as this article, my cost would have been $7,222.60!

(But the *Journal* doesn't even *sell* advertising space on the front page of Section II!)

The Wall Street Journal is sold on newsstands and delivered all over the U.S. to more than 1,850,000 business people who pay for the privilege. After the story ran, consumer inquiries about my punch increased dramatically at many office products dealers, and many new dealers were convinced they should carry it in their stores. Plus, I got many letters from big corporations inquiring about the punch for use as a promotional product.

> **❝Talk about the value of free hype! I checked the *Journal's* advertising rate card and did a little figuring. If I had to pay for a display ad the same size as this article, my cost would have been $7,222.60!❞**

The lesson here is, don't give up just because you hear a "no" or two, or because some reporter doesn't call you back. If you are told your story won't run, ask why. Try to help the media people you talk to see how they can use your story. Don't try to force your ideas of what's newsworthy on them. Instead, find what it is they think is newsworthy and try to help them. Sometimes you just have to splash around until you hit it. Your job is to keep splashing.

And one more thing, don't ever think your product isn't worthy of the big prestigious publications. Because I persisted, my little eight-dollar product was heralded in the almighty *Wall Street Journal*. I still send a copy of that *Journal* clipping out with almost every mailing. The Journal story took my invention out of the doldrums of an obscure novelty item and lifted it into the realm of a certifiable business product.

Keep the Hype Going

When your invention is new — that is, before you've got it established in the marketplace — its very existence is automatically of some interest to the media. "New" almost always equals "newsworthy," and your story about a new product will be considered by editors.

But what about later, after your new product has been out there for a while? How do you keep the hype going after the newness of your in-

THE WALL STREET JOURNAL.

© 1988 Dow Jones & Company, Inc. All Rights Reserved.   ...   WEDNESDAY, FEBRUARY 17, 1988

FORM+FUNCTION
BY STEPHEN MacDONALD

Students' Bobsled Heads for the Gold

KEEP YOUR EYE on the bobsled that the U.S. two-man team will be piloting in the Winter Olympics in Calgary this weekend. It was designed by students at Ohio State University in Columbus.

According to Attila Bruckner, assistant professor of industrial design, the project began as a classroom exercise more than a year ago. The students studied Olympic rules, interviewed drivers and surveyed existing sleds. They then designed and built 25 scale models and tested them in a wind tunnel.

Ordinarily, that would have been the end of it, but the students liked the results so much that they couldn't stop. They were determined to build a sled and get an Olympic driver to try it.

Lots of people and companies helped, including Du Pont Co., which provided the sled's Kevlar skin; Cytemp Specialty Steel Co., Titusville, Pa., which fabricated the alloy runners, and Richardson/Smith, a design firm in Worthington, Ohio, where the sled was assembled.

Brent Rushlaw, the leading U.S. driver, has agreed to use the sled this Saturday and Sunday in Calgary. He may also use a stock Italian sled on some runs.

Mr. Bruckner believes the student sled may well be faster than the "state of the art" Italian model. The OSU sled's No. 1 advantage, he says, is an aerodynamic shape that reduces drag 20% to 25%. "When you stand near the chute, you can hear the difference," he says. "Most sleds whistle—a sound generated by turbulence. Ours is much quieter."

In fact, he says the students thought up several other improvements that they didn't include.

"The effect is creepy," says Tama Starr, vice president of Artkraft Strauss Sign Corp., a New York marquee and sign company that designed and executed the outdoor touches to resemble the design of the play's original theater in London. She adds that this kind of adornment has been popular in England "and now it seems to be catching on here."

Business Cards Do Double Duty

MORE THAN 30 million business cards are exchanged each business day, according to Robert G. Merrick, a Sunnyvale, Calif., businessman, inventor and president of Merrick Industries.

That's a generous estimate. But whatever the number, it's probably safe to say that most of them are soon thrown away, perhaps after their contents have been copied elsewhere.

Mr. Merrick found that wasteful, so he used to trim cards he was given and stick them on a blank rotary-file card. When that became tiresome, he invented Exec-U-Punch, a small plastic device that chops two holes in the edge of a card. This allows the card itself to fit on the tracks of a rotary file.

The punch is made of fiberglass-reinforced plastic. "The tricky part of this was developing a mold that would produce edges that can punch cleanly and are durable," says Mr. Merrick.

One problem: Sometimes the punched holes obliterate important information on the card. Mr. Merrick's response: "It's still easier to copy a phone number on some other part of the card than it is to recopy the whole thing," he says.

But he's also encouraging business-card designers to leave a blank space where the holes go.

Figure 8-3. The *Journal* has a paid circulation of 1.85 million readers. I reproduced this clipping and used it as a sales promotion enclosure in mailings and responses for years. (Reprinted by permission of *The Wall Street Journal* © 1988 Dow Jones & Company, Inc. All Rights Reserved Worldwide.)

vention has worn off? After all, this is when you really need continuing hype— when your new product is on thousands of store shelves all over America, waiting to be discovered by the consumer. It needs to be "pulled" through the distribution channels, as they say.

The good news is, it takes a long time for the newness to wear off. There are many millions of people who would benefit from your invention who do not hear your message over the noise of all the advertising that surrounds us. To these millions your story is still new and exciting, still newsworthy. This often continues for the first 2 or 3 years, maybe longer!

The bad news is, the people of the press don't always see it that way. To many editors, your invention is old news the day after your story runs. I choose to ignore this belief. One of my practices is to re-send the same new product announcement to all the same publications every six months. Repeat runs are not uncommon, especially in the trade magazines. Sometimes—without you doing a thing—editors will run your photo story again, because they need a space filler and can't find anything else!

Later on, it becomes a little more difficult to get additional press coverage. To keep things going, you will have to look a little harder for something newsworthy to talk about.

Take a closer look at the events surrounding your work as an inventor. Chances are, you will see that something newsworthy is almost always happening: You changed the size, sold your millionth one, achieved national distribution, appointed XYZ Company to be master distributor. Maybe you landed a large order from a well-known company. Maybe there has been some legal action, say, an infringement; someone has tried to knock off your patented product and you're taking them to court. (A lawsuit is always news!) When you win the suit, that news becomes another "peg" on which to hang a story for another press release.

> **❛Later on, it becomes a little more difficult to get additional press coverage. To keep things going, you will have to look a little harder for something newsworthy to talk about.❜**

My search for the correct plastic material for my Personal Punch led me to the duPont Company and their glass-reinforced Nylon. When duPont celebrated the 50th anniversary of the invention of Nylon—*their* latest excuse to send out a press release—I joined in on their celebration when they purchased 5,000 Personal Punches emblazoned with a duPont logo to give away as a memento of the event. duPont also wrote about my punch (at my urging) in their "external house organ"—a magazine going out to the industrial customer base they serve. More free hype!

Finally, refer to the directory of *Books in Print*, and look for existing and planned non-fiction books in your field. Contact the author and see if he or she would consider mentioning your product in their text. Example: I learned of a book called *Organizing Your Home Office for Success*, by Lisa Kanarek. We spoke and she decided that two of my products would be appropriate for her readers to know about. She mentioned my business card punch and tabs with illustrations. This turned out to be valuable exposure, when her book turned into a best seller with many printings, even in foreign languages! My products were also mentioned in another book called, *The Portable Office* by Stuart Crump, Jr.

> ❝ So, whenever you print something new, draft a new literature release describing it and send it far and wide to the trade press. You'll be surprised how much pick up you will get. ❞

The New Literature Release

It's not a new product, it's just a new catalog sheet back from the printers. Nevertheless, trade magazine editors will print new literature announcements from manufacturers. Catalogs, data sheets, charts and the like are all of interest.

So, whenever you print something new, draft a new literature release describing it and send it far and wide to the trade press. You'll be surprised how much pick up you will get.

Your Inside Connection: The Space Rep

If you find you're having trouble generating editorial interest in your publicity efforts, try this: Contact the magazine's advertising department. This is especially useful when dealing with trade publications, where you are seen as a potential buyer of ad space. Connect with an ad sales representative, called a "space rep." Send him or her your release, then ask the rep to pass it along to the appropriate editor. This usually works; here's why:

Ad reps, called space reps, are after your money. They want you to spend it on advertising space in their magazines. So, it's in their best interest to help you. In many cases they are highly influential and can grease the skids and get something happening for you in the editorial department. More often than not they will be able to help you get your press

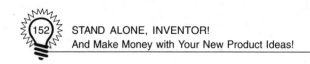
release printed in their magazines.

Later on, if your release doesn't run, you can call the space rep and nag him/her about it—something you just don't do to an editor. (Many editors become wary at the slightest hint of editorial influence by advertisers.) In general, the space reps are more likely to go to bat for you. It might be best to begin your promotional program by calling space reps. They are always great resources and you can ask them various questions about the ins and outs of the industry in general.

> ❛ You can help the writer, and yourself, by bringing the particulars of *your* invention to his or her attention. ❜

But this is not a black-and-white situation. Many times magazines keep their editorial and sales functions strictly separate. Anything that smells of promotion is reviled by those on the editorial side.

In this situation the space rep might say, "Send it to Margaret. She edits the "Tid Bits" department. But for God's sake, don't mention my name." In which case, you still found out the best place to send your press kit. The space rep can be your personal "mole" inside that publication!

One Nearly Sure-Fire Way to Get Your Name in the Paper

One of the most newsworthy stories in any inventor's life happens the day his or her invention is awarded a patent. Your patent will be listed in *The Official Gazette*—published every week by the US Patent and Trademark Office. About 2,200 patents are listed numerically in each issue. Every entry includes a drawing of the invention and at least one of the patent's claims to define the invention.

Fortunately, for Stand-Alone Inventors, there is a column called "Patents" printed weekly in newspapers across the country by the *New York Times Syndicate*. (See Resource Section) It features three or four interesting inventions that received patents recently, usually the previous week. To find these inventions, the writer of this column regularly pores over the pages of the *Gazette*, ferreting out whimsical and goofy inventions, but also serious technological breakthroughs, all of which make for interesting reading in the column.

The columnist, of course, is free to write about any of the inventions listed in the *Gazette*, but sifting through 2,200 listings per week can be a bit mind boggling.

You can help the writer, and yourself, by bringing the particulars of *your* invention to his or her attention.

I did this myself in 1989. I had discovered the "Patents" column in the *San Francisco Chronicle* and kept my eye on it. When I learned that the patent on my Personal Punch™ was about to issue, I telephoned the columnist in his Washington, DC office and told him about my impending patent. Although he didn't seem very interested, I sent him my press kit. I knew he wanted his column to be timely, so I did this a month before my patent was to issue. (You can find out in advance from the Patent Office the exact date your patent will be issued, once it has been "allowed " by the examining section.) Try this when your next patent issues.

I went out of my way to try to make my story newsworthy for him. I talked to him about the punch head being shaped like a human tooth. I gave him a statistic about the numbers of business cards handed out on an average business day. I tried to make the story of my patent interesting and give him some good stuff for his column.

> ❝ Remember, almost as important as getting the ink, is making photocopies of the news clippings and sending them to your wholesalers, sales reps and dealers, to keep the hype going. ❞

Apparently I succeeded, because my punch got about six inches in his "Patents" column, which goes out by wire to 600 subscribing newspapers worldwide. It appeared in more than 200 major daily newspapers in the U.S. The result of this exposure, though not precisely measurable, was to greatly increase public awareness of my punch. This fact was used as valuable sales ammunition for my reps, wholesalers and dealers. That is why I photocopied the "Patents" clipping and sent it to them for their sales people to use during calls. I made hay with that clipping by enclosing it with everything I mailed for about a year.

Whether or not the story of your invention appears in "Patents," send a press release and product photo to *Inventors' Digest*, which has a "Patents Issued" department. Also, your hometown daily and neighborhood weekly newspaper editors, are very likely to give you some ink.

Remember, almost as important as getting the ink, is making photocopies of the news clippings and sending them to your wholesalers, sales reps and dealers, to keep the hype going.

When You've Exhausted All the Freebies, Try This

Have you ever noticed that the inside of the front page of many major daily newspapers is a kind of catch-all page, and usually includes an off-the-wall photograph of marginal news value? Well I have. One day,

I noticed a particularly goofy photo and thought to myself, Hey, as long as they're not looking for hard-breaking news (whoever *they* are), why not

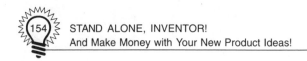

The New York Times

SATURDAY, OCTOBER 7, 1989

Patents | Edmund L. Andrews

Teeth in a Puncher
Shaped Like Molars

Simple inventions are not always simple. Witness Robert G. Merrick's Personal Punch, a finger-sized device that punches holes in calling cards so they can be put on a Rolodex.

The puncher consists of two one-inch-square plates, connected by a hinge. Two teeth are mounted on one of the plates, which cuts holes through a card when the plates are closed together.

So what's new? The teeth, said Mr. Merrick, founder of Merrick Industries in Sunnyvale, Calif. To cut holes more easily, each tooth is shaped like a human molar — edges on either side and a depression in the middle. The design allows the puncher to cut through cards with only light pressure between the thumb and one finger.

He reports brisk Sales. The United Stationers Supply Company, an office supply wholesaler, is selling 17,000 units a month to retailers. The store price is $5.95.

Mr. Merrick received patent 4,869,143.

Patents are available by number for $1.50 from the Patent and Trademark Office, Washington, D.C. 20231.

Figure 8-4. This syndicated column went out by wire to 600 subscribing newspapers worldwide. It appeared in more than 200 major dailies in the U.S. (© 1989 by the New York Times Company. Reprinted by permission.) Do you think this kind of free publicity put my product on the map? You better believe it did!

try to get an unusual picture of my invention to appear in this space?

So I began looking into this phenomenon. Where did these photos originate? How could I get my invention pictured in that spot? Eventually, I discovered that many of these kinds of news photos came from independent photo services that supplied them to newspapers through national wire services.

I approached one such photo service, called Wagner International in New York City (see Resource Section). It was operated by a retired wirephoto editor. For a fee this editor would shoot a memorable, visually-striking photograph of your product, write a brief caption, then deliver it in person to his contacts at the wire services. They also printed and circulated sheets of "clip art" photographs—stock photo stories intended for use by weekly newspapers in every state. In addition to getting my photo sent out over the wire services, as part of the package, our photo would be included on this sheet. If you can submit your own acceptable photograph to Wagner, your fee is less than $1000 for the package (as of this writing).

I decided to hire this service. The (goofy, off-the-wall) photograph they took of my punches eventually ran in several hundred newspapers across the country! Not exactly free, but more hype at an almost negligible cost compared to that of display advertising.

Another commercial news service, NewsUSA, Inc., (see Resource Section) which I discovered and used, is in Vienna, VA. It takes a similar approach. But instead of focusing on a photograph, they write a straightforward news story for you, in which you may include a photograph. Then they send the story out by wire, computer, and mail, along with clip-art sheets, to thousands of newspapers around the country who receive these stories free.

When the stories of your product are published, NewsUSA collects news clippings and sends them to you. Their fee for this package in 1994 was about $2,600. After I used this service my story appeared in many newspapers, and I was sent dozens of news clippings with labels identifying each publication, its community, and its circulation. My distributors loved me for it! I'm trying to talk News USA into giving a deep discount to Stand-Alone Inventors like us. Most of News USA's clients are big organizations like GM who can easily afford the $2600 fee. But we "little guys" need something like this we can afford, too!

And, since there are a lot of us, maybe News USA could make it up in volume.

AP Photo

Figure 8-5. This attention-getting photo, with a caption that talks about my business card punch, was sent out over the wires to newspapers all over the country. For weeks after, I received clippings from the hundreds of papers that printed it free.

Figure 8-6. These are clippings (from a newspaper clipping service) of a paid story News USA transmitted to 10,000 newspapers for us. It was picked up by literally hundreds of newspapers, as documented by News USA's clipping service. This is good sales ammunition for your reps and dealers.

Ongoing Relationships

One professional copywriter I know has a rule of thumb regarding the frequency of press releases: Send out one a month every month, whether something newsworthy has happened or not!

I'm not sure I agree with him, but as a Stand-Alone Inventor, you will certainly want more than just a one-time nod from the media; you want to develop ongoing relationships. That's one good reason to send out a press release any time you can generate one.

The likelihood that every one of your releases will produce a lot of printed news stories is next to nil, especially if you send out 12 or more a year. But when you present yourself regularly to newspeople, something else happens: they start thinking of you, not as a nagging promoter of inventions, but as a resource. Perhaps they set you up on their Rolodex under "I", and they begin to look on you as more than just the guy or gal who cobbled together a new product—you are the inventor they know. You possess knowledge and expertise useful to reporters looking for background, searching for story context, or just trawling for a quote.

This is especially true if you are helpful when they call. It's a good idea to develop and maintain a list of local editors and newspeople. Keep track of them. Let them know you're still in business and available to help them.

This attitude—this orientation to the press—was largely responsible for my accepting an engagement as a guest on a radio talk show. I was serving as the president of the California Inventors' Council when a producer at a radio station in San Francisco called me, looking for someone to talk about inventing and to answer questions on a call-in show. I recognized this as an opportunity to both promote my inventions and serve as a resource to media folks.

So I volunteered to appear on the show myself. I garnered huge credibility from that appearance, and had a great time doing it.

Networking

For Stand-Alone Inventors, the opportunity to promote inventions with free publicity doesn't begin and end with the media. To be in the right place at the right time to be able to take advantage of these opportunities, you have to get out of your home or office and do some networking. A good way to start is to join a local inventors' club, of which there are more than 400 in the U.S. (See Resource Section.)

NEWS USA
2300 Clarendon Blvd., Suite #308
Arlington, VA 22201
703-841-9500 fax 703-841-9513
KNOWN PLACEMENTS TO DATE

Page Number: 3
Report Date: March 3, 1992

Bob Merrick
Merrick Industries
690 West Fremont Avenue
Sunnyvale, CA 94087

Newspaper	City, State	Clip Date	Circulation	Published	Readers
Derby Daily Reporter	Derby, KS	09/23/91	4,350	Daily	12,180
Ponca City News	Ponca City, OK	11/13/91	14,000	Daily	39,200
Hanover Evening Sun	Hanover, PA	11/13/91	19,964	Daily	55,899
Hebbronville View	Hebbronville, TX	11/14/91	1,100	Weekly	3,080
Oyster Bay-East Norwich Pennysaver	Huntington, NY	11/20/91	12,152	Weekly	34,026
Owensboro Messenger-Inquirer	Owensboro, KY	11/24/91	34,000	Daily	95,200
Foster's Democrat	Dover, NH	11/26/91	30,000	Daily	84,000
This Week	Portland, OR	11/27/91	468,731	Weekly	1,312,447
Aberden American News	Aberdeen, SD	11/27/91	19,174	Daily	53,687
Seaside Post	Seaside, CA	11/27/91	10,000	Daily	28,000
Parkesburg Post-Ledger	Quarryville, PA	11/27/91	1,559	Weekly	4,365
Quarryville Sun-Ledger	Quarryville, PA	11/27/91	2,629	Weekly	7,361
Stanton Register	Stanton, NE	11/27/91	1,800	Weekly	5,040
Sedgwick Pantagraph	Sedgwick, KS	11/28/91	481	Weekly	1,347
Halstead Independent	Halstead, KS	11/28/91	1,700	Weekly	4,760
Atlanta Constitution	Atlanta, GA	12/05/91	285,000	Daily	798,000
Louisville Daily Record	Louisville, KY	12/05/91	450	Daily	1,260
Antelope Valley Press	Palmdale, CA	12/08/91	55,000	Daily	154,000
New Carlisle Sun	New Carlisle, OH	12/11/91	4,440	Weekly	12,432
Florissant Independent News	Florissant, MO	12/12/91	38,500	Daily	107,800
Kentucky Enquirer	Cincinnati, OH	12/13/91	17,830	Daily	49,924
Cincinnati Post	Cincinnati, OH	12/13/91	115,900	Weekly	324,520
Cincinnati Enquirer	Cincinnati, OH	12/13/91	197,000	Daily	551,600
Cincinnati Herald	Cincinnati, OH	12/13/91	25,000	Weekly	70,000
Chesnee Tribune	Spartanburg, SC	12/18/91	1,500	Weekly	4,200
Morrow County Sentinel	Mt. Gilead, OH	12/18/91	5,400	Daily	15,120
Jacksonville Journal Courier	Jacksonville, IL	12/19/91	15,000	Daily	42,000
Eatonton Messenger	Eatonton, GA	12/19/91	3,750	Weekly	10,500
Citizen Newspaper Group	Chicago, IL	12/19/91	112,000	Weekly	313,600
PRINCETON TIMES	PRINCETON, WV	12/19/91	7,010	Weekly	19,628

Six Novel Gifts for Home, Office and Car

Figure 8-7. This is page 3 from News USA's report showing us "Known Placements to Date" of another prepared story covering several products. This report is also good sales ammunition for your sales reps to use during sales calls.

These are usually nonprofit organizations whose purpose is to educate inventors and bring them together so they can network with each other and with people in associated professions. (Do not confuse these usually reputable clubs with the notorious invention marketing scams written about in Chapter 4.) There are patent attorneys, machinists, model makers, plastics specialists, investors and others who frequent inventor organization meetings for the purpose of networking.

Attending these kinds of meetings can generate valuable word-of-mouth advertising for your invention. These groups often publish newsletters with announcements and features about the activities of their members. (Another chance for more free ink!)

I served as president of the California Inventors Council for three years. Whenever I mention this credential to an editor, I automatically gain more credibility. When I include this fact in my releases, a much greater number of them get published. I've heard about other inventors who find it advantageous even if they just mention their membership in an inventor's group.

> **❝ But if you can't find the right association for your product, you could do what I did— start one yourself! ❞**

Other organizations within your own industry offer networking opportunities that are worth investigating. Once you have your product in the marketplace, you will also discover related associations within your market in which you will want to network.

I have mixed feelings about the usefulness of memberships in chambers of commerce to Stand-Alone Inventors. Chambers exist primarily to serve the needs of merchants within their local community. But the marketplace for most inventors is the nation, or even the world. I'm reluctant to spend a lot of time and money with local organizations; I'm trying to spread the word a lot farther.

I'm not saying never join your local chamber. As I always say, you never know where something might lead you. But be sure to look seriously for organizations that afford you an opportunity to reach out beyond your little community.

The "Right" Industry Association

Just about every industry has an association that you can use as a vehicle to publicize your product. (See Resource Section for directories). Almost all associations have publications that accept news releases. They also have seminars and trade shows that you can participate in.

But if you can't find the right association for your product, you could do what I did—start one yourself!

Here's what happened: I wanted to reach the thousands of people who design business cards, but they did not have an association. I wanted to educate them that a business card punch existed, and that more and more people were using this punch to organize their collection of business cards into a rotary file. But if printing appeared along the lower edge of the card, it was liable to be punched out. I wanted designers to layout cards that left a blank space where the notches go. Why put printing where it is liable to be punched out?

So I formed "NABCUP," The National Association of Business Card Users and Printers. The announced purpose of the association was to promote the standardization of business cards. If users are to file business cards in *any* kind of a file, including vinyl folders or tray files, it would help if there were no odd-size or odd-shaped cards, cards with vertical layouts or fold-over designs, etc. The "correct" card should be horizontal, 2"x3.5" and, of course, punchable! I found respected leaders in the industry who liked my idea and who agreed to join me on the board of directors of NABCUP. Their names and titles appeared on the NABCUP letterhead.

Releases went out on this letterhead about the formation of the association. (See Figure 8-8.) In the release we offered a free translucent template that designers of business cards could use when laying out cards. Many templates are in use today. If you think NABCUP is merely a public relations gimmick used to call attention to my business card punch, you are partially right. Though not very active, NABCUP still exists and provides a worthwhile purpose—it helps me answer the buyers' objection, "The punch cuts out printing at the lower edge of a card." NABCUP is taking care of my customers by doing something about the problem. The other answer to this objection is, "If, before punching, users look through the holes in the punch, they will *see* what will be knocked out, giving them a chance to jot useful data elsewhere on the card." I must admit NABCUP does help me get a lot of free hype for my punch.

Public Speaking

Another way to spread the word about your invention is to stand up and talk about it yourself. Like writing your own press releases, public speaking is another desirable skill of the Stand-Alone Inventor. In some ways it may be even more important.

If you're out there networking, public speaking opportunities will present themselves with great frequency. You may be asked to speak at seminars, club meetings, or other events. Often, these events are written up in newspapers, where your product may be mentioned (more free hype). And of course, when you are standing before a captive audience of 100 people, that's 100 more new people who learn all about your invention.

Avail yourself of every opportunity to talk about your work, whether it's at a university symposium for inventors, or your local Rotary club. The little gigs are as important as the big events because they afford you the opportunity to practice and get good at this. Most of these opportunities are of the volunteer variety, but once in a while you get expenses, perks, or even a fee. I was once contacted by a group in Puerto Rico. They were having a four-day seminar for small business development and wanted me there to give a talk. When I accepted their invitation, they flew me down from California, took care of my expenses, and I had a nice little vacation in San Juan.

But, your objective is not a tropical suntan, it's exposure for your invention. One speaking engagement I accepted started a sequence of events that led to greater exposure for my invention than I could have ever dreamed of: my appearance on national television — twice!

Here's how it happened: In 1989, Professor Bob Krolick of San Francisco State University, was teaching a class on new product design and development. Each student was required to actually invent something and do a marketing plan. He asked me to speak to his students about new product promotion, which I did. Later that year, professor Krolick himself was invited to appear on the *Good Morning America Show*, because one of his students in the '70's was the inventor of the waterbed, and the show was doing a feature on inventions. Among the inventions he took with him to demonstrate on the show was my business card punch.

As it turned out, because of time limitations, they never gave him a chance to show my invention, which was quite disappointing to me. But the whole experience started me thinking about television. I got to thinking about how many millions of people one could reach through that medium, and I got eager for that level of exposure.

So I kept my eyes open for a second chance to get my invention on national TV. That chance came a couple of years later when I learned about a new television show from a notice in one of the inventor club's newsletters. The new show was going to be called, *Why Didn't I Think of*

BUSINESS CARD DESIGNER'S TEMPLATE

Check Your Layout For Compatibility To Rolodex® And Other Card Files

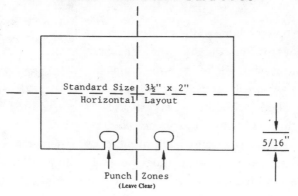

Standard Size 3½" x 2"
Horizontal Layout

5/16"

Punch Zones
(Leave Clear)

1. OVERLAY THIS TEMPLATE ON YOUR DESIGN / ARTWORK TO MAKE SURE PRINTING <u>AVOIDS</u> PUNCH ZONES. OK TO SET TYPE TO WITHIN 1/16" OF ZONES.*

   *Keep in mind that the <u>user</u> of the punch can <u>look through</u> punch <u>openings</u> in advance and avoid any printing, providing you leave punch zones clear.

2. RESULTING BUSINESS CARD CAN BE PUNCHED WITHOUT KNOCKING OUT ANY OF YOUR COPY. CARD IS NOW COMPATIBLE WITH 1" TRACKS OF POPULAR CARD FILES BY ROLODEX, AND MANY OTHER COMPANIES.

A DIVISION OF BRITISH AMERICAN BANK NOTE INC

EXAMPLE

Greg Unger
SALES REPRESENTATIVE

ONTARIO BANKNOTE
799 ISLINGTON AVE
TORONTO, CANADA
M8Z 5W8

TEL: (416) 255-2311
FAX (416) 232-1981
FAX (416) 255-3802
RES. (416) 588-9494

Example Of Layout That
Is Rotary File Compatible

BUSINESS CARD PUNCH

Figure 8-8. NABCUP offered this free transluscent template to take its message to the marketplace. It was positive, educational and free. I didn't believe we could regiment the design of *all* business cards, but we used NABCUP to call people's attention to our punch, and we are causing the "correct" design of many cards.

That? The producers of the show wanted inventors to submit home videos so they could evaluate their inventions and see how they presented them on camera.

Since putting together a home video is a lot of work, I wanted to know what my chances were before I got out the camcorder.

So, I telephoned one of the producers and told him about my Personal Punch. Right away, he wasn't impressed. "So where's the drama in watching a guy punching holes in business cards?" he asked. "Hey, this is national TV!"

> The TV show, *Why Didn't I Think of That?* is in reruns now, and is no longer being produced. But be alert for new shows of this type.

But, I didn't give up. I explained to him that my 22-year-old son, John, had produced and patented a competing invention. I suggested we appear together on the show as "dueling" inventors. He admitted he liked that idea a lot, and said we should send a video.

My son and I put together a video using a recording of the song "Dueling Banjos" as our background music. The producers saw it and liked it. Soon we were being flown to Hollywood for taping, and we appeared on one of the first episodes of *Why Didn't I Think of That?* The show aired in primetime on 140 television stations around the country. John's invention (Valuable Contacts ®) won best of the show and he took home a $2,000 prize. Both of us got the hype of a lifetime for our products, and our own "fifteen minutes of fame."

When our episode came up for its first showing, I used it as an excuse to send out a barrage of press releases. I included all of our promotional materials in it, and got the word out to all our sales people and distributors. We squeezed as much juice out of that TV exposure as we could. Releases to local papers, my fraternity magazine, you name it! The show producers assisted us in our promotional efforts by supplying photos of us on camera with the host of the show, Will Shriner. When the show we were on aired a second time just before Christmas, we sent out another PR barrage and we again noticed a sharp spike in our sales curve.

Conclusion

There's a kind of hyper-awareness—call it an obsession—that comes with taking on the task of promoting your invention, and soon you'll find you can't help but notice the many opportunities to spread the word. You receive a newsletter in the mail; you open it and immediately spot a little

Figure 8-9. That's yours truly on the right, my son, John, on the left, and show host Will Shriner in the middle. We got our 15 minutes of fame by appearing on national TV. But we also got a fortune in free exposure for our products. John's invention, the Valuable Contacts® tabs won the best-of-show prize, $2,000!

"opportunity" section in the back for new products. A friend mentions in passing that his Rotary club needs a speaker and you volunteer. You see someone on a local talk show and you wonder, "Would they be interested in talking with me?" You follow up and persist!

With no copywriters, no publicity agents, no media contacts— and with no more resources than the average Stand-Alone Inventor—I man-

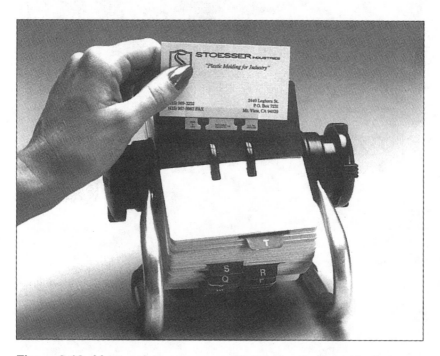

Figure 8-10. My son, John, came up with the idea for Valuable Contacts, and his name is on the patent. Royalties from it helped put him through college. This invention, which is a Mylar tab with notches that anchors to the lower edge of a business card, also makes business cards work like Rolodex® file cards.

age to get a tremendous amount of national exposure for my inventions— virtually free. A big marketing firm would charge hundreds of thousands of dollars for these kinds of results. With some solid effort, a passion to make your invention succeed, and a lot of persistence, you can get the same volume of priceless hype for your inventions—free!

The Unsung Inventor

Please permit me once again to editorialize a bit. I believe the news media industry could and should do more to support fledgling inventors.

A good start would be to quit stereotyping inventors as crackpots. Notwithstanding what I've written above, it's becoming increasingly difficult for individual inventors to launch a new product and make the public aware of it using publicity.

Compare the lone inventor's task to that of a Hollywood studio launching a new movie. It's axiomatic that the movie studios be given lots of free media exposure for *their* newest "inventions on film" regardless of entertainment value. Why? I couldn't tell you.

The American public at large is forever on the receiving end of a massive barrage of free hype for Tinseltown's latest flick—through magazines, newspapers and TV's *Good Morning America, Entertainment Tonight, Siskel and Ebert*, and many other venues. Face it, a new movie, be it blockbuster or dud, does little to create new jobs in Hollywood, compared to new jobs that can be created by commercial innovation all over the country. Why doesn't the mass media bombard the public periodically with some free hype about a truly useful new *product*? Isn't *innovation* as important as *entertainment*?

How about a weekly "inventors' corner" on the network news programs that would feature the latest patents issued to lone inventors. How about one minute on *60 Minutes*? Or, how about having two guys like Siskel and Ebert debating the merits of the best new inventions coming out each week in the Patent Office's *Official Gazette*. Imagine what "two thumbs up" on national TV would do for *your* brainchild! Even if innovation were given only a fraction of the kind of media exposure movies get, you would see many new ventures succeeding—and the hiring of many new workers. (*The New York Times Syndicate's* weekly printed feature, "Patents," is the kind of thing we need more of.)

> ❟ **Write your news media and network headquarters and send them a photocopy of this page from *Stand Alone, Inventor!* Remind TV people that we don't need anymore inventor "gong shows" that feature only goofy or useless gimmicks, and that make fun of inventing and inventors. ❟**

Write your news media and network headquarters and send them a photocopy of this page from *Stand Alone, Inventor!* Remind TV people that we don't need anymore inventor "gong shows" that feature only goofy or useless gimmicks, and that make fun of inventing and inventors.

Let's try to get the media to recognize the many serious individual

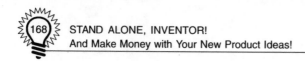
inventors out there with truly useful inventions that need only public awareness to put them on the road to success.

Note: The Resource Section begins on page 259 and is arranged by chapter to make it convenient for you to find related references.

CHAPTER 9

Merchandising Your Product

A Word About Retail Packaging

By now your free publicity is working, and articles in the media are pulling people into stores all over America looking for your new product. In a typical store in one city a prospect is wending his way down an aisle looking for, but at first not finding, your product. Finally, he asks a clerk (who happens to be aware of your product) who steers him to the section where he points to your product hanging on a J-hook. (Possibly, the clerk became aware of your product because of its attractive package.)

The clerk disappears as your would-be customer picks up your product and carefully examines it. Right away he begins making judgments about your product based on its packaging. Does he find your product better or worse than he imagined it would be from reading your publicity? (And, remember, he has yet to *open* your package, and he has yet to decide if he wants to *buy* your product.) Does the product description printed on the package promise him the benefits he wants? Does it promise a product that is well-made and durable? These and other questions are answered both directly and indirectly by your packaging. Whether your packaging looks cheap and flimsy, or classy and in good taste, it speaks volumes about the product inside. Does the information you printed on the package convince the customer that this is a product he *needs* and wants to buy? Keep these questions in mind when you select and design a package for your new product.

According to Scott Martineau, President and CEO of Servall Packaging Industries, Inc. of Torrance, CA, the job of your package is to create a reason for the consumer to stop and pick up your product off the shelf. He also writes the following in his company's newsletter: "So what is the make-up of the perfect package? The **ideal** packaging for a consumer product should make the product—even a lackluster product—look irresistible. It should take up no more space than the product itself. It could facilitate any type of display required by the merchandiser, whether it hangs, stands, stacks, etc. It should protect the product from damage in shipping, and reduce pilferage to zero. It should be environmentally friendly, and be available in any quantity. And finally, the perfect packaging would be free, adding no additional cost to the product. The challenge of the real-world packaging is how to approach the **ideal** as closely as possible."

The Institute of Packaging Professionals lists that a product package has four main functions: to contain, to protect or preserve, to transport and to inform or sell.

Your package will communicate according to its physical structure, shape and size, its color, and the typography and illustrations you use. What your package looks like and how well it presents your product's benefits are crucial to its effectiveness, because 70% to 80% of consumer purchasing decisions are made in the store. According to studies of shoppers' habits, you have only a few seconds to attract a consumer's attention with your package.

When a consumer reads the printing on your package, he is looking for two basic bits of information: 1. What exactly are you selling? and 2. What benefits, if any, does it have for me?

You'll want these two points to jump out at the consumer, because they can grab him and pull him into the rest of your copy. If you guarantee your product, say so, and explain.

The graphic design and type selection for your package are important. The largest type you use (your headline) will say what you are selling. The next largest type will tell the consumer what your product will do for him. Bullet points and smaller type will cite main benefits and give additional reasons to purchase this product.

> **" When a consumer reads the printing on your package he is looking for two basic bits of information: 1. What exactly are you selling? and 2. What benefits, if any, does it have for me? "**

Walter Soroka in his text book, *The Fundamentals of Packaging Technology,* suggests the following practices when selecting the typography for your package: "Make the type readable from a normal viewing distance, use consistent typefaces, use sans-serif type, avoid the use of reverse type, increase type size on poor-quality substrates, avoid text over illustrations, avoid long stretches of type, avoid hyphenation, maintain a high contrast and avoid text that crosses package seams."

Guy Lee of Lee Packaging Corporation of San Carlos, CA helps many novice inventors with their packaging. He always reminds them that beginning inventors cannot afford the pre-launch hoopla that the big firms use to pre-sell a new product. This is why careful attention to point-of-sale detail is so critical for the Stand-Alone Inventor. "The package and the product inside must perform most of the marketing process," says Guy. "Always remember the opera, AIDA—because it's also an acronym for Attention, Interest, Desire and Action—important functions expected from the structure and graphics of your package."

> ❛ Your package should grab a customer's attention, hold his interest, feed his desire, and move him to buy—now! ❜

Your package should grab a customer's attention, hold his interest, feed his desire, and move him to buy—now!

Often, your packaging manufacturer will have a graphic artist on staff who will prepare a design for your approval. Check it against the points suggested above. Make sure you like the design, and get the input of dealers and distributors.

What Kind of Retail Package Should You Select?

The following are seven popular methods that are used for packaging retail store products: Autobag, shrink wrap, skin package, blister card, clam shell, clam pack and shelf box. The first six are designed to give the product visibility, and to hang from a pegboard on a J-hook. (Don't overlook the possibility of creating your own category of package that can be the defining element of your product, such as the Silly Putty egg, the L'eggs egg and the Pringles potato chips can.)

Let's examine some common methods of modern retail packaging:

Autobagging

This is clear tubular polyethylene bag material that comes flat in different sizes perforated on rolls. It is used to package relatively lightweight, 3-D or flat objects that require little physical support. It is simply a sealed clear plastic bag. Autobagging machines are used to open each bag so that a product can be inserted, and to heat seal and cut each unit into a finished package. Typically, the sealed bag is identified using a printed card inside, an outside header stapled to the top, or a printed pressure-sensitive label affixed to the outside. Don't use this type of packaging if you are trying to impress anybody or charge a lot of money, because after "bulk in a barrel," it's a close second to the cheapest, and cheapest-looking, form of packaging.

Shrink Wrapping

Shrink wrapping is a clear protective wrapping used a lot on food boxes, software, audio and video tapes, CDs and pharmaceutical boxes. Observe that whatever is shrink wrapped is rigid, is in a rigid container or on a stiff card board, which is a requirement of this method. Typically, the purpose of this type packaging is to seal the product so the consumer is assured that the product is fresh and new and/or has not been opened. Some inexpensive products that are thin and/or flimsy are first mounted on a supporting cardboard, which is usually printed, and then sealed by shrink wrapping. This is probably the third least-expensive method of packaging. It is simply clear plastic material that, when heat is applied to it, shrinks to fit tightly around the object. If you choose this method, make sure your product will not be damaged by the required heat. Remember, shrink wrapping of some products says "cheap," so make sure it is appropriate for the way you are trying to position your product. You can outsource this kind of packaging, until your sales volume justifies buying the equipment and materials, and hiring an operator.

> ❢ A skin package can give larger size to small items, and is notorious for being hard to open. Retailers like these features because they deter shoplifting and tampering. ❢

Skin Pack

This method uses a clear plastic film ("skin") that is heated and draped over the product (or multiple products) and pulled skin-tight onto a stiff cardboard or corrugated board to seal it tightly against the face of it. To identify this method of packaging, examine the back of the cardboard for a porous surface or a pattern of needle holes. Air is sucked by vacuum through these pores or holes to stretch the clear plastic film over the product and seal it to the cardboard which has a clear heat seal coating over the printing. Because of the porosity of this cardboard, its surface is not ideal to print on, and might look a bit sub-standard. Because a skin packaging machine is needed to accomplish this method, I recommend that you use a vendor, such as a workshop for the handicapped, until your volume justifies buying your own machine and hiring an operator. Skin pack is an inexpensive way to package a small object so that the consumer can examine it and read about it on its card. It will cost less than the blister card method.

A skin package can give larger size to small items, and is notorious for being hard to open. Retailers like these features because they deter shoplifting and tampering.

Blister Card

Often confused with skin pack, this is a very common method of packaging that has been around for more than forty years. This is a two-piece system. The first piece is clear rigid PVC sheet material that is custom-formed into a cavity roughly the size and shape of your product. This piece is called the blister, and it has a flange all around it on a single plane. The flange is designed to be sealed to the front of a printed cardboard, which is the second piece of the system. (Look into the availability of 'stock' size blisters that will save you the custom tooling charge.)

The front of the printed card has been coated with a layer of clear, heat-activated adhesive. The back of the card, usually unfinished, is not ideal for small printing.

Sealing this package requires a press, powered by electricity and compressed air, that can apply heat and pressure to the flange from the back of the cardboard. The press operator places the product inside the blister, places the card—adhesive-side-down—on the flange of the blister and closes the press for a few seconds. Heat and pressure of the press melts the adhesive and seals the blister flange to the card. The construction just described is called a "face seal". For a more substantial blister card you can use a "fold-over" construction. This package offers good coated printing surfaces front and back; the adhesive is on the uncoated surfaces *inside* the fold. The flange of the blister is hidden inside the fold giving an overall neat appearance. Use this method to create a higher perceived value that might help justify a higher price. See Resource Section for companies that sell the PVC blisters, the printed cards, and the presses.

Clam Shell

This is a relatively recent—15 years-old or so—single-piece innovation in packaging. Think of the shell of a clam with its hinge, and how it opens and closes. Now imagine if the clam shell were made of clear plastic and it had a means of snapping closed so it could not be opened easily.

Finally, imagine that the clear clam shell closely follows the shape of your product making it fit snugly into the shell. Wouldn't this be an ideal package for you? Especially if you could integrate a J-hook hanger into its structure, or a stand for display on a shelf or counter.

> **❛ Finally, imagine that the clear clam shell closely follows the shape of your product making it fit snugly into the shell. Wouldn't this be an ideal package for you? ❜**

Once I was looking for a trailer hitch ball and I spotted one in a clam shell package that was designed with a counter stand. It really called my attention to the product in the store, and said quality all the way. I chose it over another that was merely shrink wrapped onto a cardboard.

Until very recently, if you wanted a clam shell-type package for your product it was a very expensive proposition. By definition, your clam shell would be custom shaped to the configuration of your product. This requires custom tooling with multiple cavities, usually at a cost of several thousand dollars. On the plus side, the multiple cavities mean that many clam shell packages can be molded at once, making their production cost only pennies each. Also, picture the speed and ease at which your product can be inserted and sealed into a clam shell package. Inserting the product and closing the package can be done by hand, with no machinery needed. Ideal for the Stand-Alone Inventor who can sit at home and do his packaging in front of the TV!

Clam Pack

If only the cost of this type packaging were more within reach of the Stand-Alone Inventor. Enter Placon, a packaging company in Madison, WI.

The people at Placon figured out that you could get all the advantages of the clam shell package, at an overall low cost, if you gave up the custom-shape feature.

So, in 1994 Placon introduced its Graphicbox® line of various-sized *stock* packages, that have the tooling costs amortized in their price. These are square and rectangular-shaped clam shell-type boxes with a J-hook hanger. They are designed to have a printed card inserted as a backdrop for your product, which goes inside an integral compartment. Placon has many different configurations available off-the-shelf. The question is, will your product fit in one of Placon's stock packages? Call their toll-free number and ask them. Also, check with Servall and ask about their clam pack. Lee Packaging can help you semi-customize a Clam Pack using insert tooling at a fraction of the cost of fully customized tooling. (See Resource Section.)

Shelf Box

For a more elaborate or a larger product you may want to use a shelf box. There is a wide range of shelf box styles to choose from. The least expensive is a one-piece folding carton that pops up into a three-dimensional enclosure. If you select a gray chipboard, you can print on it in a single color, but you would be better off going with a multi-color printed label to add some attractive graphics. For better printed graphics, select a white, coated stock.

A higher-quality box is the two-piece paperboard setup box. Small, slick-paper jewelry boxes—the ones that usually have two layers of cotton in them—are setup boxes. But setup boxes can be any size, up to very large. The advantages of this type box are that it is a high-quality, sturdy storage container that projects an upscale image. The disadvantages are: it costs more, it can be expensive to automate the loading of this type box, and it requires as much space to store empty as full.

Another choice is a clear plastic three-piece box. This is a custom-made box manufactured of clear vinyl. It is relatively new, and patented. The first piece is a length of square tube (shipped flat) that defines the rectangular outline of the box. The other two pieces are the end plugs, which are made of the same material. The end plugs are thermoformed into a shape that lets them snap into the ends of the tube to complete the package. The advantage of this type box is that the product inside is very visible. Also, it is suitable for a gift box

❝ The people at Placon figured out that you could get all the advantages of the clam shell package, at an overall low cost, if you gave up the custom-shape feature. ❞

merely by adding a ribbon. Usually the "labeling" is done by means of hot stamping the outer surface, or using a printed insert card. This box will probably cost less than the two-piece box described above, and it requires a lot less storage space. The only drawback is that it is somewhat labor-intensive to assemble. The originator of this style box is SLM Manufacturing Corp. of Somerset, New Jersey. We buy a 3-piece box for one of our products through Lee Packaging. (See Resource Section) Do not overlook a popular variation of this type of container: The small hanging tube with a hook on its cap that is often seen in hardware stores containing nuts, bolts or other small parts.

Other Packaging Considerations

Consultants and Brokers

For your first package, I recommend you work with either a packaging consultant or a packaging broker, also called a distributor. A consultant works for a fee. A broker does not, because he makes his income from a commission or mark-up on the packaging he sells you. These packaging professionals will help you with the selection and design of your package. You may think you know what kind of package you want, but to make sure, work with one of these pros. They will steer you to the most appropriate suppliers for your package. There are about 500 people in the industry who are trained and certified by the Institute of Packaging Professionals; they carry the designation CPP after their name, which stands for Certified Packaging Professional. Check the Yellow Pages, or contact the IoPP. (See Resource Section)

Once you settle on the exact package for your product, find out from your vendor what the minimum purchasing quantities are. Also, find out about the tooling and set up fees. If you find the total investment is substantial, and you have doubts about selling enough product to break even, stop and see if the factory will make up a prototype package. If so, order one and use it to obtain some good photo shots with your product enclosed. First, use the photos to get some free publicity (See CH 8). Next, show these photos to prospective buyers so they can see what your product will look like in the package. One sales technique I use is to offer a discounted price to a buyer if he will place a preproduction order of a certain size. If I land such an order (or orders), then I can see my way clear to place my initial package order.

Pre-booking orders in this way can help reduce or even eliminate the risk of loss on a product launch.

Pre-booking orders in this way can help reduce or even eliminate the risk of loss on a product launch.

Bar Code

In the preparation for printing your package, or the header or insert for it, you will need to obtain a UPC code number and artwork for printing the resulting bar code. A bar code is machine-readable and is needed so your product can be scanned at the cash register. An in-store computer uses the bar code number to look up the description and price of your product to be printed on your receipt.

> ❝ At your request and for a fee, this office will assign you a unique 5-digit UPC number that identifies your company in your segment of the retail industry. ❞

UPC stands for Uniform Product Code, which is administered by the UPC Bar Code Council in Dayton, Ohio.(See Resource Section).

At your request and for a fee, this office will assign you a unique 5-digit UPC number that identifies your company in your segment of the retail industry.

It will also provide you with one or more 5-digit numbers to identify each of your products. Together, these ten digits determine your product bar code, and are printed along its lower edge. Call for current fees. Try to have the second 5 digits the same as your stock number for that product, so you will have fewer numbers to keep track of.

Your next step is to obtain the custom camera-ready artwork and/or film needed for the printing of your bar code on your package. There are several sources that will charge about $35 for the negative and a couple of white prints. Alternatively, there are computer programs that will crank out bar codes, too. But bar codes must be printed with precision so they are "readable" by a laser scanner, so you must use sharp original art. Ask your printer to test scan his printing of your bar code to make sure it reads. (See Resource Section)

Package size

Think of shelf space in a store as a piece of real estate that the store may or may not decide to rent to you for the sale of your product. It is very difficult—sometimes impossible—to come by, because there is a finite amount of it available in each store. One way to increase your chances of getting shelf space is to have your package take up as little space as possible. If you choose a blister card for example, make it only as wide and as long as it needs to be, so it won't waste precious store display space. Rows of J-hooks are spaced according to the *biggest* card in the row. Make sure it's not yours. However, you should not make your package

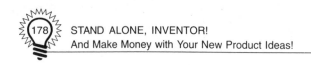

178 STAND ALONE, INVENTOR!
And Make Money with Your New Product Ideas!

any smaller than, say, 3X6 inches, or it may be rejected as too pilferable.

Counter Displays and Clip Strips

When you are launching your product in retail stores, you certainly don't want it to be hidden away on a shelf. And the store management will want to find a prominent spot for it, too. Often, your best approach is to invest in a counter display and/or a clip strip for your product.

A counter display (pictured on next page) is a paperboard container that holds say 12 to 24 blister cards or units of your product. Usually it is printed with appropriate point of purchase copy that lists the main user benefits of the product. Store management usually finds a place for such a display on a countertop near the cash register. This container can double as your inner carton in

> **❝If you use clip strips, its important that you prehang your product units on them, and pack them pre-assembled so when they arrive at the store, clerks can quickly unwrap and hang them. ❞**

a master carton of say 48 or 72 units. Make sure all containers are properly labeled as to contents, because they will be handled separately in warehouses along the way. Inquire to your packaging vendor as to the design and cost of a counter display.

Clip strips, another way to spotlight a new product, are just what the name implies: A strip of plastic designed to hang vertically, having a series of clips onto which say 12 or 24 overlapping blister cards or other units can be hung. A hook at the top of the strip enables the strip itself to be hung on the right or left edge of a store shelf.

If you use clip strips, its important that you pre-hang your product units on them, and pack them pre-assembled so when they arrive at the store, clerks can quickly unwrap and hang them.

Or, get your sales reps to set them up. Don't expect store personnel to take their valuable time to set up your clip strips or other displays. (Please see Resource Section for sources of clip strips.)

Use counter displays and clip strips during the first year or so of launching. After that time, if your product is moving, the store will want to find a more permanent spot for it, and make room for other new product counter displays.

Packing and Shipping Containers

You will need to pack your product in inner containers of about a dozen units, several of which are packed in what are called "outer car-

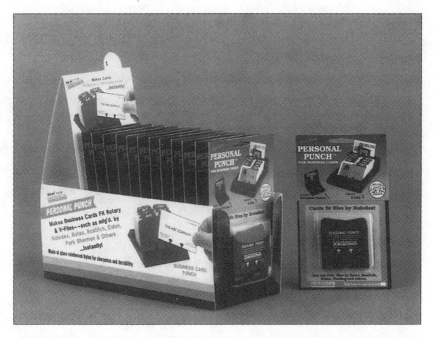

Figure 9-1. This is a counter display for merchandising blister-carded units. The display does double duty as an inner pack that holds 12 units. Retailers love you to put your new product in a display like this because they don't have to make shelf space for your item until it proves it will sell from the counter.

tons", "cases" or "master cartons". The reason for this packing is to protect the product against damage in transit, and to facilitate the counting and handling of your product by warehouse workers and storekeepers. Get some advice from your sales rep about how many units you should pack in an inner container and in a master carton. You must publish the counts, weights and dimensions of these containers on your price list. But, be careful what you decide to print, because these numbers will end up in everyone's computers, and it will cause great difficulty later if you try to make changes.

An inner container is usually a plastic bag or a chipboard box. Or, as mentioned above your counter display itself can be your inner container. Inner containers must be labeled clearly with the name of the item, its item number (and SKU number, if different), the quantity, often a special bar code and a purchase order number, if requested by the buyer.

The same kind of information goes on the master carton label, but it must also state the number of inner cartons, and the unit total, inside. The

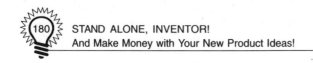
master carton is usually made of corrugated board that is sealed using re-inforced packing tape. Larger bar codes may be required on inner contain-ers and/or master cartons by certain customers. They can be printed by the carton maker, or applied later as a label. These bar codes are scanned at the buyer's warehouse to record receiving, shipping and inventory counts. Contact the UPC Bar Code Council to obtain the

> **Note: The UPC bar code num-ber is often used as the SKU (Stockkeeping Unit number), but some manufacturers always as-sign a separate SKU number.**

additional unique bar code numbers for your inner and outer containers, and to find out the correct size and position. (See Resource Section.)

Packaging for Mail Order

If you begin by selling your product only via mail order and mail or-der catalogs, you won't need a retail store package. Most likely an inex-pensive plastic bag or a paperboard box will do, provided it has a label that identifies its contents. Or, if you develop your retail package first, it may be more practical to simply use your retail package for both markets.

Note: The Resource Section begins on page 259 and is arranged by chapter to make it convenient for you to find related references.

CHAPTER 10

Advertising and Sales Promotion

Getting the Word out

One of the most important jobs you'll have with your new invention is getting the word out to potential buyers. A word of caution: Stay away from advertising agencies. As a former partner and account executive in an ad agency, I can tell you from personal experience that an advertising agency is much too expensive for the beginning independent inventor. The professionals who work at advertising agencies are like other professionals: They do valuable work and are paid well for it. If they take on the project of getting the word out on your new product, they will propose a program that will cost you a minimum of several thousand dollars.

> **❝ Unless you are one of the rare people who has invented a "killer" product, and you are certain you are doing all the right stuff with it, you simply can't justify the expense of having an ad agency working for you. ❞**

Unless you are one of the rare people who has invented a "killer" product, and you are certain you are doing all the right stuff with it, you simply can't justify the expense of having an ad agency working for you.

Wait until you have built up a hundred thousand dollars or more in working capital before you start thinking about ad agencies.

Your Do-It-Yourself Advertising Agency

Fortunately, as a Stand-Alone Inventor, you don't need an advertising agency to create effective sales tools, ads and marketing materials. In this chapter you will learn how to get the job done at savings in the thousands of dollars. I will also show you how you can track your advertising to make sure it is working. First let's look at answering inquiries, and sampling.

Assuming you've done a good job with your press release per Chapter 8, various newspapers and magazines will have printed an announcement about your new product. When you generate free publicity in print, the notices will produce inquiries. That is, people who read the article will contact you requesting additional information about your product. So, you must prepare for this and be ready to reply.

The recommended way to respond to an inquiry is to mail an attractive 8-1/2" X 11" catalog sheet on your new product, along with a cover letter, and, if practical, a sample.

Sampling—A Secret Weapon to Hook Customers

If your product is small and inexpensive, you may want to include a free sample in those responses that go to potential distributors or stores. Do not send free samples to consumers or end-users, because this is your market—the people you want to *pay* cash money for your product. The exception to this "rule" is when your product is a low-cost consumable. A consumable is a product that gets used up, and therefore must be periodically re-purchased. You should sample this type product freely. Post-It Notes™, the little yellow stick-on notes from 3M, became a huge success after free samples were put in the hands of thousands of secretaries who became hooked on using them.

I used this strategy when I learned about an organization called the National Association of Professional Organizers (NAPO), which has 250 chapters around the country. Members of NAPO make their living organizing people's messy offices and homes. "How about organizing people's collections of business cards using my punch?" I thought.

I contacted the president of the group and offered to provide each of her various chapters with a free demonstration sample of the Personal Punch. She thought it was good that this punch could help organize a collection of business cards, and NAPO members should know about it so they could include it with their recommendations. I also offered to provide NAPO, at cost, a quantity of punches with their group's name imprinted for their national convention. She thought it sounded like a

❝If possible, you should personally attend the seminar or conference and give a presentation; it's the best way to make sure you get what you want. ❞

good idea and purchased 400 punches with the NAPO logo. We used the exact same strategy with great success when we collaborated with a group called Professional Secretaries International (PSI) that has 850 chapters.

A year later we had another new product. We contacted NAPO and PSI again, and set up programs to provide free samples of our business card adapter tabs, called Valuable Contacts, to all of their members at meetings and conventions. Since this is a consumable product, we were much freer about providing samples. Each packet, which contained six tabs, was printed with the message that for availability information, phone a certain 800 number—our master distributor.

> **❝ Keep in mind that if your product is truly novel, it will be a "mystery" to your market. No one will have ever seen it before. So, it requires you to *educate* the people in your market as to what it is, how to use it and why it is so important and valuable to have around. ❞**

This is a good way to build awareness for your invention, but be sure to follow up. Talk to the group leaders and make sure they are going to distribute your materials as you intended. Try to get assurances that your samples and/or literature will be put in a packet given out to all attendees at registration. If it's not practical to give away your product itself, providing your catalog sheets will still do a good job.

If possible, you should personally attend the seminar or conference and give a presentation; it's the best way to make sure you get what you want.

The lesson here is, identify the various membership organizations in your target market and promote, promote, promote!

Your Catalog Sheet

The purpose of your catalog sheet is to communicate the good news about your product. Your goal with your catalog sheet is to convince readers that your product is something that they really need because of what it will do for them.

You will want your catalog sheet to show a very flattering photograph of your new product. Inventors frequently make the mistake of not paying enough attention to the quality of this photograph. Very often they try to get by without hiring a professional photographer, and end up with a poor-quality photo that makes a bad first impression. A good photo is the first step to making a quality catalog sheet. (See photography section in Ch 8, "How To Get Free Hype.")

Keep in mind that if your product is truly novel, it will be a "mystery" to your market. No one will have ever seen it before. So, it requires you to *educate* the people in your market as to what it is, how to use it and why it is so important and valuable to have around.

Your main photograph can help with some of this educating, but you also may need additional step-by-step photographs or drawings to help show how it works, or the various ways it can be used.

Besides the photos and illustrations you will need to write some text, or what is called "copy". The copy talks about your product. It should clearly articulate what your product is, how it works, how long it will last, what are its advantages over previous products or methods, and how or where it can be obtained or purchased.

Basic Rules for Good Catalog Copy

Abe Lincoln once said, "Writing... is the great invention of the world." As an inventor yourself, you should be able to come up with reasonably effective copy ideas that will help sell your product. After all, who knows more about your product than you?

Your headline and sub-headlines must explain in a simple, clear manner your product's main benefits to the user, and why someone would need it. Don't use clever, exaggerated or confusing headlines. Avoid adjectives such as "Exciting!", "Best!" or "World's First . . ." Unless you can back up these kinds of adjectives with fact, stick to the plain "unvarnished" truth. One adjective that is always advantageous to use is the word, "NEW". Although overused, it is still a very powerful attention-getter, especially when a product is truly new to the market. So is the word , "FREE" when you are able to work it into your headline, such as when offering a "free sample" or "free demonstration."

> ❝I'm sure you can think up a slogan for your product more sensible than, *"Engineered Like No Other Car in the World!"*❞

Use a Slogan

Your headline, or sub-headline could also be your product slogan or what today is called a theme line. A theme line to an advertiser is what a sound bite is to a politician. Both are sayings that are repeated again and again in an effort to etch an idea into the public's consciousness.

I'm sure you can think up a slogan for your product more sensible than, *"Engineered Like No Other Car in the World!"*

The problem with this car builder's slogan is that there is no *value* assigned in it, or *exclusivity* about it. Any car maker can say the exact same thing about its car.

Although the car manufacturer used this "Engineered..." slogan for many years, in 1995—for better or for worse—it switched to a jingle, "*Oh*

Lord Won't You Buy Me a Mercedes Benz?.." Why not use more creative and provocative slogans like, *"Just Slightly Ahead of Our Time"* (Panasonic), or, Hertz' slogan *"Exactly,"* which relegates all of its competition to *"not exactly."* I used the following slogan as the headline for a recent advertisement for my punch. Under a photo of the punch being squeezed it read:

MAIN SQUEEZE!

**People *love* this punch. It makes business
cards work like Rolodex® cards!**

Bullet Points

* These are subheadings, usually with a dot (or "bullet") at the left setting off each one. They are capsulized features that sing the praises of your product and what it will do for the buyer. They catch the reader's eye and make your point quickly. Examples are:
  * quick and easy to use
  * pocket size
  * economical
  * disposable
  * biodegradable
  * recycled

Main copy—Stress The User Benefits, Not Just The Features

In your main copy, you should highlight and list the *benefits* that your new product will deliver to the end-user. Explain why this product is needed by the consumer. Will it save him/her time, money or stress? Will it make him/her thinner, richer or happier? How will it do this? If you state a *feature* here, such as "chrome plated," explain what the benefit of that feature is for the consumer: "chrome plating keeps rust away so the product looks good and lasts longer."

Just tell your story as honestly and simply as you can and stop. Long copy or short copy both get read (or not read) depending on what the reader understands your product is going to do for him. Don't try to sell your reader here, just educate him.

Technical stuff

In a separate box, in smaller type, list all the sometimes boring, but necessary, technical facts and features of your product. Size? Weight? Colors? Compatibility? etc. These are needed by the end-user to enable him to make an intelligent decision whether this product can do the job and what's required to use it.

Test Your Copy

Try out your copy on typical people who would be likely to want your product in whatever industry it serves. If they understand immediately what your product is and what it will do for them just by reading your copy, you've done a good job. If they are confused by what you have written, keep rewriting or get some help from a professional copywriter.

Your Price List

Whether you include pricing on your catalog sheet will depend on how much money you invest in its printing, weighed against how soon you may want to adjust your pricing. If you include pricing, a future price change will make your supply of catalog sheets obsolete.

Therefore, if you produce a 4-color printed catalog sheet, I suggest you omit any reference to pricing or anything else that might change. This is because 4-color printing jobs are relatively costly and are necessarily done in fairly large quantities. It would be an expensive waste if your catalog sheets became obsolete and you had to re-do them.

Prepare an accompanying price list on a separate sheet, and print only limited quantities as you need them, picking up any changes as you go. Photocopying or runs at the quick print shop will do fine for this.

On the other hand, if you produce a small quantity of "quick and dirty" black and white preliminary catalog sheets, you might as well include the pricing, because if it changes it is not an expensive matter to revise and re-do.

The Sign-Off

The last, but also important, element of your catalog sheet is the "sign-off." This is usually at the lower edge of the sheet and is comprised of the name of your company, or your logo (if you have one), your complete address, phone and FAX numbers, the URL for your web page and E-mail addresses. (Find out from your reps if you should include your company's identification. In some markets, your distributors and dealers prefer you omit your identification. Your reps will know.) Footnote elements such as industry ID numbers, legal notices of patents, trademarks, copyrights, etc. can be in small type near the lower edge of your sheet. It is a good idea as a minimum to include a copyright notice, which takes

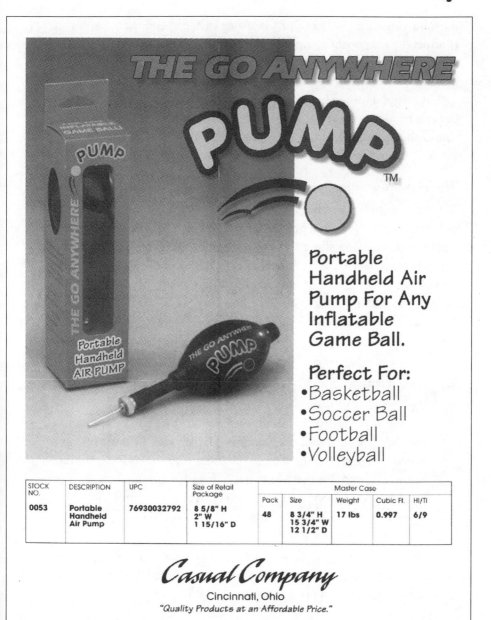

STOCK NO.	DESCRIPTION	UPC	Size of Retail Package	Master Case				
				Pack	Size	Weight	Cubic Ft.	HI/TI
0053	Portable Handheld Air Pump	76930032792	8 5/8" H 2" W 1 15/16" D	48	8 3/4" H 15 3/4" W 12 1/2" D	17 lbs	0.997	6/9

Casual Company

Cincinnati, Ohio

"Quality Products at an Affordable Price."

Figure 10-1. This is an inexpensive full-color catalog sheet produced by a "turn-key printer." Notice the headline, sub-head, main illustration, bullet points, technical stuff and sign-off. Line drawing clip art is printed on the reverse side.

the following form: © 1999 XYZ Co. After all, if someone knocks off your product, he may want to rip off the wording in your catalog sheet, too. Always put a date or a unique code number in the lower corner so you can easily distinguish it from revised editions later on.

It's a good idea to leave some blank space near your sign-off that can be used by a sales rep, distributor or dealer to put his company name, address, phone number, etc., in this space. Usually a label or rubber stamp is used. A space about 1.5" x 3" is satisfactory.

The Reverse Side

You might be wondering about the back of the catalog sheet. I suggest that on your very first product that you try to keep everything on the *front* of your catalog sheet and leave the back *blank* to help keep your printing costs down. Nevertheless, since you've left the back blank, later on you can always print or photocopy additional information as appropriate. For example, I have used the space on the back of catalog sheets to print various things, such as:

1. A letter or letters from satisfied customer(s) who have already bought and used this new product.

2. Longer lists of companies who have already purchased this product from us.

3. If your new product is sold through retail stores, the store owners will be pleased if you use the back of your sheet to print what is called "Clip art" and "slicks." These are reproducible graphics, drawings or photos that he can use in his advertising merely by clipping them and dropping them into his layout, or scanning them into a computer file. Original clip art can be prepared by an artist either manually or electronically.

Now that you know what to include in your catalog sheet, you may be wondering exactly how you are going to execute all this, and actually end up with a supply of printed catalog sheets in your hands.

Getting Your Catalog Sheet Printed

I have good news for you. Because we live in the United States *(what a country!)* we are fortunate to have a lot of excellent printing companies that offer you a complete package for producing four-color catalog sheets.

What I call "turn-key printers" have all the facilities under one roof to do your layout, artwork, photography, copy writing, typesetting, film

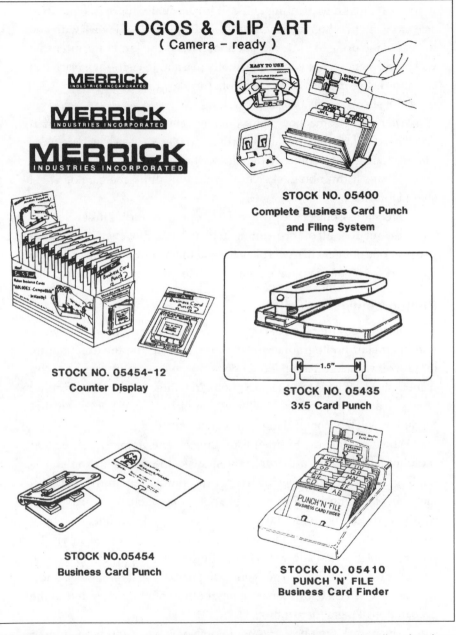

Figure 10-2. This is a sheet containing reproducible logos and product line drawings called clip art. Dealers and wholesalers use line art to "drop" illustrations into catalogs and ads. You need this to get others to advertise your product.

work, plate making, printing and drilling. Usually there is a qualified sales consultant who will be your project leader and will work with you to get the job done to your satisfaction. This is the kind of printer that will help you get what you need usually in a single visit—at a price you can afford. Recently, I've seen ads from turn-key printers offering "2,500 full-color sheets, $495."

After giving some thought to your new catalog sheet, before you start you'll need to pull together all the props and pieces. These include some photogenic samples, some written descriptions, line drawings or clip art and perhaps a thumbnail sketch of what you think the catalog sheet should look like.

Direct Press, one of the printers I use, operates studios in several major cities, but does all of the printing in New York. But, even if you don't live near one of their cities, it's okay to send them your materials and they will work with you via phone, fax and mail to get your sheet produced.

Photography

During your first visit or contact with the printers you should work with their staff photographer to help him/her capture the exact photograph you want. You are the only person who can specify the way you want to show off your product in a photo. You must tell the photographer what you are trying to do, and what you think you want. Often the photographer will have helpful ideas for you to consider.

When shooting my Business Card Punch, for example, I insisted that the photographer get a picture that showed the punch in someone's hands *in use*, punching a business card. (In contrast, an uninspired "still life" shot of the punch sitting on a table, not in operation, would have been nearly worthless, no matter how attractively the photographer may have composed it.) I felt a second shot was needed that zeroed in on the punched notches that allow it to fit in a Rolodex® file. It's OK to use one or more additional shots to get your point across. Just remember, additional shots will cost additional money, both in photography and in the preparation of them for printing.

I always ask the photographer to put some black and white film in the camera after he/she shoots the color photos, because I know that eventually I will need black and white photos for publicity and for my advertising slicks. Alternatively, you can have your color transparencies scanned into a computer as black and white files.

Copy

Now that you have completed the photography, talk to your printer about your copy—the written text (also called "romance copy") describing your product. Some turn-key printers will help you write the copy, but in my experience it is better to have all that done beforehand. Often, beginners will write too much copy to fit on a page, and it won't be readable or look right. I suggest you first look at some sample catalog sheets, find a layout style appropriate for your product, and then keep your word count the same. Give them a finished manuscript for the text that you want them to print This saves much time and avoids unnecessary rewrites after the type has been set. After you have prepared your catalog copy, which should explain all the important benefits and features of your product, you can take the next step, that of laying out your catalog sheet to look "attractive."

Layout

The printer's layout artist will work from your thumb-nail sketch that shows how you think you want your catalog sheet to look, or he will suggest several layout sketches for you to choose from. He will also "spec" the type, that is, choose the type styles and sizes, making the printing larger for headlines, etc., to produce a professional-looking, very readable catalog sheet. You must highlight those sentences and headings of your copy that are the most important, so he knows what he should make stand out.

Logo

Pay a graphic designer to create a distinctive logotype, called a "logo", that will be the symbol of your company. Tell the designer that you want a simple, one-color logo, because you want to be able to reproduce it in various sizes and in many places without difficulty. Do a trademark search at the USPTO to make sure you are not infringing a trademark owned by another. Use the ™ superscript to claim rights to your new logo. Give your printers a clean camera-ready black and white copy of your logo for them to drop into your sign-off. Also, tell the printers exactly how you want your address stated, and give them the exact numbers for your phone, fax and patent numbers, and include your trademark and copyright notices.

Now you are finished dealing with the printers for a while.

Proofing

In a week or ten days you will receive a black and white "proof" of the mechanical that the printer has composed or pasted up for the printing of your catalog sheet. The proof is usually a photocopy of the mechanical that you can mark up if you want changes made. Or, there may be no mechanical, in which case your proof will be a computer-generated proof from electronic files.

The "mechanical" itself is usually a stiff cardboard sheet containing a paste-up of the exact layout, usually at 100% size, for an 8-1/2" x 11" catalog sheet. The printer also will send you the transparency of the color shot(s), which you can check for cropping, color, sharpness and overall quality. The mechanical will show where the photo is to be printed and it also will have the actual type pasted down in place exactly where it is to appear on the catalog sheet. This includes the text, sign-off, legal notices, etc. Modern techniques have all the components of the layout in a computer file.

The purpose of this proof is to show you how all the elements are laid out on the sheet, and to enable you to proofread the type for accuracy and make any final changes you want. To indicate you want to change something, simply cross it out and make notations in the margin as to how you want the copy to read. It is a good idea to send this back to the printer with a request for another proof reflecting your changes for your final OK before he goes into production and prints your sheets.

The printer uses the mechanical as the original from which he shoots photographic negatives. Or, if he is up-to-date, he will scan the mechanical and the photos into a computer file, manipulate them to finally convert them to produce the color-separated negatives needed for the next step.

Next he uses the negatives to etch the printing plates for each color to be printed on the press.

If for precautionary reasons you want to see a pre-production proof in color, for an extra charge you can order a proof in the form of a "color-key" or "chromelin." These are relatively faithful renditions of how your color photograph(s) and printing will actually appear on the sheet. Most times this is not necessary because the color printing will look very much like the color transparency, and the printed type will look exactly like the type pasted down on the mechanical that you checked and approved. But it is a good way to make sure the headline, sub-heads, background, etc. are the colors you expect them to be.

Should you be disappointed with the quality of the finished printed sheet, it could be the printer's fault, and then the job would be subject to rerun at the printer's expense. If, however, your finished sheet equals the quality represented to you in the printer's other work, you must accept it. If the sheet contains errors that you did not catch, *you* would be responsible for the cost of any re-do.

After the sheets are printed, I always have the printer drill three holes along the left hand edge of the sheet, making it easy for my sales reps and distributors to keep this catalog sheet in their three ring binders. Also, for this reason it is best to use a standard "portrait" format, 8-1/2 x 11 inches.

What to Do With Your New Catalog Sheets

When you have completed your catalog sheet don't forget to send one out to the appropriate trade magazine editors accompanied by a new literature release, as described in Chapter 8. Trade magazines are those written for persons in the trade, which (for you) might mean store owners and distributors in whatever industry your product can be sold. Doing this could produce free publicity notices in various magazines describing your new literature as available from you. The result: more sales leads and sales.

Make Your Catalog Sheet Do Double Duty

It's very likely your catalog sheet could serve as a powerful ad in a magazine. As the advertiser, you can provide umteen thousand catalog sheets to a magazine to be inserted, or bound in, as a paid advertisement. The next time you flip through a magazine, look for a thicker page with a full color ad on it. This is called an *insert*. Keep this in mind as you prepare your catalog sheet. For example, make the headline arresting. Use headline words that make a "promise" about your product that will pull readers into your ad. And, finally, make your text *answer* the promise, but keep it brief and conversational. All this makes for a good catalog sheet, *and* a good advertisement. Inserts are only practical in magazines with a circulation of about 25,000 or less; otherwise it may be more economic to buy a four-color ad that is printed with the magazine.

Other Sales Literature and Materials

Good looking business cards, printed stationery and order forms cost no more to print than amateurish or cheap looking ones. But the first impression they can make on your customers is huge. Whether or not you make a sale can depend heavily on the image your company presents on paper. If your printed materials make you look like you are a small startup (who may not be in business tomorrow), you will find it much harder to win customers or obtain business credit from vendors.

In the past it took considerable money to design and print business cards, stationery, order forms, price sheets, sales letters, product descriptions, catalog and data sheets, news releases, and other marketing materials. But today with the advent of computer desktop publishing you can generate your own printed sales materials for a fraction of what it would cost to hire it done. Most of the new word-processing programs even provide style sheets and sample letterheads, brochures, etc., so that your printed materials will look as good as if they were created by a professional designer. Even if you don't get into it yourself, desktop publishing is economical when you hire it out.

Your Display Ad

By the time you have refined your catalog sheet and have used it a while, it will be very useful as the basis for creating a small-space advertisement. Very often the same headline can be used in your ad. Some of the same bullet points can be used. However, you will need to add a sentence in your ad asking the reader to take some kind of action—Write for sample or further information—Available at your local drug store—or whatever.

A display ad can be a full page unit or a fractional page unit in size. For openers, I always go for the smallest, least expensive unit the magazine will sell me, just to get my message out there and to see what happens. (Run it up the flagpole and see if anyone salutes!) After all, if your product is a legitimate innovation, the right headline in a small ad should be enough to pull a lot of readers into it.

Often, you can get trade magazines to do the graphic preparation of your ad for you at no charge. Just ask the space rep about this. If they balk, I say, "If you set it up for me, I'll pay you to run it." Once agreed, I send the magazine a sketch layout with a photo and some typed copy. In a week or so they send me a photocopy of the mechanical for my revision or approval.

Breaking the Rate Card

As a stand-alone inventor, don't be afraid to ask for deep discount pricing for your ads. Doing this the publication will be "breaking" their rate card. Their rate card being their published list of prices, along with specifications for placing ads. A few trade magazines will be receptive to cutting deals, while nearly all consumer publications will vehemently refuse.

When I talk to a space rep, or more often, the publisher, I always let them know I would be interested in last-minute "standby" ads and "filler rates". What are these? Thumb through any magazine, and often you will see public service ads for United Way and other charities. These organizations have an ad standing by at the magazine to be run at no charge in the event the publisher hasn't filled all his space, or at the last minute needs a filler ad to substitute for a canceled ad. My pitch to the publisher is: "Why not accept my ad to be run at your convenience, but at a fraction of the price listed on your rate card?" Generally, they are not too keen on doing this, but

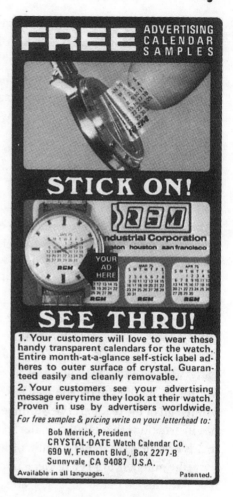

Figure 10-3. This small space ad ran in airline magazines and business publications and pulled very well. The two illustrations tell the story and the copy promises benefits to the user.

they realize that it is a better deal for them than running the free public service ad. At first they are usually non-committal. But sometime later they might call me on deadline with an offer I can't refuse. They realize (because I have told them) that I am a stand-alone inventor with a single product, and that I truly cannot justify paying full price, even for their smallest ad. Some publications simply accept this and run a contract schedule with me at half price or less.

Sometimes you will find a magazine that is so well-targeted you decide to bite the bullet and pay their full rate card price to be in it , even though it's a stretch for you to do so. Surprisingly, I've even had one or more of these magazines call me on deadline and offer to repeat my ad, at no charge, because an ad my size was needed to fill some unsold space. I make it a point to let magazines know that I am open to filler ads.

Reader Service Cards

Most trade magazines use a reader service card or "bingo" card system to elicit and to facilitate handling reader requests for more information. A typical reader service card system works like this: The magazine publisher prints a unique reader service number below each display ad, each new product listing and sometimes at the end of each article. The reader service card itself is a large post card, bound into the magazine, and perforated so the reader can tear it out. On the back of the card the reader is instructed to print his/her name, job title, company, address and phone number. There is usually a brief questionnaire to further qualify the person as a potential buyer. Also on the back are printed all of the reader service numbers used in the magazine. The card has instructions that tell the reader to circle those number(s) pertaining to ads or articles that interest him or her. (Sometimes there are boxes to write the numbers in.) The reader completes the postage-paid card, which is self-addressed to the publisher, and mails it.

> Magazines use the bingo card system as a marketing tool to show you how much response you'll get, in hopes you'll begin advertising, or advertise more.

Sales Leads

When the cards reach the magazine, reader data is processed and the resulting sales leads are printed out on mailing labels that are sent to the appropriate companies. Keep in mind these inquirers are valuable qualified sales leads. They are asking for information about your product!

Your response should include your catalog sheet, possibly a sample, and a cover letter signed by you. Keep copies of the sheets of labels so you can follow up with a phone call to each sales lead after a few weeks have passed. Also, if you have sales reps, you should send them those sales leads that are located in their territories so they can follow up with a sales call and hopefully close a sale.

Your best bet is to begin by advertising directly in trade magazines

Figure 10-4. I negotiated with McGraw-Hill Publishing to run this ad at a "filler" rate in many of their various trade magazines over a three month period. Not only was it a great media buy, but the program was successful in motivating my ad specialty distributors to sell more of my Crystal-Date product. As a result, we did nearly $1 million in Crystal-Date business that year.

Sales And Marketing
STRATEGIES & NEWS

PROCESSING DATE 08/14/96   ADVERTISERS COPY
PAGE NO. 1
ADVERTISER 37251
SALESMAN

THIS SIDE IS A COPY OF THE NAMES AND ADDRESSES SUPPLIED TO YOU ON THE HANDY, EASY-TO-MAIL LABELS. THE ISSUE DATE AND ITEM DESCRIPTION ARE LOCATED ON THE FIRST LINE OF THE LABEL. DEMOGRAPHICS ARE LOCATED TO THE RIGHT OF EACH LABEL.

07/18/96 AD   PERFECT GIFT FOR ANY
IRV MARSTERS
BANGOR LETTER SHOP
193 STATE ST
BANGOR ME 04401
ITEM 120 / PRIMARY BUSINESS / JOB FUNCTION / # OF EMPLOYEES
TEL 207-945-9311   FAX 207-942-9914

07/18/96 AD   PERFECT GIFT FOR ANY
MARGIE M WEILER
MSW TRAVEL GROUP
630 FIFTH AVE STE 3000
NEW YORK NY 10111
ITEM 120 / PRIMARY BUSINESS TR AG,MIC FNS / JOB FUNCTION SLS/MRKTNG / # OF EMPLOYEES 50-99
TEL 212-332-1242   FAX 212-399-6277

07/18/96 AD   PERFECT GIFT FOR ANY
FEELDMAN
IND OFFSET LITHOGRAPHERS
920 23 BAYCHESTER AVE
BRONX NY 10475
ITEM 120 / PRIMARY BUSINESS WHSL,DIST,JB / JOB FUNCTION CORP MGT / # OF EMPLOYEES 50-99
TEL 718-671-3691

07/18/96 AD   PERFECT GIFT FOR ANY
RONALD C THEISS
HILLS
3010 GREEN GARDEN RD
ALIQUIPPA PA 15001
ITEM 120 / PRIMARY BUSINESS RETAILER / JOB FUNCTION SLS/MRKTNG / # OF EMPLOYEES 1000+
TEL 412-378-0511   FAX 412-378-7144

07/18/96 AD   PERFECT GIFT FOR ANY
HOMER ROSS
CITY HOSPITAL INC
DRY RUN RD
MARTINSBURG WV 25401
ITEM 120 / PRIMARY BUSINESS OTHER / JOB FUNCTION OTHER MGT / # OF EMPLOYEES 100-499
FAX 304-264-1255

07/18/96 AD   PERFECT GIFT FOR ANY
R SMITH
MIDWEST MGMT CORP
109 NEW PERRY RD
GREENVILLE SC 29609
ITEM 120 / PRIMARY BUSINESS AD AG,MKT RES / JOB FUNCTION CORP MGT / # OF EMPLOYEES 50-99
TEL 864-246-1087

07/18/96 AD   PERFECT GIFT FOR ANY
MARVIN ROSS
TEMPACO
1701 ALDEN RD
ORLANDO FL 32803
ITEM 120 / PRIMARY BUSINESS WHSL,DIST,JB / JOB FUNCTION SLS/MRKTNG / # OF EMPLOYEES 25-49
TEL 407-898-3456   FAX 407-898-7316

07/18/96 AD   PERFECT GIFT FOR ANY
C L WHITE
WHITE AND ASSOCS
2920 MOSS SPRINGS
ANTIOCH TN 37013
ITEM 120 / PRIMARY BUSINESS WHSL,DIST,JB / JOB FUNCTION CORP MGT / # OF EMPLOYEES UNDER 25
TEL 615-361-5921   FAX 615-361-4509

07/18/96 AD   PERFECT GIFT FOR ANY
JACK PAPPAS
PEERLESS
3240 DUEBER AVE SW
CANTON OH 44706
ITEM 120 / PRIMARY BUSINESS / JOB FUNCTION / # OF EMPLOYEES

07/18/96 AD   PERFECT GIFT FOR ANY
ALLAN SHOFF
ADVANCED SIGN & BANNER
6435 TOPANGA CANYON BLVD
CANOGA PARK CA 91303
ITEM 120 / PRIMARY BUSINESS RETAILER / JOB FUNCTION CORP MGT / # OF EMPLOYEES UNDER 25
TEL 818-346-2142   FAX 818-346-2263

07/18/96 AD   PERFECT GIFT FOR ANY
NORMAN POLLITT
KITS CAMERA
6908 RICHMAN WAY
SACRAMENTO CA 95828
ITEM 120 / PRIMARY BUSINESS RETAILER / JOB FUNCTION SLS/MRKTNG / # OF EMPLOYEES UNDER 25
TEL 916-444-6080   FAX 916-444-7935

07/18/96 AD   PERFECT GIFT FOR ANY
DICK DOYLE
DOYLE COMMUNICATIONS GROUP
591 RIVERCREST DR
SACRAMENTO CA 95831
ITEM 120 / PRIMARY BUSINESS AD AG,MKT RES / JOB FUNCTION CORP MGT / # OF EMPLOYEES UNDER 25
TEL 916-391-1748   FAX 916-391-1354

03/20/96 AD   PERFECT GIFT FOR ANY
MARJNE SCHWARTZ
OWNER
ENFRA TRADING CO
381 PARK AVE S
NEW YORK NY 10016
ITEM 194 / A 4 4 7 / NO. OF CIRCLES
TEL 212-684-3072   FAX 212-725-4932

03/20/96 AD   PERFECT GIFT FOR ANY
M COHEN
CEO
COBBO INS
385 BROADWAY
BETHPAGE NY 11714
ITEM 194 / 1 1 C 5 / NO. OF CIRCLES 10
TEL 516-681-1540

03/20/96 AD   PERFECT GIFT FOR ANY
JOSEPH A LAWN
PRES
LAWN BROKERAGE
4779 MAKYES RD
SYRACUSE NY 13215
ITEM 194 / A 2 A 7 / NO. OF CIRCLES 3
TEL 315-492-1605   FAX 315-492-6945

03/20/96 AD   PERFECT GIFT FOR ANY
MORTON F MARKLEY
CHAIRMAN
MARKLEY FINANCIAL SERVICES
615 WASHINGTON RD #401
PITTSBURGH PA 15228
ITEM 194 / B 2 F 6 / NO. OF CIRCLES 8
TEL 412-343-2900   FAX 412-343-8690

03/20/96 AD   PERFECT GIFT FOR ANY
DEBBO HAIRE
XK DESIGNER
COLLINS & AIKMAN CORP
BOX 32665
CHARLOTTE NC 28232
ITEM 194 / A 2 / NO. OF CIRCLES 4
TEL 704-548-2263   FAX 704-548-2098

03/20/96 AD   PERFECT GIFT FOR ANY
MARTIN ALKERMAN
DIR MKTG
PALLET PALLET INC
4 COMMERCE PK SW #555
CLEVELAND OH 44122
ITEM 194 / A 2 C 7

The Perfect Gift For Anyone with a Rolodex® Brand Card File!

Millions have discovered the best way to organize business cards: *Punch them to make them work like Rolodex® Brand Cards!* No more trimming, taping or retyping cards. You can find the Merrick Punch in stores such as Office Depot, OfficeMax, Staples, Inc. *and 3,000 others.* Also, it makes an ideal business gift with your company logo imprint. If you're the one who buys your company's promotional products, mail or fax us your business card for a **FREE** random imprinted sample punch.

MERRICK INDUSTRIES INCORPORATED
Box 2277
Sunnyvale, CA 94087
FAX 408/739-4351

Figure 10-5. This sheet of mailing labels, sent to me by the magazine, is made up of readers who responded to my ad using the bingo card system. The address labels make it easy for my company to respond to these potential customers. This print-out also has marketing data for my company, such as primary business, job function, and phone and fax numbers for follow-up.

only, without help from an advertising agency. Consider hiring an agency to prepare ads for consumer magazines and possibly TV, when your potential reaches the megabuck range.

Note: The Resource Section begins on page 259 and is arranged by chapter to make it convenient for you to find related references.

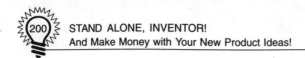

200 STAND ALONE, INVENTOR!
And Make Money with Your New Product Ideas!

CHAPTER 11

How to Set Up Distribution

New Products Wanted!

The introduction of new products in US retail stores has accelerated at a dizzying pace for the past thirty years. In 1964, according to *New Product News* magazine, only 1281 new products showed up on the shelves of supermarkets and drugstores. Contrast that with 1994, when manufacturers introduced 20,076 new SKU's—Stock Keeping Units having a unique UPC bar code.

New SKU's are anything from completely new products to existing products with new colors, flavors or sizes, etc.

This long-term escalation has resulted in an increasing number in the variety of products in supermarkets, for example. In the past twelve years the average assortment in supermarkets has gone from about 13,000 products to more than 30,000.

> ❝New SKU's are anything from completely new products to existing products with new colors, flavors or sizes, etc.❞

One of the reasons for these product increases is that retailers believe—rightly so—that they must innovate or die. This is good news for you because your new product, providing it has merit, is in demand by wholesalers, retailers—and consumers.

Tradeshows

Every industry has one or more tradeshows each year. This is where people in the industry gather to learn about the latest products and services available. Exhibitors and attendees use tradeshows to talk to competitors and line up potential distributors This is why tradeshows are rated as one of the most cost-efficient ways to market products. When launching your product, look into renting or sharing a tradeshow booth.

Use it to demonstrate your new product, distribute sales sheets and to meet potential customers and distributors.

There are inventor exhibitions that you might look into if you want to license. (See Resource Section.)

Support Your Local Merchant

If your product goes to the consumer market, you need to embark on a learning journey that begins with one small step. That first step is a trip to a

❝ Outside of retailing, it's a little-known fact that a unique or specialty product, new or not, needs to sell at a rate of only one or more units per week to be kept on the shelves and to be considered a "keeper." This is a rate of "one turn per week," as they say in retailing.❞

nearby retail store of the kind you hope will be selling your product all over the country. The following is a basic method of test marketing your product to determine the potential of what you have.

Let's say you invent a product that you believe would sell in hardware stores. Go talk to your local hardware merchant. Try to find an independently-owned store where you can speak to the owner. Remind him that you trade at his store, and explain that you would like to show him a new product. Since you are his customer, he will probably feel obliged to spend at least a few moments with you to see what you have.

Test Market

Show him your product or prototype and explain that it is a brand new invention. Ask for his candid opinion of it. Is it the kind of thing he thinks his customers would buy? Regardless of his reaction, tell him you would like to have him put a few in his store on consignment as a market test.

A way to encourage him to do this is to offer him "memo billing." You'll need to prepare an invoice that simply records the fact that you put a quantity of your units in his store. Customarily, this invoice is not payable unless and until the store is successful selling the test batch and places a reorder.

If he agrees to the test, don't be discouraged later on if his sales are poor. He may have put your product in a bad location, marked it with the wrong price, or whatever. Try to get your product into three or four other stores at the same time for a more meaningful test. Try to persuade each merchant to include your product in his advertising mailings, or in his newspaper ads. Keep track of which stores run ads, and correlate this data with the sales results at those stores. If sales are spotty or weak, ask each merchant about your packaging. Can they suggest changes? If your product is really new, you may want to invest in a counter display, shelf-talker or other point of purchase aid. (See Chapter 9 on Merchandising.) Or, your pricing may be the problem.

On the positive side, it's encouraging to know that a retail store need not sell huge volumes of your product to make a go of it. As a novice, I assumed that a retail store must sell about twelve units of my product each month, or they would discontinue it. Not so.

Outside of retailing, it's a little-known fact that a unique or specialty product, new or not, needs to sell at a rate of only one or more *units per week* to be kept on the shelves and to be considered a "keeper." This is a rate of "one turn per week," as they say in retailing.

❝ If your product is to sell in retail stores, set the retail price at a minimum of ten times your cost to produce it. Your price should be as much as the traffic will bear. Visit a retail store and check the prices of other products like yours. ❞

Test your product in a few stores, and even if it sells at only one unit per week, you could have a winner. There are other factors involved that influence whether management wants to carry your product in the first place. For example, if your publicity brings people into stores asking for your product, management will want to have it in stock. Or, your particular product may be needed by the store, for example, to round out the kitchenware line they carry, or another product line.

Pricing and Discounts

It's not an easy job to set a retail price on a new product. First-time inventors ask themselves whether they want maximum financial return, or maximum distribution, feeling they can't have both. Usually they wind up with a price that is too low and a garage full of inventory they cannot afford to market effectively. Why? Because without a sufficient price, there is not enough money for advertising and distribution discounts. And without these, the product will not sell.

If your product is to sell in retail stores, set the retail price at a minimum of ten times your cost to produce it. Your price should be as much as the traffic will bear. Visit a retail store and check the prices of other products like yours.

Talk with your local merchant about your pricing. He will want to know your suggested retail, or what is called "list price." It is customary that the manufacturer is the one who sets this price. This is most obvious in the automotive industry where you have the Manufacturer's Suggested Retail Price, "MSRP," or "sticker price." The retail list price, or price to the end user, is the so-called manufacturer's "published" price in almost every industry.

These days we all know the published retail price for established products has little to do with reality. No one pays retail anymore, unless one is shopping at an airport or hotel gift shop or at an isolated store. We all look for the "street price". But when all is said and done, the retail list price does perform a needed function: It is the primary benchmark from which discounts are taken by various classes of buyers. For example, the retailers' and wholesalers' cost, is usually calculated by taking certain discounts off the retail price.

> **Generally, a new product does not need to be discounted in the stores. It can usually command the full price, which gives store management a good reason to put your new product in.**

Ask the retail merchant what kind of discount he is getting on merchandise similar to your product to see what he says. Probably he will tell you that usually he gets about 40-50% discount off the manufacturer's suggested list price. He also probably gets some kind of terms, such as 2% net 10 days. These terms mean that if he pays promptly within a certain number of days he can take an additional 2% off the invoice. A retailer might buy a $10 item for, say, $5, less 2%, or $4.90. To be competitive he will price it in his store at $8.99, or even less, because nobody wants, or expects, to pay full retail, unless perhaps it's a new product.

Let's go back a bit and say you have not yet established your list price. But, since you want your income as manufacturer to be about $5 per unit for your new product, you figure you need to set your suggested retail price at around $10. This will provide for the 50% discount expected by retailers. This reasoning is fine if all your sales will be directly to individual retail stores.

But, in further discussions with merchants, or others, you learn that retailers do not normally buy directly from manufacturers. Retailers usually buy most of the products they sell in their stores from wholesalers, sometimes called distributors or jobbers. These are companies that operate warehouses and who sell to retailers in a certain region or regions.

You do some more nosing around and you learn that wholesalers in a certain industry are accustomed to receiving what is referred to as, say, a "50/25/10%" discount off the manufacturers' list price. This is a string of arbitrary percentage discounts that has been used in price negotiating for years.

As you can see, there is a learning process going on. You are finding out by talking to the retail merchants (and perhaps to manufacturers' reps and others in the industry) that you, as manufacturer, must give up a lot more than 50% of retail, and you need to provide for it.

For example, take a new product that you think should retail at $10. As manufacturer, you must sell it to the wholesaler at, say, a 50/25/10% discount, or $3.38. (The calculation is, $10, less 50% equals $5, less 25% equals $3.75, less 10% equals $3.38.) Next, subtracting 2% terms, equals $3.31. In addition, you may have to pay a manufacturers' rep's commission of 10% (of the $3.31), leaving you with a take of only $2.98!

Therefore, as manufacturer, if your target is to keep (not $2.98 but) $5 for yourself, you employ your high school algebra and find you must set your suggested retail price to about $15. Next, you must try to determine if $15 is a price that traffic will bear. If it turns out to be too high, you must find ways to lower its cost to make, or decide if you want to lower the $5.00 income to yourself, say to $4.00, to see if that might work.

> **❛Before you do anything, however, keep in mind that the suggested retail price you set will go by the boards if you get your product into the warehouse clubs or superstores.❜**

Before you do anything, however, keep in mind that the suggested retail price you set will go by the boards if you get your product into the warehouse clubs or superstores.

They may discount your $15 retail price to $10.99 or even $9.99! And this could turn out to be a price that the traffic *will* bear!

Your Product Price Lists

My consultant, Bob Sherman, taught me how to set up price lists for the office products market that would look professional. As the manufacturer, he said, I needed to prepare two separate confidential price lists:

1. <u>Wholesalers' Price List</u>—for my manufacturer's reps to leave with buyers at various regional and national wholesalers around the country. This list includes the product cost to the wholesaler from

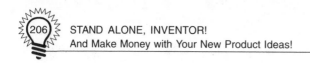

206 STAND ALONE, INVENTOR!
And Make Money with Your New Product Ideas!

the manufacturer. In addition, I would need:

2. Dealers' Price List—that the wholesalers' sales people could leave with the buyers at office products dealers. This list includes the product cost to the dealers from the wholesaler.

The format and quality of these price lists is important. They shouldn't look much different from the price lists of other manufacturers in the industry. If they are not clear and complete, they could make you look like an amateur, and could be a reason for a buyer not to place an order.

Bob Sherman also taught me that a complete price list should include:

- The manufacturer's SKU number
- A description
- A suggested retail or list price
- The applicable discounts for the wholesaler or the dealer
- The price list should tell how the product is packaged
- Is it in a blister-card? A shelf box? Or a bag?
- Is there a counter display?
- How many units are packed in an inner box or display?
- And, how many inner boxes or displays are contained in a master carton?
- Also, it should list the dimensions of the inner box and the master carton, and their weight. The Wholesale Price List should include your prompt payment terms.

Warehouse Clubs or "Category Killers"

In recent years, in almost every retail category we have seen the arrival of warehouse clubs and superstores, also called megastores, category killers or power retailers. As you probably know, these are national chains of large stores that deal mainly in one category or industry, and that offer a broad line of products in a no-frills setting. Price Costco, Home Depot, Home Club, OfficeMax and Petco are examples that are established nationwide.

This superstore trend has shut down all kinds of mom-and-pop shops all over the country. No longer do we have many handy corner grocers or neighborhood hardware or stationery stores. Now you must travel a greater distance to a huge store with a huge parking lot where customer service is usually lacking, but where many of the prices are lower. Much lower. (It's for you, the consumer, to figure out *which* in the mix are the truly low-priced products.)

You could argue that advanced marketing strategy built the megastore phenomenon. But you could also argue that none of it would be possible without the use of computers to orchestrate the logistics. Or, you could simply ask, is this progress?

If you are skillful and/or lucky enough to get your product into one of the warehouse clubs, or superstore chains, you will learn that their buyers play hardball with you when it comes to the discounts they demand. Because of their tremendous purchasing power, these clubs and superstores can buy directly from manufacturers at better than the basic discounts given to national and regional wholesalers who resell to other smaller groups and independent stores.

Typically, in addition to a 50%, 25% and 10% discount, they will require a series of extra discounts. For example possibly a 3% discount for returns or damaged product, a 5% discount as an advertising allowance, plus a 4% discount just because they are the retail powerhouse they are! Then, another 10% for your sales rep, unless you've negotiated a lower commission with him. This means that the $15 list price you just set which you thought would yield $5 for you, now yields you only $4.03. But, you quickly agree to all their discount demands, and anything else they want such as drop shipments, because these clubs and superstores could move your product by the carload!

> You could argue that advanced marketing strategy built the megastore phenomenon. But you could also argue that none of it would be possible without the use of computers to orchestrate the logistics. Or, you could simply ask, is this progress?

Unfortunately, there is a downside to the warehouse/superstore phenomenon for the independent inventor:

a) It's difficult for you to "pioneer" a new invention through these stores. Why? Because the success of these stores is predicated on their handling mainly *proven* products that will deliver considerable sales volume from day one.

Your product must have a proven record of solid sales before many buyers for these stores will even think about putting it in. They have been criticized by marketing professionals for "not fully participating in the marketing process."

Many power retailers are without programs for introducing new

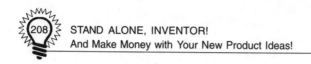

products, unless they are the new products of their existing big vendors.

The impact of the megastores leaves the independent inventor with limited avenues for introducing his new product: The inventor can still pioneer a new product by selling to direct marketing catalog houses, and via radio and TV, possibly the Internet, and by going dealer-direct (to what's left of the mom-and-pops). What you must do today is build a distribution success story, and hook up with a master distributor that will present your product to the megastores.

b.) Once you sign on with warehouse clubs and superstores and commit to sell to them, you've in essence put all of your eggs in one basket. The risk is that a megastore could suddenly cut you off—discontinue your product immediately at any time, for any reason. This would slice a big chunk out of your sales and income, leaving you with the huge problem of trying to regroup and recover. In addition because these big stores sell your product so cheaply, it could hurt your other sales in the mom and pop stores.

In summary, if you understand the positive and negative aspects of the megastore phenomenon you can prepare your company to deal with them.

The Author's War Story

The first day I had my business card punch ready for market, I jumped in my car and went down to my local stationery store, which is called McWhorters. Very proudly I presented my new product to the store manager and asked him what he thought. He said, "What is it? And how does it work?" So I gave him a demonstration, inserting a business card and squeezing it. The squeeze cut a pair of notches in the lower edge of the card. I then asked him if we could go over to his Rolodex© section, where I demonstrated how the punched business card would fit on the tracks of a Rolodex® rotary file.

Luckily, the store manager liked the idea. But he said that his store was only one of twelve McWhorter stores, (today they have 21!) and all the buying was done "downtown". However, I persisted and asked if I could put some punches in *his* store on consignment to try to build up a success story to take downtown to the buyer. He agreed, and in a couple of weeks he had sold a half a dozen punches.

Armed with this fact, I went downtown and talked with the buyer, whose name was Jerome Davis. Jerome liked my presentation and eventually gave me the first real order for my new product. He ordered one

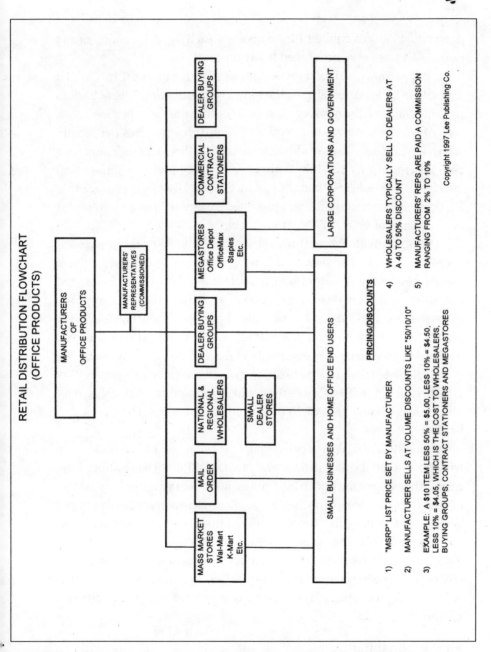

Figure 11-1. This chart shows the various ways office products flow from the manufacturers through distribution to the end users.

dozen punches in a counter display box for each store, for a total of 144 punches! I was very encouraged to say the least.

At that time I had set a retail price of $8.95 for this punch. On that first sale to McWhorters, I gave the typical 40% discount. I went back to my office and ran the numbers to see if I could retire yet. Let's see . . . if each of Jerome's twelve stores could sell one dozen punches per month, which would be consistent with the market test, then over the course of a year he would buy 12X12X12 punches or 1,728 punches times $8.95 which equals $15,465.60. Next, if I deduct the 40% discount, plus another 2% prompt payment discount, I projected my annual revenue from this one customer of $9,093.77. Not too shabby!

Next, if I divide the total annual revenue for these stores by twelve, I get $758. per store per year. Suddenly, I'm very anxious to find out just exactly how many similar office products stores there are in the United States. The year was 1986, and I found there were, at that time, approximately 14,000 stores listed by the National Office Products Association (NOPA), which was located in Washington, DC. (I found this resource at my local library, using the *Encyclopedia of Associations*. It's now the BPIA.)

I calculated that if in the first year I could achieve a 10% penetration into this market (sell 1400 stores), I could expect annual sales of just over one million dollars! ($1,061,200). I could almost retire! Or at least kick back a bit!

Initially, all this was very exciting . . . but when I came back down to Earth, I found it was much too early to be making such ambitious forecasts. After we got the punch into numerous other stores, we learned that instead of twelve dozen punches, the average sales rate (per store per year) was closer to four or five dozen. Though this is still considered acceptable for a new specialty product like this, it wasn't going to make me millions overnight! Nevertheless, an early ten per cent market penetration still meant several hundred thousand dollars in annual revenue for my company. A promising start for the newest product of a Stand-Alone Inventor!

Find a Consultant

My advice to new Stand-Alone Inventors is to find a distribution consultant. You might want to inquire at SCORE, which is the Senior Corps of Retired Executives. These veteran businesspeople volunteer to consult to small businesses under the sponsorship of the Small Business Administration of the Federal Government. Here's a way to get some free help from experienced corporate executives.

See if you can find someone within that organization who has experience in distribution within your target retail industry. If you can't find someone through SCORE, try your target industry association, checking for them in the *Encyclopedia of Associations* in the library. Or, simply take a proactive stance and "network" the industry, starting with your local merchant. Find a retired executive in your target industry who may not be associated with SCORE. You may want to sign a simple letter agreement with your consultant and agree to pay him by the hour for specific services. Or, you could work out some kind of retainer payment so that you can call this person for help when you need it. If, through his contacts, the consultant can get you sales, pay him a small percentage of your gross sales, say 2%, as an incentive for the first couple of years.

Let's go back again to the day when I made that first sales call on Jerome Davis at McWhorters. Let's find out how I happened to be so well prepared to present my new product so smoothly with the correct pricing, etc. It was because I *didn't* go in cold: I made a point of knowing the basics of what I was trying to do.

Most of the credit for preparing me goes to a friend (mentioned earlier), Bob Sherman, whom I met when we were college students at Berkeley. After graduation I followed Bob's career. I knew he had his own business, called Marathon Office Supply, and that it was a wholesaler of office products. Marathon had a central warehouse in Benicia serving northern California.

When the idea for the business card punch came along, and it seemed like such a natural to sell in office products stores, the first person I went to see with a prototype was Bob Sherman. He encouraged me to go ahead with the project, saying he thought it was something he could sell. Also, he suggested I use a blister card type package for it. Years earlier I had taken my transparent calendar for watches to him and he had helped me with the distribution of that product. This is one of my success secrets—keeping in touch with people I meet through the years and staying aware of their lives and careers. It's related to today's "networking", but perhaps longer term. The time I've spent interacting with people has often produced good business relationships like this, in addition to great friendships. A few years later, after he sold Marathon and retired, Bob agreed to serve as marketing consultant to me for my office products.

Once you find your consultant, he will be able to help you with putting together the kind of price sheet that will keep you from looking amateurish.

As mentioned earlier, the price sheet must be presented in the customary fashion expected within your target industry, and your consultant will know the format. Also, this consultant will be a wealth of information about which trade shows you might want to attend and/or exhibit in, which magazines that are read by the retailers that you might want to advertise in, and how to find sales representatives. Take him to trade shows with you, and pay his expenses. He will get you the introductions you need, teach you trade secrets and show you the ropes. He's your mentor.

> ❬Once you find your consultant, he will be able to help you with putting together the kind of price sheet that will keep you from looking amateurish. ❭

Find a Sales Rep

Whether or not you are able to find a consultant, I suggest you talk further with your local merchant and ask him for the names of some of the sales reps who call on him, especially those selling items similar to yours. Once you have identified an appropriate sales rep, he should be interested in talking to you, because reps are always looking to pioneer a new product that could become the next big seller.

Hopefully, this sales rep will decide to be your sales rep for your new product. Ask him for a complete rundown on how the industry is organized with regard to distribution. Find out as much as you can. Are there wholesalers who would take your product on? Is it possible for you, as the manufacturer, to start things rolling by selling directly to the retail stores? How much commission are reps like him paid? Can he help you find reps in other regions of the country? Incidentally, you will do well to pay your sales reps 15% (instead of 10) to pioneer your new product. They will expect it, because they must spend extra time to show and promote your product before the volume picks up. You might consider paying "spiffs", which are extra $2-$25 cash bonuses per dozen units paid directly to reps who close orders during a certain promotion time frame. Spiffs have the effect of stirring up reps so they focus their attention on *your* product, which is the name of the game when you deal with reps.

Going back to the day I landed the first order from the McWhorter stores, I had asked the buyer if he would refer me to a local sales rep who called on him selling this kind of product. Jerome gave me the name of Chuck Vanderwege who was the Northern California salesperson for a sales rep organization based in Los Angeles. He sold writing instruments and several desktop specialty items.

When I talked to Chuck and told him I had sold my product into the group of twelve stores, he was immediately quite interested. He said he could take that story to all the dealer stores and wholesalers he called on in Northern California. So I appointed Chuck my first manufacturer's rep and promised to pay him 15% commission for *all* sales shipped into his territory (regardless of whether or not he personally caused every sale.) This was a typical arrangement for any product, but because it was a *new* product, I set the commission at 15% instead of 10%. Also typically, our written agreement was cancelable by either party for any reason on 30 days' notice.

In the next few months, Chuck sold my product into 30 or 40 more stores in his territory. Before long we had a case history with many stores that showed each store would sell an average of 3 or 4 business card punches per month, which was a fine rate of sale.

When Chuck related our new product story to his counterpart in Los Angeles, he was very interested. Soon, I appointed him as my manufacturer's rep for the Southern California territory under the same terms as Chuck's.

Manufacturers' reps, like any other affinity group, network at industry conventions and meetings. This is why Chuck was able to refer me to other manufacturer's rep companies all over the country for me to contact, which I did. By now we had built up a very good track record for the business card punch. The punch was selling through office product stores throughout the state of California. In a matter of months, this track record enabled me to sign up 19 rep organizations in other regions that collectively employed about 80 sales people who called on virtually every office products dealer in all fifty states. I used a very simple appointment letter for contracting with rep groups.

Price Reduction

After the second year, I lowered the price of the business card punch from $8.95 to $5.95. The reason: Sales seemed to be slowing a bit, and I was getting feedback from distributors that their sales people were encountering some price resistance during calls on dealers. I surmised that

MERRICK
INDUSTRIES INCORPORATED

RON SMITH & ASSOCIATES
Attn: MR. RON SMITH
23 MOON BEAM DRIVE
SAN RAFAEL, CA 94043   June 1, 1993

Subject: Sales Rep Agreement

Dear Ron:

This letter will serve as the agreement between Merrick Industries, Inc. (Manufacturer), and Ron Smith & Associates, Manufacturer's Representatives, (Rep) with regard to sales and services rendered to Merrick Industries, Inc. The effective date of this agreement is June 1, 1993.

The Rep will assist the Manufacturer in the marketing of new and existing products (Product) to the office products industry (Market). The Rep will give best effort assistance in obtaining orders from the Market and servicing the market to promote maximum sales and repeat orders.

The Market includes contract stationers, all retail stationery dealers, office supply wholesalers and dealers.

Territory: BPIA District 9: Northern California and Northern Nevada.

Compensation. Manufacturer agrees to pay Rep 10% of net sales of all orders to the Market shipped into Territory. For purposes of this agreement "Net Sales" is defined as Manufacturer's total invoice amounts for the Product to the Market in the Territory, exclusive of all discounts, allowances, taxes and transportation. Payment will be made at the end of the month following month of invoice.

Rep agrees to pay all his own expenses in the performance of services rendered under this agreement, except as other wise agreed to by Manufacturer. Samples and catalog sheets will be supplied at no charge to Rep.

This agreement is subject to cancellation on 30 days' written notice by either party for any reason.

If all of the above terms and conditions are agreeable to you, please execute a copy of this letter; the original is signed by the Manufacturer for your file.

Submitted: Accepted:

_____   _____
Robert G. Merrick, President   Ron Smith
MERRICK INDUSTRIES, INC.   RON SMITH & ASSOCIATES

Date:_____   Date:_____

BOX 2277 ● SUNNYVALE, CALIFORNIA 94087 ● (408) 738-2200 FAX (408) 739-4351

Figure 11-2. Use a simple one-page letter like this to appoint your sales reps.

most of the people who would shell out $8.95 for this punch had already done so.

Initially, I had introduced the punch at $8.95, knowing it was rather high. My rationale was that this was a new and useful time-saving product that I believed could fetch a premium price, at least for a while. (This is a pricing strategy called "skimming" or "creaming" the market. You see it everyday in the computer and software business, except those prices continue to drop almost by the month.) Also, I needed the extra dollars in the beginning to help recoup the $40,000 development costs I put into the plastic injection molds used in manufacturing the punch. (Note: Because this was not my first invention, I did not need to keep my cash investment small per my Rule #8. The $40,000 was funded from accumulated profits.)

> ❝ In the third year I lowered my reps' commission to 10% because the pioneering effort from them was no longer required, and the volume was such that 10% was a decent income for their efforts. ❞

In the third year I lowered my reps' commission to 10% because the pioneering effort from them was no longer required, and the volume was such that 10% was a decent income for their efforts.

Today, ten years later, the price of the punch has crept back up to $7.98, owing to inflation and other factors. (I must admit that perhaps I shouldn't have lowered the price so much in the first place!)

Flashback

A couple of months following my first order from McWhorters, the office products dealer, I returned to Marathon Wholesale to show my friend, Bob Sherman, the finished product, tell him of our successes, and hit him up for an order. He agreed right away that Marathon should inventory the business card punch in its warehouse. After all, my McWhorters success story would make powerful ammunition for *his* sales people to use during sales calls to other dealers. Having the punch in stock at Marathon meant that any dealer in Northern California could phone in his order and get punches delivered the next day. And in smaller batches, even singles, to be combined with other items in their order. (Before Marathon took it on, a dealer could buy punches from me, but my minimum was necessarily 12 to make up an order of reasonable size.) Marathon, as my first wholesaler, took over my ongoing sales to

McWhorters and others, and began serving all the dealers in Northern California. This meant that I would have to give an extra discount on my sales to Marathon, but it would be worth it, because it also meant that Marathon would be increasing the number of dealers carrying my punch in northern California. And, my job would be made much easier because I would ship fewer, but larger, orders to just one customer—Marathon. Meanwhile, Chuck Vanderwege was very happy with this development, because it meant that much more product would be shipping into his territory.

How a Wholesaler Works

Bob's company, Marathon Office Supply, was a regional wholesaler. It had a large warehouse with inventories of thousands of SKU's (Stock Keeping Units) These are individual items with unique stock numbers from hundreds of manufacturers such as ACCO, Avery, 3-M, Rolodex, Rubbermaid, Pentel, Pendaflex, etc. He had five sales people on the road calling on office products stores in Northern California who were his customers. The function of a wholesaler like Marathon is to provide a nearby supply of merchandise available in small quantities and delivered to individual dealer stores in a timely manner—usually overnight.

> ❟ Buying from a wholesaler, the dealer can get the laundry list of items he wants, when he wants it, and in the desired quantities down to a single unit. ❟

Hypothetically, without the wholesaler, dealers would have to contact far flung manufacturers every time they ran out of something. But, dealers would find that the manufacturers would sell to them only in large batches, more than a dealer needs. And, it would take many days to get delivery. These problems are solved by the wholesaler who provides an indispensable logistical service to the dealer.

Buying from a wholesaler, the dealer can get the laundry list of items he wants, when he wants it, and in the desired quantities down to a single unit.

(Dealers must order a certain dollar size order before the wholesaler will pay the delivery costs.)

Sell the Sales People

With Bob Sherman's concurrence I provided each of his sales people with dealer demonstration samples of the business card punch imprinted with the Marathon logo. I also provided a supply of catalog sheets and the all-important price sheets on which they would rubber stamp with their Marathon name—as distributor. The sales people liked the idea of leaving a sample with each dealer after making a sales call. It provided reminder advertising for the punch, and for Marathon.

Also, with Bob's permission I put out monthly memos directly to Bob's salespeople to help remind them to show and sell my product. After all, my product was competing for their attention against all the other thousands of items Marathon carried. I felt it was my job to sell the sales people and keep them thinking about my product as much as possible. And, I still do this to this day.

Bob Sherman had cautioned me that dealers are a conservative lot who would not put a new product in their store unless several people had come in asking for it. This is not to say that sales to those casual inquirers would be lost. Hopefully, the Marathon salesperson had made the dealer aware that the new product existed and was in stock at Marathon. The dealer could special order it (even one at a time) overnight from Marathon anytime a customer came in and wanted to buy it. Later, following some of these onezie-twozie kinds of sales, the dealer would usually decide to buy and display a small quantity of the product in his store. He would do this on a low-risk basis, because he now had good reason to believe that the product would sell.

Consider, however, a situation where no one is coming into stores asking for the new product. In this case dealers do not want to stock it, and there will be no sales through these stores. What to do? Simple. You, the manufacturer, need to do some publicity for the product that will reach the consumer (end-user) and bring him into the store looking for this new product. When he buys, it's called *pulling* the product through the store. This is many times more effective than trying to *push* the product through by promoting exclusively to the wholesaler or dealer. (See Chapter 8, "How to Get Free Hype.")

You should provide dealers who agree to stock your new product with statement stuffers, which are small printed advertising fliers that can be inserted by the dealer in his mailings to customers.

Often, if you can show a dealer that you are doing some measure of consumer advertising, this will be enough to persuade him to put the product on display for sale in his store. (See Chapter 10, "Advertising and Sales Promotion.")

Advertise to Your Dealers

Look into running a small ad in a trade magazine that will reach the dealers you are trying to sell. This kind of advertising will help build dealer awareness of your product, and will show the wholesalers that you are giving them support. Hopefully, the ad will be seen by the dealer by the time the wholesaler calls on him. Don't forget to supply reprints of your ads to all reps and salespersons.

Why Appoint a 'Master Distributor?'

When starting out, try setting up your own distribution network in at least your region of the country. Once having done this, and provided your product is selling well through the stores, you are now ready to look for a "master distributor," a manufacturer who distributes products in the same category as yours. This should be a manufacturer *other* than the one that makes your product.

Your goal is to delegate the distribution function to him exclusively. Having a master distributor will simplify your life, because you ship everything to that one "customer". Make sure you have a well-written appointment agreement that ensures he performs to your satisfaction.

If you are successful, you will find a manufacturer who will take on your product and treat it as *incremental* business. This is extra business (sales) that will not produce the full profit margin that the manufacturer is used to, yet it is immediate business that will add extra profit to his bottom line.

> ❝ In addition there may be a strategic reason for this manufacturer to add your particular product, like adding an exclusive product, or filling out a line. ❞

In addition there may be a strategic reason for this manufacturer to add your particular product, like adding an exclusive product, or filling out a line.

The master distributor will increase your sales, because his customer and prospect list will include the entire industry. His relationship with important outlet companies will result in increased sales of your product.

Finding a Master Distributor

Wholesalers will tell you that they love to do business with large vendors who offer a line of several hundred products. Buying long lists of products at a time from a large vendor, buyers told me, took about as much time and paperwork that it took to buy a single product from me. Wholesalers want to do business with as few vendors as possible, while

Figure 11-3. Have your reps clip them, and make a montage of your dealers' ads that appear in catalogs and local shopping newspapers. Use this sheet to tip off other dealers as to how they might advertise your product.

avoiding small ones. Since extra administration costs companies money, they try to reduce it whenever they can. My company was looked upon as "a single-product vendor," which I learned could be a dead end, unless we could do something about it.

My company added additional products, but we were still considered a "single product vendor", even when we had a line of seven products. I found that manufacturers need at least 40 to 50 products—with at least a dozen of them producing substantial volume—to justify being set up as a vendor by a big wholesaler.

One of the buyers at a major wholesaler told me that he liked my product, and he would be willing to take it on if it were part of a broader line, such as that of Keene Manufacturing, a vendor in Wisconsin from whom he bought on a regular basis. As a result of his suggestion, I started talking to Keene and to some other vendors to see if I could work out an arrangement whereby I could sell my product to them. This would make my product part of his line, which would be sold by *his* manufacturer's reps instead of mine.

⸂ And, instead of getting many small orders every week, I got one large order every month or so. ⸃

Before long, I decided that Keene Manufacturing would be an ideal "partner" to toss in with. Keene had a 48-page catalog containing several hundred products in the category of my product, office accessories. Wendell Keene, the CEO, told me he was very interested in adding my Business Card Punch to his line. He saw it as a it novel product without competition that could draw in extra business for his regular line of stationery items.

Keene foresaw a scenario whereby if a retail dealer could obtain the Business Card Punch only through Keene, it could mean new customers for Keene, and additional sales to his current customers. For example, say Keene's prospect (a dealer he does not currently serve) orders some Business Card Punches from Keene. The buyer will probably look to see what *else* Keene has to offer so he can include additional items at the same time. He wants to make it a reasonably-sized order for which Keene would pay the freight.

I was in a good bargaining position with Keene since I already had good sales momentum in the marketplace with my product. By now, my reps had succeeded in getting my product into several thousand office products dealers around the country. And, the product was moving through the stores at a decent pace.

Soon, Keene and I entered into a simple two-way exclusive agreement that I drafted. From then on, instead of having several hundred customers I had one, Keene Manufacturing, who I had appointed my master distributor.

And, instead of getting many small orders every week, I got one large order every month or so.

It was now my unpleasant duty to discharge my nineteen manufacturer's rep organizations, after three years of loyal service, because I would no longer need them. As mentioned above, the agreements I had with them were all cancelable upon 30 days written notice by either party. I thanked them all for their wonderful help. (Some were not affected because they were also Keene's reps) All of the reps were professionals and understood this was a normal happening in the growth cycle of a successful product. They wished me well.

The new agreement I had with Keene required me to extend to him an extra 15% discount, which from my vantage point was a net 5%, since I no longer had to pay my manufacturer's reps their 10% commission. If you're thinking this smacks of a "sweetheart deal," realize that Keene was the beneficiary of some 2000 dealers already buying the punch, many of whom were not yet (but soon-to-be) customers of Keene. Keene was now the sole source of a synergistic product that he could use to add accounts and increase sales of other items.

The written agreement I entered into with Keene Manufacturing contained what I believed was a unique clause that I wanted in it. That clause permitted me to be in direct contact with all the Keene manufacturing sales reps so that I could send them monthly memos, etc. as I did with the Marathon reps. The memos would advise them of certain promotions we were doing, and I would give them ammunition to use during their sales calls. My main objective was to position my product in their minds, and to keep some of their attention focused on my products so they would not forget to talk about them during sales calls. I would try to get a newsy memo out each month with some interesting success stories about the punch. I continued with my memos after Keene was acquired by Newell Office Products Company.

I highly recommend appointing a master distributor to keep your market penetration increasing. We noticed that making this change transferred a huge workload of administration and bookkeeping out of our office, and freed up our time for doing product promotions and developing more new products. Best of all, sales boomed, because our master distributor got our product into many new places.

Looking back, I am thankful that I initially rounded up my own team of sales reps, and set up my own distribution, taking it as far as I could. This decision enabled me to pioneer this new product myself. I don't think anyone else would have put forth as much careful and concentrated effort as I did.

Later on it put me in a strong position when the time came to spin off my product line to a master distributor. It even turned my company into an acquisition target. More than once we had companies sniffing around. They knew we owned a patented product in their field that had national distribution. But they were too late, because we had everything handled, and did not need a merger. The lesson here is, if you develop your product far enough along to prove it can be successful, it becomes attractive to master distributors, to corporate buyers and to potential licensees, giving you several options.

Summary

1) Visit your local merchant in the appropriate industry.

2) Talk to sales reps and find out how distribution is organized in your industry.

3) Try to find a personal consultant to help you learn the distribution patterns of your industry. (Check with SCORE)

4)· Sign up manufacturer's reps progressively, until you have the entire national market covered.

5) Advertise to the retail dealers to help increase their awareness and acceptance.

6) Conduct publicity and advertising to the consumer market to help build awareness and demand by end-users in the stores.

7) If possible, sign up a master distributor and communicate directly with its sales force.

Note: The Resource Section begins on page 259 and is arranged by chapter to make it convenient for you to find related references.

FR: **MERRICK**   TO: All Sales Reps

K05454

ABC COMPANY

K05480

K05410

BACK-UP AND SALES SUPPORT FROM THE MANUFACTURER!

1) **DIRECT MAIL:** Merrick has just completed a mailing to some 3,000 independent office products dealers (which is about all there are now).
    The mailing included a free store demo Business Card Punch that attaches to the counter. We also included a strip of Valuable Contacts K05480, so when customers inquire, the dealers will be aware of this product, which **they are told is available through regional and national wholesalers.**

2) **MAGAZINE ADVERTISING:** Merrick runs a continuing schedule in the NOPA Business Products UPDATE MAGAZINE featuring the Punch, the Punch N' File, and the Valuable Contacts. Free samples are offered and filled to dealers by Merrick. We plan to begin a similar schedule in THE SECRETARY MAGAZINE in 1995.

3) **CONSUMER PULL-THROUGH:** Professional Secretaries International (PSI) is a group that has chapters in every state with more than 20,000 members. Merrick has provided free samples to be demonstrated to attendees of chapter meetings and conventions who are referred to O/P dealers for purchase.

4) **PROMOTION TO LEADERSHIP:** The American Management Association has a Secretaries and Administrative Assistants branch that had its annual meeting meeting in San Francisco this year. Merrick provided all 1500 attendees with a free business card punch and strip of Valuable Contacts. This is the same group 3M sampled its first POST-IT Notes to. These " centers of influence" set trends within their companies and industries.

5) **BOOKS:** The Merrick Business Card Punch and the Valuable Contacts are recommended in a new illustrated book called, "Organizing Your Home Office for Success". This a very popular book in its sixth printing, which should help increase awareness across the board. In addition to book stores, Office Depot, and other office products stores sell this book.

6) **ORGANIZERS:** There are about 2,000 individuals in the U.S. who are professional organizers. They consult to business people and others and often recommend certain office products that help people get organized. Many belong to NAPO, The National Association of Professional Organizers, which has chapters in major cities. Merrick provides free demo samples and literature for NAPO meetings and is often mentioned its magazine and newsletters.

Figure 11-4. Sending newsy memos to your sales reps each month is a good way to keep them thinking about *your* product instead of someone else's. It also gives them ammunition to use during sales calls.

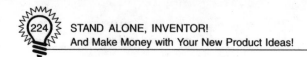

CHAPTER 12 | Mail Order, Direct and Internet Marketing

Mail order is only one aspect of direct marketing. Direct marketing is what a manufacturer does when he sells his product(s) *directly* to his end-user customer, bypassing wholesalers and dealers. There is no law against this, written or otherwise, but the practice should fit a company's distribution strategy. The manufacturer can market its product directly by mailing its own flier or catalog, by using telemarketing, or by using electronic media, which includes radio and TV, and now the Internet.

If you enter into an agreement with a master distributor, make sure it provides for exploiting mail order markets, either by him, or by you.

Catalog Companies

Mail order in general is a system that typically uses a catalog that is sent to developed lists of end-users who are known to purchase products directly from "sources" via mail. Mail order can also pull in customers if you run advertisements in newspapers, magazines, card decks in electronic media and even on bookmatches. The sources mentioned above, for example, could be actual manufacturers of goods.

> **❝ If you enter into an agreement with a master distributor, make sure it provides for exploiting mail order markets, either by him, or by you. ❞**

But more often the source is a *catalog company*, called a "catalog house", that is simply a reseller of others' goods. Later you will see how some of the goods for sale by catalog houses could be *your* goods.

Mail Order vs. Mailings

Many inventors who see me for advice have a product they want to sell using mail order. Usually, what they have in mind is running a little ad in a magazine or newspaper hoping to generate a bag full of mail containing orders and checks. Except perhaps for a unique offer of a rare product, this is usually a waste of time and money. A decent ad requires a tremendous response just to bring enough money to cover its cost to produce and run.

In the world of mail order the consumer is analogous to the commercial wholesaler, described earlier, who does not want to set up a single-product vendor.

Consider this: Almost every day the typical female consumer receives several beautiful full-color catalogs in her mail box. If she is so inclined, she can pick up one of these catalogs and pore through it to see if there is anything in it she might want. Chances are, if she finds one item she wants to buy, she says to herself, "While I'm taking the trouble to place an order, is there anything else I might need?" Finally, with her list complete, and her credit card in hand, she telephones the direct marketer's 800 number, places her order, and in a matter of minutes she is done.

I tell novice inventors, compare this with *your* hypothetical customer tearing your ad out of a magazine. She puts the tearsheet aside to be attended to later, when she has time to prepare an order to send to you. Finally, if she ever gets around to it, she sits down, begins to write you a check and thinks about mailing you an order. Meanwhile, she begins to wonder. Who *are* you? Why don't you take Visa or have an 800 number? Can she really *depend* on you to fill her order? What about a money-back guarantee?

The big direct marketing firms refund your money, no questions asked. Finally, she changes her mind, and decides not to order from you.

> **❝The big direct marketing firms refund your money, no questions asked. Finally, she changes her mind, and decides not to order from you.❞**

Because you are a "one product" company, you probably cannot justify the cost of having a toll free 800 number or setting up for credit card sales. Therefore, to buy from you your customer must write out a check, address an envelope and go to a lot of trouble just to place an order for one of your products. Compare this to marking up a full color catalog with several items, calling toll free and reading off a credit card number.

Even though you can't expect much from mail order *ads*, it could be advantageous for you to test your product using mail order *mailings*. New products can be introduced in mailings faster and at a lower cost to the manufacturer than by selling through retail stores. This is because fancy and expensive store packaging is not required in mail order, and the product goes direct—from you to the buyer—with no middleman. But, don't run an ad to find customers—buy a mailing list!

> **❛ Along the way, you can use your mail order success story to persuade catalog houses to put your product in *their* catalog and buy it bulk from you. ❜**

You can buy a test or sample list of known mail order buyers in your market category. Use it to do a small trial mailing to see what happens. In this way, you can start small and test different lists, prices, and approaches until you find what works. It is a terrific way to start and run a business on the side of your regular job, until it grows enough to support you.

Along the way, you can use your mail order success story to persuade catalog houses to put your product in *their* catalog and buy it bulk from you.

Use the Catalog Houses

Fortunately, there are hundreds, perhaps thousands, of consumer catalogs that could appropriately list and sell your invention. If your invention is not a consumer product, there are hundreds of trade and industrial catalogs that you could potentially sell through. There are several ways to identify and deal with catalog houses.

Not surprisingly, there is a trade magazine, *Catalog Age*, that is directed to and read by the managers and buyers at consumer catalog houses. The publisher of this magazine relies on the fact that many of these managers and buyers are on the lookout for new and exciting products to put in their gorgeous catalogs. Advertisers and potential advertisers in this magazine are not just inventors, but manufacturers and others who want to get their products listed in as many consumer catalogs as possible.

To get started in mail order without advertising or marketing costs:

1. Identify mail order catalogs that carry products similar to your invention.

2. Call and talk to the buyers at these mail order catalog companies and find out if and how they want you to present your product to them for consideration.

Mail order companies are very receptive to new products—but only if the products are targeted to their audience. Remember, the company that publishes a mail order catalog usually is not the manufacturer of any of the products contained in it. Very often it is a mail order company skilled in direct marketing that makes money introducing and distributing the new products of others by mail. They buy their products from many manufacturers, and perhaps they would be happy to consider yours. But keep in mind they usually require hefty profit margins—selling your product for two or more times what they pay you for it. This means that you may have to reduce *your* selling margin to keep the retail price point attractive.

You will have to convince them that you are established, and have the means to supply your product to them in sufficient quantities, and in a timely manner, should they list your product and it takes off.

Sometimes the catalog company will require you to send a color or black and white photograph of your product. But, more often they want to do their own photography to keep it consistent with the style of the other graphics in their catalog.

How to Find Mail Order Houses

1. One good way is to check the Sunday newspaper supplements and look for advertisements soliciting direct orders for products similar to yours. If yours is a household product, for example, there is usually a supplement in every Sunday paper listing items for the bathroom, kitchen and automobile. Contact the buyers for these companies and find out their required procedure for submitting a product.

2. Go to the library and check the *National Directory of Catalogs* (Oxbridge Communications/Gale) that describes 7,000 catalogs and lists the addresses of the publishers.

3. *Catalog Age* (mentioned above) accepts new product publicity releases for possible publication. This magazine is mailed to thousands of direct mail catalog publishers who are looking for new products. Later, if your publicity pulls well, you may want to place an advertisement in this magazine

> **❟You will have to convince them that you are established, and have the means to supply your product to them in sufficient quantities, and in a timely manner, should they list your product and it takes off.❞**

Once you are selling several direct mail catalog houses, you are probably covering the mail order category pretty well. However, it is a continuing job to keep an eye open for appropriate catalogs you may have missed. I think you will find that this method of participating in direct mail/direct marketing is far easier, and that it makes more sense, than trying to set yourself up in the mail order business as a one-product company. (See Resource Section for data on the publications mentioned above.)

Passive Mail Order

At any given time my company markets a dozen or so different consumer products. Frequently, we get phone calls from individual consumers who have learned about one of our products and tracked us down. (Usually they have seen our publicity, or have taken our company name and city off our product package, and called the Information operator.) Usually they want to buy only one or two items for their own personal use. We handle these inquiries by sending them our mail order "catalog." Ours is simply a legal-size sheet of paper with product descriptions illustrations, and prices. We mail it (folded) in an envelope to the caller. He or she fills out the order form printed on it, and mails it. (The sheet is designed to be folded into a self-addressed mailing envelope that will contain their check.)

> ❮ This system produces enough income to pay our electric bill, and then some. At the same time we are spreading the word about our other products, and we are satisfying that all-important person—our customer. ❯

I call this a passive mail order program, because we do not mail it to lists. (A test mailing told us this would not be profitable.) We mail one only when someone calls about one of our products that they can't find in a store. This way we get nearly a 100% response!

This system produces enough income to pay our electric bill, and then some. At the same time we are spreading the word about our other products, and we are satisfying that all-important person—our customer.

Mailing List Brokers

Mailing list brokers have catalogs of the lists they offer to rent or sell. One entry might read, "Service stations........33,000," and then in another section be broken down by state, . (See illustrations) (See Resource Section for lists of brokers.)

Mailing list brokers can provide two kinds of lists based on their sources. The first kind include lists of people grouped by "demographics." that is, where they live, or the kind of work they do, their age, income,

COMPILED

SAD-SOC

S

Quantity	List	Price
3,641	Saddlery & Harness Shops	
3,708	Safe & Vault Wholesalers	$45/M
3,847	Safety Equipment Whls.	$45/M

SALES

Quantity	List	Price
92,520	Executives, All	$50/M
72,690	At Leading U.S. Corporations	$50/M
1,977	Fortune 1,000 Cos.	$150/F
1,579	Sales Promotion Services	$150/F
2,759	Salvage & Surplus Stores	$150/F
1,319	Salvation Army	$150/F
13,177	Sand & Gravel Whls	$45/M
10,489	Sandwich Shops	$45/M
5,312	Sand Blasting Service	$45/M

Sanitation Services

Quantity	List	Price
23,296	Disinfecting & Exterminating	$45/M
13,101	Garbage & Trash Collecting	$45/M
9,306	House Cleaning	$45/M
28,368	Janitorial Services	$45/M
3,148	Maid Services	$150/F
6,327	Snow Removal	$45/M
6,715	Window Cleaning	$45/M
3,598	Savings & Loan Assn Headquarters (See Banks)	$50/M
5,707	Sawmills & Planning Mills	$45/M
2,088	Scaffolding Contractors & Steeple Jacks	$150/F

SCHOOLS

Quantity	List	Price
15,027	School Board Presidents	$52/M

By Type of School

Quantity	List	Price
160	Agricultural	$150/F
1,342	Allied Health Sciences	$150/F
119	Architectural	$150/F
490	Art Instruction	$150/F
3,479	Auto Driving Instructors	$45/M
2,237	Aviation	$150/F
2,729	Beauty Schools	$150/F
185	Business Administration (MBA)	$150/F
1,170	Business Schools, Collegiate & Private	$150/F
7,397	Business & Secretarial	$45/M
4,363	Colleges & Universities (See Colleges)	$60/M
11,685	Dance	$45/M
2,483	Data Processing & Computer Training	$150/F
287	Engineering	$150/F
250	Journalism	$150/F
156	Medical	$150/F
314	Medical & Dental Assistants	$150/F
5,716	Music Instruction	$45/M
66,835	Nursery & Day Care Centers	$50/M
1,158	Nursing	$150/F
163	Photography	$150/F
255	Commercial Art	$150/F

Quantity	List	Price
276	Physical Education	$150/F
397	Preparatory	$150/F
71,643	Public, Private & Catholic, Elementary	$45/M
38,871	Public Private & Catholic, Middle	$45/M
24,959	Public, Private & Catholic, Senior High	$45/M
1,178	Real Estate & Insurance	$150/F
653	Self Improvement	$150/F
244	Social Work	$150/F
609	Speech & Drama	$150/F
1,261	Teacher Education	$150/F
252	Theology	$150/F
3,490	Trade & Technical	$45/M
19,251	Vocational/Trade	$60/M
16,630	School Districts	$60/M
10,223	Under 2,500 Enrollment	$60/M
2,938	2,500-10,000 Enrollment	$60/M
931	10,000+ Enrollment (also see Education, Educators)	$150/F
2,005	School Supplies Wholesale	$150/F

SCIENCE, SCIENTISTS

Quantity	List	Price
90,302	Leading Scientists	$50/M
5,522	Agricultural & Forest Sciences	$50/M
27,590	Biological Sciences	$50/M
33,052	Chemistry	$50/M
34,906	Computer	$50/M
19,181	Engineering	$50/M
31,247	Environmental	$50/M
7,458	Mathematics	$50/M
16,961	Medical & Health	$50/M
25,352	Microbiology	$50/M
35,819	Physics	$50/M
17,069	Scrap & Waste Whls.	$45/M
3,143	Screw Machine Product Mfrs.	$150/F
25,710	Secretarial Svcs.	$45/M
34,983	Security Dealers	$50/M
3,680	Seeds & Bulb Dealers	$45/M
1,925	Semiconductor & Related Device Manufacturers	$150/F

SENIOR CITIZENS

Quantity	List	Price
990,357	High Income Prime-Timers	$55/M
14,000,000	Senior Citizens	$50/M
7,123	Organizations	$45/M
9,821	Retirement Communities, Homes	$45/M
12,435	Septic Tank & Sewer Contractors	$45/M
20,853	Surgeons, General	$50/M
95,496	Service Stations, Gasoline	$45/M
2,359	Service Station Equip. Whls	$150/F

SERVICES

Quantity	List	Price
1,904,982	Services, Personal & Business, All (See page 36 in SIC Section)	$45/M
1,519	Sewerage Systems	$150/F
10,487	Sewer Contractors	$45/M
4,972	Sewing Machine Dealers	$45/M
3,942	Repair Services	$45/M
18,584	Sewing, Needlework & Piece Goods Stores	$45/M
12,363	Sheet Metal Contractors	$45/M
6,975	Sheet Metal Work Manufacturers	$45/M
3,228	Sheriffs	$50/M
1,004	Ship Building & Repair	$150/F
6,393	Shipping & Freight Forwarding Companies	$45/M
4,172	Shock Absorber Replacement Services	$45/M
39,207	Shoe & Footwear Stores	$45/M
11,338	Repair Shops	$45/M
17,036	Siding Contractors	$45/M
2,137	Sightseeing Tour Companies	$150/F
31,413	Sign & Advertising Display Manufacturers	$45/M
2,413	Sign Maintenance & Repair	$150/F
15,614	Silk Screen Printers	$45/M
1,220	Skate Boards & Equipment	$150/F
1,194	Ski Centers & Resorts	$150/F
2,665	Ski Equip. Retail	$45/M
1,834,000	Small Business Owners, Presidents and Managers	$65/M
1,307	Smokers Information & Treatment Centers	$150/F
2,365	Snowmobile Dealers	$150/F
6,327	Snow Removal Services	$45/M
719	Soap & Other Detergent Manufacturers	$150/F

SOCIAL SERVICES

Quantity	List	Price
228,155	Organizations	$45/M
827	Abortion Info & Svcs.	$150/F
1,025	Adoption Agencies	$150/F
14,841	Alcoholism	$45/M
4,217	Birth Control & Family Planning	$45/M
67,570	Child Care Services	$45/M
6,635	Counseling Services	$45/M
2,370	Crisis Intervention	$150/F
9,764	Drug Abuse Treatment	$45/M
17,085	Job Training Svcs.	$45/M
40,174	Marriage & Family Counselors	$45/M
14,206	Mental Health Services	$45/M
1,436	Mental Retardation Services	$150/F
4,104	Recreational Centers & Services	$45/M
11,307	Rehabilitation Services	$45/M
11,843	Residential Care for Children & Adults	$45/M
6,939	Senior Citizen Organizations	$150/F
5,022	Social Workers	$45/M

Call Toll Free 800-ALC-LIST (800-252-5478) FAX 908-874-4433

Figure 12-1. Sample page from a list broker's catalog of "compiled" lists. These are demographic lists usually drawn from public records such as the census, surveys, yellow pages, etc.

Figure 12-2. Sample page from a list broker's catalog of "direct response" lists. These are lists of known buyers by mail that let you target your offer to those most likely to buy.

religion, etc. This is called a "compiled" list and is usually drawn from public records (such as Yellow Page listings, surveys, census, etc.). It is the least expensive type of list, (about $50/thousand addresses) but is usually not as effective in producing responses as the second type of list, called a "targeted buyer" or "direct response" list, which is obtained as follows:

When someone subscribes to a magazine, buys something from a mail-order company, joins a club or organization by mail, or makes a charitable donation, his or her name probably will be sold to a broker so it becomes available on a list. These are lists of known buyers that let you "target" your offer to the people most likely to want your new product. For example, if you have developed a great new weed killer, mailing an offer to a list of people who have bought seeds by mail will very likely get a good response. Lists of known buyers can pull five times better, and don't cost much more ($75 to $85 per thousand addresses) than compiled lists.

> **❝Some list brokers will give you free of charge a limited number of names from a list (say 100-300) in an effort to sell you a larger quantity. Be sure to ask about this, because you may be able to use the free short list for your test mailing.❞**

Normally, when you order, there is a minimum dollar amount or quantity of labels required by the list broker. ($150-$500, or 5,000 labels is typical.) Rather than risk a larger sum of money by initially mailing to an entire list, buy a small portion of the list and do a test mailing using a sales letter accompanied by other materials describing your new product. Within a few weeks you'll know whether your product and your letter are pulling. You can then decide if you want to mail to more of the list (called "rolling out") and if you are successful, rent more lists to try.

Some list brokers will give you free of charge a limited number of names from a list (say 100-300) in an effort to sell you a larger quantity. Be sure to ask about this, because you may be able to use the free short list for your test mailing.

Direct Marketing Using Radio and TV

We've all seen the ads for the new gadgets on late night television. The "Ginzu" knife sold millions from such 60-second commercials. And who hasn't seen at least one "infomercial"—those half hour or hour rave sessions that look like popular talk shows. If you have a new invention that can be demonstrated, or talked about with enthusiasm, TV or radio advertising can be the fastest and least expensive way to market your product. Although network advertising on TV and radio can costs thousands of dollars for a few seconds, local advertising can be low cost—even free—making this the best medium for beginning to market your new product.

Once there were only three networks, and almost everyone watched certain popular shows, such as "I Love Lucy." Today, because of the "cabling of America," there are many more channels, programs, and networks, resulting generally in fewer viewers for any particular show. While this is bad for large national advertisers, making it both difficult and expensive to get their message in front of everyone, this segmenting of the TV viewing audience is a golden opportunity for the "little guy" trying to launch a new product.

> **❝With a computer and a reasonably fast modem you, too, can rocket into cyberspace. The Internet is a huge and chaotic "media swamp" growing at a dizzying rate.❞**

A simple but effective TV ad can be professionally produced and tested for a few thousand dollars on a small cable station to see if your product is "hot." If orders roll in, usually to an 800 phone order-taking service, you can then roll out your advertisement from cable group to cable group, growing as you go. To test an ad on radio costs even less. Also, there are many local cable TV and radio stations that will run your ad on a per inquiry (PI) basis. You pay only for response inquiries or orders they generate for you.

Direct Marketing on the Net

With millions of people owning computers capable of accessing the Internet and other on-line computer services, such as CompuServe, America On-Line and AT&T WorldNet, you'd think that this is a good place to market your new product—and you'd be right!

With a computer and a reasonably fast modem you, too, can rocket into cyberspace. The Internet is a huge and chaotic "media swamp" growing at a dizzying rate.

There are thousands of different groups, agencies, services, web sites and databases, each with their own specialized interests and ways of doing things.

Some groups welcome new product announcements. Other groups would like to tar and feather you for trying to hawk your wares. But most groups and on-line services have special areas where you can advertise free. In fact, commercial areas are the fastest growing segment of the information superhighway. Little wonder that the largest corporations are now opening new marketing departments solely dedicated to marketing on the Net!

But the beauty of marketing on the Internet at this point in its early development is that no matter how small your company is, you can compete against the big guys pretty much on an equal footing! At present, nearly all ads look the same on the Net. Mostly we are dealing in printed text, with a smathering of still images. There are no million-dollar production video ads with superstar models. It's facts, benefits and price that count. What a place for a young David to take on a Goliath, and come out a winner!

For a fast-moving, small company with a better "widget," the Net provides a window of opportunity to go even where the big corporations have never gone, and to carve out a market niche. For the inventor of an exciting new product who has little or no marketing budget, electronic marketing is worth a go! But be quick—as communication technology improves, this golden window for the 'little guy' may not stay wide open for long!

To get started, sign up with one of the many ISPs (Internet Service Providers), such as AT&T WorldNet, NetCom or others. (See Resource Section). [Find one with access via a local phone call.] This will get you your own electronic mail box address, free Web-browsing software, and unlimited Internet access for a flat monthly rate of about $20 or less. America Online and CompuServe offer hundreds of additional valuable services and support.

Once connected, you will want to search the Internet to find marketing sites that will help you promote and sell your new product. In the Resource Section of this book you will find sites that will let you have free ad listings, and free postings of new product releases. But before you send your first message to the millions of other users out there, I suggest you check out sites like the *Web Digest for Marketers*, which are on the Web. Their URL addresses are listed under *Internet Resources* in the Resource Section. (Along the way, make sure you learn proper "netiquette" so as not to disturb or offend others.) As I mentioned before, you are welcome to post your promotional notices at many sites, but at some sites the users might "flame" you for being inappropriate and inconsiderate. "Flaming" is when people send angry messages to your e-mail account.

One advertiser dropped his ads indiscriminately ("spammed") at various web sites. He got so many thousand angry flames sent to his mailbox, that it totally blocked the normal business of everyone else on his ISP's server computer. So you can't just go promoting your product helter skelter on the Internet.

But, if you limit the sending of your ads or press releases to those places that have specific sections for marketing, and to special interest groups that would clearly be interested, you are not likely to get flamed; but you are likely to get some valuable exposure.

For starters you can post free classified directory listings and send out press releases to selected news groups. Also, be sure to call ABI at 402/593-4593 and order your free listing in the *Net Yellow Pages*. Interested individuals who see your listing will e-mail or call you for further information about your product and/or its purchase. You will be surprised how many business newsgroups and special interest groups there are on the Web——thousands! And your e-mail message or posting will often be seen by a CEO or key purchasing officer. If you had sent the same release via the US Postal Service, it would probably never make it to key people with buying authority before getting thrown out as junk mail. Moreover, Postal mail costs you 32 cents, while e-mail is virtually free!

After you have surfed a few weeks and see how others are using their web site to promote their business and sell products, you will want to have a Home Page for your company. The benefits are many: visitors to your web pages will see pictures of your product, read your sales literature, and possibly order, either by calling your 800 number, or sending you e-mail. If you are set up to handle credit cards, you can complete entire transactions online without even being there! Another approach is to accept checks electronically, using a service offered by ExpressChex (see Resource Section, Ch 6).

If how-to-create your own web site is a mystery to you, check out the many helpful folks on the Web dedicated to teaching you—at no cost—how to do it. Start at **http://www.yahoo.com** and **http://www.netscape.com** and go to their "computer/web page design" sections. Also, many local community colleges, even libraries, are starting to offer courses on creating web pages. If you would rather have someone do the whole job for you, contact your nearby college and you will find talented students, "computer geeks," who can, usually for a fee, build your

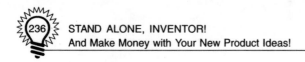
page for you.

Another approach is to sell your products through others' web sites. These web sites usually have many other products listed and promoted. Check out the Internet Shopping Network (**http://www.internet.net/**) hosted by the same people who produce the Home Shopping Network on TV.

Or you can purchase "space" at an existing commercial site or Web shopping mall, such as Sparky's Web Site Service (**http:// CyberZine.ORG**.) They will often design and maintain your Web page for you. (Sparky only charges $10 per month!)

Note: The Resource Section begins on page 259 and is arranged by chapter to make it convenient for you to find related references.

| CHAPTER 13 | **Selling Your Invention as a Promotional Product or a Premium** |

Insider Terminology

The promotional products industry has three important definitions that will help you understand it.

Suppliers: Manufacturers—like you and me—that make imprinted promotional products.

Distributors: Independent sales companies that buy imprinted promotional products from suppliers, and resell them to advertisers.

Advertisers: End-user businesses and organizations that buy imprinted promotional products for use in various internal and external programs.

Promotional Products Defined

Promotional products, which were called "advertising specialties" for nearly a hundred years, are items of nominal value—usually imprinted with a sponsor's logo and message—that are given away.

> **❝Promotional products, which were called "advertising specialties" for nearly a hundred years, are items of nominal value—usually imprinted with a sponsor's logo and message—that are given away.❞**

Typically, these items are given away free to customers, prospects, distributors, salespeople, vendors or employees, depending on the program. These items are used by the advertiser or sponsor as a reminder advertising tool to promote sales, goodwill, safety, and other causes.

Bookbags and bookmatches are said to be among the oldest forms of promotional products. Pens, pencils, coffee mugs and key tags are examples of the most common promotional products, along with calendars. Wearables, like T-shirts, caps and jackets are also in this category, and the most popular by survey.

Figure 13-1. This handle for a 2-liter soft drink bottle, invented by Remberto Carranza, is an example of a promotional product. Notice the advertising imprint on it. It can also be sold as an on-pack premium with or without imprint.

Starting out selling your new invention solely as a promotional product has important advantages. The risk-reward ratio favors going to this market first—before you tackle the retail market. Why? First, you don't have to invest in retail store packaging (which can be expensive), because promotional products are usually shipped in bulk with little or no individual packaging. Second, a minimum order for a promotional product is usually one hundred to two hundred and fifty pieces, whereas the typical order from a retail store is a dozen units or less. These bigger-volume orders from the outset put you up and running and in the black faster, and they will let you accumulate the extra cash you will need later for your retail launch. Third, unlike the retail market, because each order is custom, you do not produce an order until after you sell it.

❝ Actually, for this reason it's possible for a product that would fail to sell in retail stores, to succeed very well as a give-away promotional product. ❞

Best of all, you will never have an order of promotional products returned to you with the excuse, "It wouldn't sell," because these products are always given away!

Actually, for this reason it's possible for a product that would fail to sell in retail stores, to succeed very well as a give-away promotional product.

Generally, there is the same amount of paperwork involved in shipping one dozen units of your product to a retailer, as in shipping one thousand imprinted units to a buyer of promotional products.

The greatest advantage to offering your product as a promotional product is—the "sky's the limit" in terms of the size order you might land. If your product really appeals to a major corporation, it is not uncommon for the quantity ordered to be in the hundreds of thousands of units or even in the millions of units! Retail sales will hardly ever ramp up this rapidly.

Recalling my own experience with windfall orders, the largest imprinted order we had ever filled for my watch calendars was for 100,000 pieces, until. . . One day I was contacted by a San Francisco bank marketing executive who had seen our ad for the calendar in an airline magazine. He said his bank did monthly mailings statewide to all its depositors, and the mailings usually contained an imprinted item of nominal value. He thought my calendar would be just right for his next mailing, but we'd have to move fast. He requested that I quote price and delivery in two weeks for a quantity of 3.5 million watch calendars! I had to quickly negotiate my cost for this quantity directly with president of my vendor company, and get his guarantee for an airtight production schedule. The bank liked my proposal, and the resulting rush order went smoothly. It added a huge sum to our bottom line that year.

❝ The entire transaction took only about four hours of my time. Beautiful orders like this are always possible when you are selling promotional products. ❞

The entire transaction took only about four hours of my time. Beautiful orders like this are always possible when you are selling promotional products.

How to Sell Promotional products

This market will have great potential for you, assuming your product is of nominal cost, and that you can offer it custom-imprinted with an advertiser's logo and message on it. The reason for the great potential is that almost all of the 15 million businesses in this country buy promotional products, even if they are only key tags or calendar cards. I think this is one of the easiest markets for you to start selling because, as an industry, it is very well organized. We can thank the Advertising Specialty Institute, (ASI) of Langhorne, PA, for having the vision to first organize this market in the 1940s.

The ASI has put together an international network that enables the many companies that manufacture advertising specialties (*suppliers*) and the many sales organizations that sell these types of products (*distributors*) to communicate with each other—efficiently.

There are approximately 2500 suppliers in the US whose main activity is the manufacture of imprinted promotional products—there are more than 50,000 items. There are approximately 14,000 distributors that have salespeople—about 40,000— whose main activity is calling on the millions of end-user businesses and other organizations that use imprinted promotional products. (See Promotional Products Industry Flow Chart.)

If you manufacture and start selling your product as a promotional product, ASI will offer to "list" you as a supplier in its data base. Cost: $185. Once you are listed, they will offer to sell you such things as credit services, mailing lists of distributors and advertisements in ASI magazines and product catalogs that are sold to the distributors.

The ASI has a competitor, called Impact Advertising, located in Dunedin, Florida. This is a younger company that does not offer as wide a range of services as ASI, but has some very good advertising programs that suppliers can use to good advantage.

As mentioned above, one of the best things about the promotional products industry is that it is very well-organized. For example, it has a uniform pricing system that everyone in the industry understands and uses religiously. It goes like this: All catalog sheets, advertisements and listings include pricing that is intended for the eyes of the end user, who is called the "advertiser." Printed price lists show the MSRP, or the

manufacturer's suggested retail price. This is the price per unit the distributor charges the advertiser. Most suppliers give the advertiser price breaks for increased quantities.

The distributor, through a secret coding system, is given a discount off the advertisers' price that is his margin of profit on each sale.

Once you are listed with ASI, they will give you specific details on their confidential price coding system. For example, a supplier's catalog sheet may show that one thousand pens cost the advertiser one dollar per piece, including imprinting. The distributor, who has field sales people selling these pens, lands an order for 1,000 pens at a dollar per piece. The supplier uses the industry discount code to communicate a certain percentage discount to the distributor, say 30%. In this instance the distributor buys the pens from the supplier at $1.00 less 30%, or seventy cents, and resells them to the end user at one dollar. He makes a gross profit margin of thirty cents per unit, or $300 on the sale. Usually this profit is split equally between the distributorship and its field sales person who closed the order.

> **The distributor, through a secret coding system, is given a discount off the advertisers' price that is his margin of profit on each sale.**

Discounts range typically from 20% to 50% at the discretion of the supplier, depending on the product price point and quantity. As a rule, the smaller the quantity, the greater the discount. As a supplier of a promotional product you must structure your pricing to provide whatever discounts you want to extend across the quantity band. Be sure to leave enough margin to realize the profit percentage you want to make on your sales. Look up ASI-listed promotional products similar to yours, and study the prices and discounts used as a clue to how you should structure yours.

Many distributors tell me that they won't show a product that doesn't have at least a 40% discount. (But this doesn't mean that they won't *accept* an order for a product that the advertiser discovers on his own, even if it has only a 25% or 30% discount!) Personally, I feel that 30% is sufficient for the higher-quantity orders.

Promotional product distributors are always looking for new products to show and sell to their customers. This is where you come in. I would suggest you contact some of these distributors in your area (to be found under Advertising Specialties or Promotional Products in the Yellow Pages). Show them or tell them about your product to get their reaction. If their reaction is encouraging, make up some samples with a random imprint or a "Your Company Name Here" imprint, to be used by this distributor's sales people.

Also, you will need to print a simple price sheet describing the product and listing the prices and discount codes at various quantities, ranging from, say, one hundred to 2500 pieces. Put some catalog sheets and samples in the hands of this distributor and ask him to kick it off at his next sales meeting. Hopefully, his salespeople will present your product to appropriate advertisers to see what happens.

> ❝If this procedure produces just one order for one hundred pieces, I'd say you have what is very likely to become a successful promotional product.❞

If this procedure produces just one order for one hundred pieces, I'd say you have what is very likely to become a successful promotional product.

Imprinting Your Product

Usually the firm that makes your product has the capability of imprinting large quantities of it economically. But, when you sell promotional products, the typical orders you'll get will range from 100 to 5000 units. Getting these smaller quantities imprinted economically can pose a problem. One solution is to outsource the imprinting to a firm that specializes in this. You can start with "screen printers" in the Yellow Pages.

Also, ask around about "pad printers" and "hot stamp printers" until you find the best method for imprinting your product. Also, there are job imprinters who are ASI listed suppliers.

If your product is made of molded plastic, like my punch, you may want to copy my method of imprinting, which works very well. I use a pressure-sensitive label that is hot stamped and has a Mylar lamination on top for durability. This label looks best when it is recessed into the plastic, as it is on my punch. I had my mold maker design a shallow, recessed area in the punch slightly larger than 1.5 X 1.0 inches, which is the size of the label I use.

If you use my method, you must find a label maker (preferably local) who can hot stamp labels, and who is willing to work with you until you get your volume built up. This kind of label printing requires a minimum run of about 3,000 to get the price to about $0.10 each. The beauty of this method is that within the 3,000 run you can have numerous copy changes

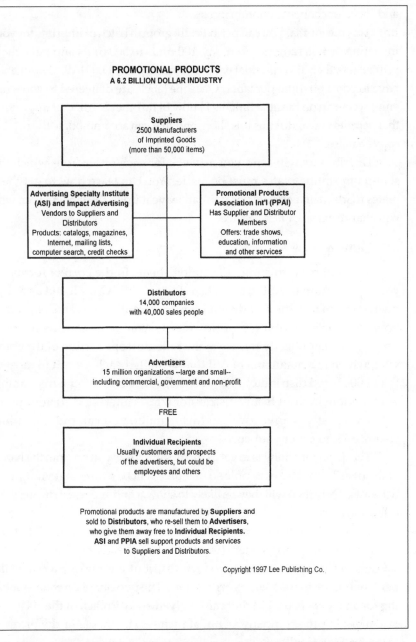

Figure 13-2. Chart shows how imprinted promotional products flow from the manufacturers through distributor sales organizations and finally to the advertiser who gives them away. If your product fits, it's better to try to market it through this channel, *before* you try to sell it through retail stores.

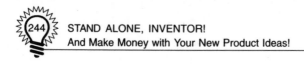
and/or color changes at nominal cost.

This means that you can periodically group a batch of imprints for your incoming orders ranging from, say, 100 units to 500 units and have them printed together. If your initial batches total only, say, 1,000 to 2,000, you may have to pay a bit more per label. Once the labels are delivered to you, your employees can do the attachment. I know of no other method of imprinting that permits you to do runs this short, and that can accommodate the needed copy changes.

Distributors will send you artwork for each order from which hot stamp imprinting plates must be made. You can learn how to get these plates made at an engraver, or you can leave it up to the label maker, who will charge extra for this service.

ASI Listing

You will need to sumit 10 catalog sheets in the correct format in your application to ASI to be a "listed supplier". Once listed as a supplier, you can run ads and do mailings to the entire universe of promotional products distributors worldwide. I recommend starting out with a new product publicity release to the Kaleidoscope section of the *Counselor*, which is a magazine of ASI that is mailed each month to most of the 14,000 listed distributors. If practical, you should offer a free sample with random imprint to any distributor who is interested. If your product is too costly to give away in this manner, you can put a nominal charge on it to cover your costs.

The important thing is to get as many samples as you can into the hands of the distributors' sales people so that they will be aware that your product exists. Only then will they be likely to show it and suggest it during sales calls to advertisers.

Let's say you invented a hollow plastic exercise dumbbell that can be filled with drinking water. (Sorry, this has already been invented.) A salesman from a promotional products distributor is making a call on the personnel director of a large corporation. The personnel director is looking for an inexpensive gift that can be given away to each of the 900 families attending the company's annual picnic. The theme of the picnic is "Stay Fit, Stay Healthy."

The salesman, remembering that he saw your new product blurb in the *Counselor* magazine, tells the personnel director that he thinks he has exactly the right product for the picnic and that he will come back next week with a sample!

At this point the salesman has his office staff "research" this product, locate and contact your company, order a sample and check your current pricing. The distributor's research person searches for your company in the ASI's Media File, or does a computer search, so he can order the sample. The next week the salesman shows your sample to the personnel director who agrees the product ties in very well with the theme of the picnic, and he places an order for 900 units.

> **ʕ The lesson here is that your publicity is working. The salesman saw and remembered your blurb in the *Counselor* that enabled him to suggest your product and eventually land the order. ʔ**

The lesson here is that your publicity is working. The salesman saw and remembered your blurb in the *Counselor* that enabled him to suggest your product and eventually land the order.

As a supplier you also must advertise to the end user. A good way to do this is by placing a small ad in one of the many condensed catalogs published both by ASI and Impact. Your ad will appear in a small catalog that fits into a letter-sized envelope. Roughly ten percent of the distributors (about 1,000) purchase quantities and mail them to their customers. The targeted circulation of these catalogs is several hundred thousand known buyers of your kind of product. I invest the greater part of my advertising dollars to reach the end user, rather than the distributor.

Selling promotional products "direct"

When you are beginning to sell your invention as a promotional product, your natural inclination will be to try to sell it yourself, directly to the advertisers/end users—the banks, the airlines, etc. But once you become listed with ASI you will learn that the promotional products industry considers "direct selling" a taboo for suppliers. Understandably, ASI-listed distributors want all the sales of listed suppliers to go through them. Some of the big-name pen companies and others do not always adhere to this, and I do not think it is a necessity for all suppliers—all of the time.

As a practical matter you need to get started, and you are legally and ethically free to sell to anyone you choose. The listed distributors expect you to set them up to sell your product on an exclusive basis, but they cannot force you to. My advice is to structure all your pricing to provide for the distributors' discount. Next, be sure that if and when you land a direct order on your own, you sell it at the full list price. Also, never accept an order that should rightfully go through a distributor. In this way distributors can never complain that you are undercutting them by selling at a lower price, or that you are selling to their customers.

Although it is true you will want and need the support of the distributors in the long run, it is also true that it is not in your best interests to always rely one hundred per cent on distributors to show and sell your product. After all, there are 50,000 promotional products out there. What are the chances that any given distributor will present *your* product to an end user on any given day? Some distributors may not even *like* your product, and will never show it. My strategy is to advertise to end users in hopes they will like my product and ask the distributor who calls on them about it. Advertise in the distributor-sponsored catalogs and magazines that reach the buyers of promotional products. Also, advertise in the independent *trade* magazines that reach the market.

> **❢ Nearly any product can be used as a premium, and perhaps yours can, too. Knowing this, you can probably figure out a premium use for your new invention. ❥**

I always state in my trade ads, "for more information contact your ad specialty distributor, or us." My objective with trade ads is two-fold: a.) To elicit sales leads from those companies who perhaps do not have an ad specialty distributor calling on them regularly, and, b.) to cause other end users to bring my product to the attention of their favorite distributor. Usually that distributor will locate my company and land an order for my product.

Premiums Defined

If your new product would make a nice gift, I recommend you explore the premium market. Broadly speaking, a premium is defined as a gift that is given to you if you do something. The sponsor gives the *premium* to his customer in *consideration* of some act: Visit our store (the consideration), and we'll give you a calendar (the premium). Open an account at our bank, and we'll give you a waffle iron. Open a jumbo CD account and we'll give you a car in lieu of interest. Various manufacturers will cajole their dealers into increasing their inventory of a product by offering to give them a free TV when they place a larger-size order.

It is best if the premium ties into the sponsor's product or into a theme. Example: A ski manufacturer gives customers a special ski cap in consideration of the purchase of his skis. Historically, premiums did not carry the sponsor's imprint, but in recent years more and more pre-

miums, especially wearables, are logo-imprinted.

Nearly any product can be used as a premium, and perhaps yours can, too. Knowing this, you can probably figure out a premium use for your new invention.

For example, an inventor came to me one day with his new, improved trowel for finishing cement work. He had prepared a good, simple black and white catalog sheet, but he said that he was having difficulty getting his product placed in lumberyards and hardware stores. However, he said when he had given his trowel to concrete finishers they liked it and used it a lot.

I asked him if he had tried to sell the trowel as a premium, and he asked me to explain. I said, "Have you taken it to any of the ready mix delivery companies to see if they will buy some from you?" He said, "Why would *they* want to buy the trowel?" I told him that concrete delivery— like every other business—is competitive and it always needs a better way to promote business. "So you could offer a ready mix company a quantity of trowels," I told him, "suggesting they give one away to concrete contractors and finishers in consideration of a truck load of ready mix cement ordered from *them*, rather than from their competitors."

Later, I found out from the inventor that this idea worked very nicely for him, and that he was expanding his premium sales to other concrete delivery companies. The last I heard from him he had successfully established his product as a premium, and was starting to launch it as a retail product in hardware stores. I hope this example will spark some idea in you as to how your product can be positioned as a premium, before you consider selling it as a retail store product.

How to Sell Premiums

How do you go about getting your product sold as a premium? Start by contacting banks or selected large corporations where your product might be appropriate. Talk to the advertising manager and/or the sales manager and explain what you have.

One inventor came to me with her novel paper towel holder. It was a single spindle that attached to a flat surface, such as a counter, and held a roll of paper towels vertically. I advised her to contact the makers of paper towels to see if this could be sold as an "on-pack premium." (This is a premium that is visibly attached to a retail package to induce impulse buying.) She did this and was successful in writing her first order—a good one—for $80,000 from Kimberly Clark. They attached her holder to

STAND ALONE, INVENTOR!
And Make Money with Your New Product Ideas!

248

a double pack of paper towels as an on-pack premium. Later, she went on to sell the product as a store item, but it didn't do as well as its premium sales.

Another way to reach premium buyers directly is to try to place a publicity notice by sending a press release to the two principal magazines going to premium buyers: *Potentials In Marketing* and *Premium Incentive Business*. (See Resource Section)

If one or both magazines run your story, probably you will hear from scores of companies who want to know more about your product. These companies may be considering using your product as a gift to employees, as an incentive for sales people, or as a premium to promote sales to their distributors or end users.

Your story will also be seen by premium sales reps who may inquire about selling your product. You can also seek out premium reps to sell your product by checking the listings in the back of these magazines and in their annual directories. These reps will sell your product in great quantities with the purchase order coming directly to you. They expect you to pay them a sales commission of between 5% and 15%, per written agreement. (Some promotional advertising distributors buy and re-sell premiums.)

Before you publicize to this market, be sure that you have the means to produce large quantities, that you know your costs, and that you have large-quantity pricing ready to quote. You could be thrust into business in a big hurry, and in a big way, if a national company wants to use your product as a premium.

Note: The Resource Section begins on page 259 and is arranged by chapter to make it convenient for you to find related references.

CHAPTER 14

How to Set Up Your "Virtual Office"

Clear the Kitchen Table!

Setting up an office for a new business today can be easier and cheaper than ever before. You no longer need to rent office space or hire an office staff in order to look like a 'real' company. Thanks to the digital age, now you can have a "virtual office." It looks and functions like a regular business office at a fraction of the cost. You can get started literally on your kitchen table!

A Place To Work: The Home Office Option

Keeping rent and other overhead expenses low is important for all businesses, but especially if you are launching a new product as a Stand-Alone Inventor. Every dollar saved from overhead is one you can put toward developing and promoting your product.

Starting a business from home is the American way! After all, Hewlett and Packard and Jobs and Wozniak started their companies at home (albeit out of their garages!). A 1993 annual Work-at-Home Survey conducted by LINK Resources, a New York based market research firm, showed 41.1 million Americans work full or part-time from their homes. Of this number 9.2 million were employed by corporations. The trend is definitely toward a stay-at-home work style.

The Virtual Office

Using a fax machine, answering machine, automated voice mail, plus E-mail, your company can take orders, answer inquiries and send sales literature automatically, whether you are in your office or not! Your new 'electronic office staff' can help you, as a part-time entrepreneur, meet your customers' needs even while you're away holding down your day job.

Let's see how you can set up a 'virtual office' that to the outside world looks and acts like a regular company.

Business Communications

Someone once defined a business as "an organization designed to create and keep customers." If this is true, then it's important to keep in mind that customer communications can make or break your business. Customers (and vendors, too) become very disillusioned and anxious if they can't get through to your company. Fortunately, your ability to tell the world about your product is limited only by the different means of communication you can tap into. Here's how to set up your 'virtual office' so that the lines of communication are always open.

Your Telephone

The minimum you need to get started is one extra telephone line just for your business—not for your 4-year-old to answer, and not for those long romantic chats by your teenager.

On this line hook up an answering machine (preferably a combination fax/phone/answering machine), and use it for *incoming* business phone calls and faxes only. Use your original personal line for *outgoing* business and all personal calls. If you find you are using the Internet a lot, you will need *another* line just for your computer. More about this later.

Your Fax /Phone/Answering Machine

Today you can find combination fax/phone/answering machines that cost less than fax machines alone used to cost (now as low as $129!). These combos are easier to set up and work better than connecting a fax machine to an existing phone/answering machine. Features that make your communications go smoother: speed dialing, automatic redialer, automatic sheet cutter and speaker phone.

Note: Don't have "call waiting" on either your business line or your personal line because it can cause your fax/ phone/answering machine to behave erratically. Incoming faxes or voice messages may be disrupted by call waiting clicks. If you must have call waiting, limit it to your personal line. If you want to avoid getting the clicks, call waiting provides for a blocking on out-going calls you select. Ask your local phone company how to block. (But, on incoming calls interrupting clicks can make you look unprofessional.)

If you have a computer, there are software programs that will allow it to take calls and faxes, and even let your clients request sales sheets or other information to be faxed to them. The one problem with having your computer play fax/answering machine is that should your computer lock up when you are doing other work, you risk your customer communications 'going down' as well. Best keep the fax/phone/answering machine separate from the computer until you can dedicate a second computer totally to this function.

Business Listing?

If you set up your phone for incoming calls as a *business line* you pay more each month to the phone company than if you are set up as an *individual*. Which way you go depends on several factors. Will you want a listing in the telephone directory under a fictitious business name, or will you be doing business under your own name? Will potential customers be looking for you in the yellow pages? The business listing may cost more, but with it people are able to look you up in the yellow pages.

Voice Mailbox Service

Busy signals can cost you money. You can't get the order if your customers can't reach you or your answering machine. And, of course 'call wait' is not a good solution. Big companies don't use call wait, so you'll look like an amateur if you do. What to do? Now for less than $25 per month you can rent a *voice mailbox service*, which acts like a super answering machine!

Your own voice answers the calls, just like a regular answering machine, but the voice mailbox service can handle many calls at the same time. So, if two or more customers call you simultaneously—and they almost always do—no one gets a busy signal, and each one can leave you a message or an order. Some voice mailbox services can actually handle up to 10,000 customers calling your company at once. This can be important if you are advertising your product on the Home Shopping Network or QVC, and when your free media publicity kicks in.

Many voice mailbox services can automatically beep you when you are on the road to let you know a message is waiting, or will even forward the number you are to call. And most voice mailbox services can get you set up within a day or two with a new business number or, if you prefer, an 800 number.

A new arrival on the virtual office scene is the *fax mailbox*. It, too, can handle numerous incoming calls at the same time. At present, these fax mailboxes can only receive faxes, not voice messages, but in the near future a combination service should be available.

If you use a voice mailbox service, should you worry that your customers will catch on that you are not a 'real' company with a receptionists, etc.? No—because so many large corporations now use voice mailbox systems, your customers have no way of knowing whether you are one of them, or the one-person company that you are.

Will your potential customers be put off if they get a voice mailbox instead of a human receptionist? Only if your system asks them to press many buttons and work their way through menus to leave a message. When setting up yours, respect your customers' time and patience. Make it easy for them to leave you a message or an order.

A voice mailbox system in some ways is better than a live operator. It never gets your message wrong and it never puts you on hold. The most important thing is to always *return calls* to your customers as soon as possible. The number one and two complaints by customers everywhere: That companies don't return their calls, and that getting help requires too much effort.

E-Mail: It's Here, It's Now

More and more, rather than using the telephone or postal system, people are communicating, buying and selling through their computers. It's the new world and you better just dive in. With a computer, a modem, software and an access service, you too can use E-Mail (electronic mail) to retrieve and send messages from computerized mailboxes, on-line databases and user groups. E-mail is a million times faster than mailing a real letter via the U.S. Postal System (now known as 'snail-mail'). And, because E-mail is so fast and uses a *local* telephone access number, it is much cheaper than phoning or faxing long distance. And once you get setup on line, your electronic mailbox will automatically take and deliver messages, orders and sales literature 24-hours a day—anywhere in the world—even if *your* computer or phone line goes down!

Long Distance Discounts

Talk may be cheap, but it is getting even cheaper to talk long distance. New companies in competition with the big three, AT&T, MCI and Sprint, offer some very competitive and innovative alternatives. Some of these companies charge a flat 14 cents a minute day rate and 9 cents a minute evenings for any domestic long distance call. (vs. 18-29 cents for the big three) These rates will undoubtedly be even less by the time you read this. Plus, they charge in one-, not six-second increments or by the minute. You will find that many fax messages can be sent in less than 30 seconds, so why get charged for a full minute!!

Record Keeping

An essential part of good communications is good record keeping. Set up record keeping systems tailored to your particular business activities. My kind of business calls for a folder or "docket" which we set up for each order as we receive it. We use a 9 x 12 craft envelope, paste a docket sheet on its front, and use it to keep track of extra charges, scheduling and work in progress. We also use it to store all the paperwork for that job as a permanent record.

Other Office Essentials

Your Computer

Buy last year's model or even a used computer and put the savings into a good laser printer (or at least an inkjet). For most business purposes, a good quality printer will serve you better than a more powerful computer. At one tenth the cost of the latest 'cutting edge' technology, the old 486 IBM compatible computer is a steal, and it can handle most of your needs. (Note: Apple Macintoshes are great computers, but there are a whole lot of 486's around, and they are going dirt cheap. Still, if your computer frustration threshold is low, pay more and get a Mac.)

When you buy a used computer, pay close attention to what used programs and user manuals are included with it. Don't think that an older program is less desirable than the latest version. These older programs were designed to run on the older machine and they will run faster and with fewer bugs than their newer versions.

(Note: It almost never pays to 'upgrade' an older computer system. Use it for what it was designed to do, with the software of its time to avoid aggravation. When you outgrow the old system, you will want to buy up into the next level.)

Your Printer

Get a laser printer, or one of the less-expensive inkjet printers. The inkjets are slower and more expensive per page to operate. If you are like me, you will print a lot of "misses" until you get your printed piece "just right". Waiting for the inkjet printer to slowly finish printing is one of the least-fun wastes of time. (The one exception is if you frequently need full color printing for mockups, etc. This the inkjet can deliver at a very reasonable price.) Previously in printers, it was important to get a Post Script laser printer for any real use of graphics or art. But with the advent of Windows, almost any good laser printer will work for you. Hewlett-Packard makes two good ones. The entry level HP printer prints at around 4 pages per minute, has a good quality of printing (resolution of 300 dots per inch) and uses a single replaceable toner/drum cartridge. If you are going to be doing a lot of graphics work you may want to spring for the more expensive HP which will give you 600 dots per inch. A clever method we use to gain the higher resolution using a 300 dpi printer is to print at double size and then reduce it on a good quality copier. The result is the same.

Your Copy Machine

You do need one. Maybe even more than you need a computer. For reproducing a large number of copies running over to the local copy or quick print shop is fine; but for day-by-day operations you will constantly be put on hold as you run out to make copies of a receipt or agreement or extra sales sheet needed. You can get by on occasion by using your fax machine to spit out a copy. A fine plain paper machine is put out by Canon, although they ask an outrageous price for toner cartridges. Fortunately, there are many companies now recycling them at half the cost of new ones.

Your Software

You'll need a word processing program to write letters, sales materials, catalogs, create forms, and do simple graphics and ads. You'll need a database or mailing list program to keep track of your customers names, addresses and other vital information, and to print labels for mailings. A spreadsheet program is handy for keeping track of inventory and sales, and performing other calculations. A communications program allows you to connect on-line to other computers, to send electronic mail, and download or upload programs. A Personal Information Manager (PIM) is useful for scheduling appointments, keeping track of projects, or finding a phone number. You can buy each piece of software separately, or save a bundle and get all of the above functions in an integrated package such as Microsoft Works or ClarisWorks. Both programs are excellent and can handle most of your business needs for under $100.

An excellent word-processor and page layout program is AmiPro by Lotus. It is much easier to use than MS Word. Another good choice for desktop publishing is Serif DrawPlus and PagePlus.

A good low-cost source for all kinds of software is Shareware. This is software that you can try for a nominal fee and then only if it proves of value to you are you obligated to send the program's author a stated royalty fee. The cost is usually much less than "packaged" store bought software since you are buying directly from the author. Shareware has the basics such as word-processing programs, but really shines when it comes to specialized and hard-to-find software.

(See Resource Section.)

Your Typewriter

Yes, even in this day of computers, you will find a typewriter is still faster for doing most mundane items. Dashing off a mailing label, filling in an order form or tax form, and especially multi-copy forms. You probably already own one, or know someone who will sell you their old one. In any event, get the cheapest machine with the least features you can find. You will find the more things a typewriter can do, the more frustrating it is to use! A used IBM Selectric is a joy to use, but they're pricey and expensive to repair. The new daisy wheel machines by Brother give better type quality, are quieter, and can be discarded when they wear out in a couple of years (which they will).

Fictitious Business Name

Life is a lot easier if you initially do business under your own name. You won't need to file and publish a fictitious business name, register your name with governmental agencies, open a new checking account, etc. But having a company name different from your own does gives the appearance of being more than a one-person business. A good name is one that is easy to spell and remember, and easy to pronounce (especially over the phone).

Permits and Taxes

If you are operating your company as a sideline business, won't be having customers or big truck deliveries coming to your home, and can keep a low profile while promoting your product to the world, you may choose to put off getting a city business license and/or use permit, etc. Let's face it. Some cities are very receptive to "at home" businesses, and some are not. Regardless, you will still need to get certain permits and licenses from your state (such as a tax exempt resale permit) if you are going to be buying materials for resale in your product.

Bank Accounts & Taxes

Keep a separate bank account and a separate credit card that you use only for the business. This will help keep your records straight when it comes time to file your income taxes (that's IRS Schedule C). Choose an accountant who specializes in small businesses.

Accounting Program

Get an accounting program like *Quicken*, *MS Money* or *Mind Your Own Business* and start using it as soon as you can. It will allow you to write checks and to keep track of all your expenses, making it easier for you to see how profitable you are. An accounting program will also be of great help when tax time rolls around.

Product Liability Insurance

Don't even consider trying to market a product unless you have product liability insurance. If someone is harmed by your product, no matter how safe you believe it to be, you must have adequate protection. Some distributors and store chains will require proof that your product has liability coverage before they will be willing to sell it.

Liability brings up whether you should incorporate your business? The real value of incorporation is not so much the tax savings, but the limitation of your liability. Suppose your new product accidentally wipes out Cleveland? Or the twenty thousand widgets from your company all cause fractured pinkie fingers? If you are incorporated, and your worst nightmare happens, your company might be lost, but not your home, your first born child or future hopes and dreams. Thus, proper insurance and legal protection is a must. A new form of incorporation available in some states is called the LLC or "Limited Liability Corporation." They are much easier to set up and require less paperwork. Ideal for small start-ups. Best consult an attorney about incorporating.

Other Insurance

Check with your insurance agent about a Business Pursuits Endorsement to your regular homeowner's or renter's insurance. This will add coverage for your business equipment, supplies and inventory. If you have a computer and software, you will need a separate policy, a rider, to cover them as well. Also, you must arrange for the required Workers' Compensation Insurance before you hire an employee.

Business Help

Free Office Research Staff

Where can you find free office space, the latest reference materials and highly trained, information specialists willing to help you without charge? The public library of course! Here you can access the same information for free that major corporations pay big bucks for. You may also find typewriters, copy machines, and even computers for your use at a nominal charge.

Small Business Help

The U.S. Small Business Administration (SBA) and SCORE (Senior Corps of Retired Executives) provides expert consulting help and a huge range of printed materials. Many cities have Small Business Development Centers (SBDCs) that provide courses for startup businesses. They are often associated with local colleges which offer courses and workshops to help businesses get started.

On-Line User Groups

By going "on-line" through such services as Dialog, CompuServe, or the Internet, you can search immense libraries of data and download all the latest facts, information, advice and gossip you desire. And you can get free help from experts on starting up your business! If you are on-line a lot, make sure you can access your service via local phone numbers, and that you use a phone line that allows unlimited usage. Telephone bills and on-line access charges add up quickly, and if you can't pay you could be cut off from most of your customers.

STAND ALONE, INVENTOR!
And Make Money with Your New Product Ideas!

258

Your "Virtual Address"

If you feel uneasy giving your home address as your business address, or you would like to have a more prestigious "uptown" address, you can rent a business address through such services as Mail Boxes, Etc. Although housed only in a rented mailbox, your business address will have a suite number (not a PO Box number). To the outside world, your company actually has a physical address. There you can send and receive UPS packages, mail, and faxes.

Other companies like Kinko's provide complete copying and bindery services, as well as rental computers with the top rated software programs, art boards and supplies for doing graphics, and more. Kinko's has begun adding telephone-video rooms you can rent for teleconferences with vendors or clients. The virtual office is happening now!

Business Incubators

For most Stand-Alone Inventors, beginning your business from your home is the way to go. But if you feel you must have a "real" business location, instead of your kitchen table, or you find you can't get started without office help, copiers, or laboratory space, you will want to look into "incubators". Not exactly the same as those used to hatch eggs but similar in concept, incubators are private companies and organizations that provide office space, equipment and support personnel at an "affordable" price to help you "hatch" your new enterprise.

Executive Suites

Another alternative is the executive suite or part-time shared office. Why pay for an office 24 hours a day, 7 days a week if you need one only occasionally to see someone or to receive packages? Executive suite services provide you with a part-time office for a much lower cost per month than a full-time one costs. The price usually includes receptionist and voice mail services, use of a conference room and office suite when needed, and having your company listed in the building directory.

Note: The Resource Section begins on page 259 and is arranged by chapter to make it convenient for you to find related references.

RESOURCE SECTION
Arranged By Chapter Topic

This section lists helpful books (many are in public libraries), key contacts, organizations, services, Internet web sites, and other resources to help you move your idea from concept to marketplace. Special listings with light bulbs are resources that I have mentioned specifically in the book. A $ designates companies with whom we have negotiated special price considerations or discounts for Stand-Alone Inventors.

(Note: The listing of a company or service here is not necessarily an endorsement by the author. Use your best judgment before entering into any business arrangement. Also, though accurate at the time of printing, addresses and phone numbers change rapidly.)

Ch. 2 — Some Successful Stand-Alone Inventors
Books:

100 Inventions That Shaped World History, Bill Yenne, Bluewood Books, 111 Pine St., Suite 1410, San Francisco, CA 94111 (1993, 112p, $7.95).

Edison's Electric Light, Robert Friedel & Paul Israel, Rutgers University Press, 109 Church St., New Brunswick, NJ 08901 (1986, 263p, $16.95). Well told story with rare photos of the great inventor at work.

How The Cadillac Got Its Fins, Jack Mingo, Harper Collins Pub., 10 East 53rd St., New York, NY 10022 - 212-207-7000 - Fax 800-822-4090 (1994, 228p, $15). The true histories of *Spam*, Apple computer, the Walkman and more.

World of Inventions, Bridget Travers, Ed., Gale Research Inc., 835 Penobscot Bldg., Detroit, MI 48232 - 800-877-4253 - http://galenet. gale.com, (1994, 767p). A tremendous amount of research went in to this volume that chronicles history's most significant inventions and the people behind them, including the first eraser on a pencil!

Zipper, an Exploration in Novelty, Robert Friedel, WW Norton & Co., 500 Fifth Ave., New York, NY 10110 (1994, 288p, $23). The history of the ubiquitous invention was both ingenious and snarled.

Internet:

Community of Science Inventions - http://medoc.gdb.org/work/ invent.html. A searchable database of inventions by institution, inventor, invention or patent status.

Dead Inventors' Corner - http:// www.discovery.com/DCO/doc/ 1012/world/technology/ technology.html. Discovery Channel Online bi-weekly profiles of late great innovators.

Invention Museums:

The Edison Institute & Henry Ford Museum, Box 1970, Dearborn Village, MI 48121. Henry Ford used his tremendous wealth and influence to purchase the original laboratories and homes of many famous inventors and innovators of his time and have them moved and preserved in this village from the late 1800's. Here you can actually walk into Edison's lab where he invented the lightbulb, the Wright Brothers' bicycle shop where they built the first airplane and of course here is Henry's collection of historic automobiles.

The Edison Ford Winter Estates, 2350 McGregor Blvd, Fort Myers FL 33901 - 941-334-3614 - http://edison-ford-estate.com/. Edison's winter estate and laboratory where he spent a fortune finding a substitute for rubber.

National Inventors Hall of Fame - St. Anthony Productions, 1540 W. Market St., Suite 302, Akron, OH 44398 - 800-865-8859 - Fax 330-865-6701 - http://www.invent.org.

CH. 3 — A World of Inventors
Books & Software:

The Inventor's Bookstore, 37 Seneca Road, Danbury, CT 06811, 203-797-8955, Fax: 203-792-1377. Suggests and sells by mail top notch references for the aspiring inventor.

💡 *A Goal Is A Dream With A Deadline*, Leo B. Helzel, McGraw-Hill, 1221 Ave. of the Americas, New York, NY 10020 - 800-262-4729 - http://

www.osborne. com/ (1995, 197p, $12.95) Pithy sayings and savvy insights on making your ideas a reality.
A Whack on the Side of the Head, Roger von Oech, Creative Think, Box 7354 Menlo Park, CA 94026 (1983, 186p). How you can be more creative.
The Creative Problem Solver's Toolbox, Richard Fobes, Solutions Through Innovation, Box 1327, Corvallis, OR 97339 (1993, 345p, $17.75). Hundreds of examples of how to use your creativity to tackle age old problems.
The Innovators' BookSource Catalog, Aspen Books & Software, 908 S. Tracy Ave., Bozeman, MT 59715 - Ed Verry, 800-319-2665, 406-586-3798 - Fax 406-585-3412 - E-mail: 73757.421@ compuserve.com. Mail-order catalog of resources for innovators in all fields.
Millions From The Mind, How To Turn Your Invention Into A Fortune, Alan R. Tripp, Amacon, 135 West 50th St., New York, NY (1992, $24.95). Provides 50 success stories of inventors who turned their creativity into cash.

Trade Magazines & Newsletters:

Inventors' Digest, 310 Franklin St., Boston, MA 02110 - Joanne Hayes-Rines, Ed-Pub., 800-838-8808, 617-367-4540 - Fax 617-723-6988 - E-mail: InventorD @aol.com ·http:// www.inventorsdigest. com. (6x yr, $22). Chock-full of informative articles covering all aspects of inventing.
Dream Merchant Magazine, 2309 Torrance Blvd., Suite 104, Torrance, CA 90501 - John Moreland, Ed., 310-328-1925 - Fax 310-328-1844. (Bimonthly, $15.95). **Special subscription rate of $9.95 for our readers.**
Eureka! The Canadian Inventor's Newsletter, 156 Columbia St., W, Waterloo, ON N2L 3L3, Canada - 800-265-4559 - Fax 519-885-5729.
Invention Connection, and *Inventor's Voice Journal and News Service*, Box 93669, Los Angeles, Ca 90093 - Stephen P. Gnass, Pub., 800-458-5624, 213-469-7533 - Fax 213-962-8588.
The Light Bulb, Inventors Workshop International, 1029 Castillo St., Santa Barbara, CA 93101 - Arthur Tratner, 805-962-5722. Magazine for members of IWI, since 1971. **Ask about special discount for Stand-Alone**

Inventors.

TV Shows:

Today's Inventor TV Show, Business Network National Magazine - 800-269-2648 - http://www.mgl.ca/~invent/tvshow.htm. Features inventors and new products.

Internet:

Alliance for American Innovation - http://www.nttc.edu/aai.html.
The Canadian Innovation Centre - http://www. innovationcentre.ca/.
DaVinci's Inventor Homepage - http://sulcus.berkeley.edu/Invention. A list of Internet resources of use and interest to inventors and entrepreneurs.
Ideas, Inventions & Innovations Forum - CompuServe-Go IDEAS. Research, marketing, financing, prototyping, promotion and more.
Intellectual Property Creators - http://www.best.com/~ipc.
Inventnet - http://www.inventnet. com. Assistance for inventors and free advertising of inventions for sale.
Inventus - http://www.sgn.com/ invent.html. Forum for presenting your ideas, asking questions and talking shop.
InventorWorld - http://inventorworld. com/. Anything and everything to do with inventing.

Contests:

Great Idea Contest, Inventors Workshop International Education Foundation, 1029 Castillo St., Santa Barbara, CA 93101 - Arthur Tratner, 805-962-5722. Prizes for 17 categories of innovative ideas including arts, construction, transportation, food, medical, toys and ecology. Prizes of up to $1000 and awards of trademark searches and patent registration.

INVENTOR CLUBS & ASSOCIATIONS

National Associations:

Inventor Assistance Source Directory, Battelle Pacific Northwest Laboratories, Innovative Concepts Program, Box 999, K8-11, Richland, WA 99352 - Dr. Robin Conger, Ed., 509-372-4328 - Fax 509-372-4369 - ipn_sii@pnl.gov. Encourages and assists inventor associations and offers a directory of inventor clubs and organizations that assist the individual inventor.

Affiliated Inventors Foundation, Inc. (AIF), 902 N. Circle Dr., Suite 208, Colorado Springs, CO 80909 - John T. Farady, 800-525-5885, 719-635-1234. Founded in 1975 this national organization offers free educational materials for beginning inventors. It also provides invention evaluation, low-cost patent and trademark services, and marketing services on a commission-only basis.

American Inventors Council, Box 4304, Rockford, IL 61110 - Nicholas G. Parnello, 815-968-1040.

Houston Inventors Association, 204 Yacht Club Lane, Seabrook, TX 77586 - Charles Mullen, 713-326-1795. Provides printed materials and video tapes to help you set up your own local inventors organization.

Inventors Assistance League, 403 So. Central St., Glendale, CA 91204 - Ted DeBoer, 800-846-3228, 818-246-6540.

Inventors Clubs of America, Box 450261, Atlanta, GA 31145 - Alexander T. Marinaccio, 770-938-5089 - Fax 770-355-8889. Founded in 1935. Yearly inventor awards Shows inventions on TV programs.

$ **Inventors Workshop International**, 1029 Castillo St., Santa Barbara, CA 93101 - Arthur Tratner, 805-962-5722. Founded in 1971. Offers workshops, patent services, annual Great Idea Contest, *The Lightbulb Journal*, book store, and InvenTech tradeshow. Dues $139 initial and $59 annual. **Ask about special discount for Stand-Alone Inventors.**

United Inventors Assoc. of the USA, Box 23447, Rochester, NY 14692 - Carol Oldenburg, 716-359-9310 - Fax 713-359-1132.

Regional Associations (Listed By State):

Alaska

Alaska Inventors & Entrepreneurs, Box 241801, Ankorage, AK 99524 - Pamela Middaugh, 907-276-4337 - Fax 907-278-2982 - inventor@arctic.net.

Inventors Institute of Alaska, Box 876154, Wasilla, AK 99687 - Al Jorgensen, 907-376-5114.

Arkansas

Inventors Congress, Box 411, Dardanelle, AR 72834 - Garland E. Bull, 501-229-4515.

Arizona

Inventors Assoc of AZ, 2201 N Camino Principal, Suite 4, Tucson, AZ 85715 - Susan Moore, 520-296-4464 - Fax 520-290-8164.

California

Central Valley Inventor's Association, Box 1551, Manteca, CA 95336 - John Christensen, 209-239-5414.

Contra Costa Inventors Club, 295 Stevenson Dr., Pleasant Hill, CA 94523 - Sherm Fishman, 510-934-1331 - Fax 510-934-1132.

Intellectual Property Creators, 101 First St., Suite 425, Los Altos, CA 94022 - Paul Heckel, 415-948-8350 - E-mail: ipc@best.com http://www.best.com/~ipc

Inventors' Alliance, 5666 Arboretum Drive, Los Altos, CA 94024 - Martha Regan, 415-967-0220 - Fax 415-967-0720. Meets twice monthly at Cal State, Hayward.

Inventors Assistance League, 403 So. Central St., Glendale, CA 91204 - Ted DeBoer, 800-846-3228, 818-246-6540.

Inventors Forum, Box 8008, Huntington Beach, CA 92615 - Jim Mitsuoka, 714-253-0952 - Fax 714-836-5609.

Inventors Forum of San Diego, 11190 Poblado Road, San Diego, CA 92127 - Greg W. Lauren, 619-673-4733 - Fax 619-451-6154.

$ **Inventors Workshop International**, 1029 Castillo St., Santa Barbara, CA 93101 - Arthur Tratner, 805-962-5722. Founded in 1971. Offers workshops, patent services, annual Great Idea Contest, *The Lightbulb Journal*, book store, and InvenTech tradeshow. Dues $139 initial and $59 annual. **Ask about special discount for Stand-Alone Inventors.**

Invention Workshop Paradise, 5909-D Clark Rd., Suite 120, Paradise, CA 95969 - Harold J. Bingaman, 916-872-6559.

National Congress of Inventor Organizations, Box 93669, Los Angeles, CA 90093 - Stephen Paul Gnass, 213-878-6952 - Fax 213-962-8588. Founded 1977. $75 yr. Co-sponsors Invention Convention, publishes newsletter.

San Diego Inventors Group, 11190 Poblado Rd., San Diego, CA 92127 - Greg W. Lauren, 619-673-4733.

Santa Clara County Inventors Club, 340 Rosewood Avenue, San Jose, CA 95117 - Buck Buchanan, 408-248-1059.

Colorado

Rocky Mountain Inventors and Enterpreneurs Congress, Box 36233, Denver, CO 80236 - Hal Linke, 303-670-3760.

Connecticut

Innovators Network of Greater Danbury, 37 Seneca Road, Danbury, CT 06811 - Jack Lander, 203-797-8955 - Fax 203-792-1377. Offers book catalog of inventor interest.

Inventors Clubs Of America, 57 Walnut St., Enfield, CT 06082 - Mark Marinaccio.

Florida

Edison Inventors Association, Box 07398, Ft. Myers, FL 33919 - Dr. Gary Nelson, 941-275-4332 - Fax 941-267-9746.

Inventors Council of Central Florida, 822 E. Wallace St., Orlando, FL 32809 - David Flinchbaugh, 407-859-4855.

Tampa Bay Inventors' Council, 2420 Seneca Court, Palm Harbor, FL 34683 - Dave Kiewit, 813-789-1915.

Georgia

Inventors Clubs of America, Box 450261, Atlanta, GA 31145 - Alexander T. Marinaccio, 770-938-5089 - Fax 770-355-8889. Founded in 1935. Yearly inventor awards. Shows inventions on TV programs.

Idaho

E. Idaho Inventors Forum, Box 452, Shelley, ID 83274 - John Wordin, 208-346-6763 - Fax 208-346-6763.

Illinois

American Inventors Council, Box 4304, Rockford, IL 61110 - Nicholas G. Parnello, 815-968-1040.

Inventors' Council, 431 S. Dearborn, Suite 705, Chicago, IL 60605 - Don Moyer, 312-939-3329 - Fax 312-922-7706.

Triple I Inventors, 1851 165h St., Moline, IL 61265 · Cathy Mallary, 309-764-4508.

Indiana

Indiana Inventors Association, 5514 South Adams, Marion, IN 46953 - Robert Humbert, 317-674-2845.

Indiana Inventors Association, Inc., Box 2388, Indianapolis, IN 46206 - Randall Redelman.

Inventor & Entrepreneurs Society, Purdue University, Box 2224, Hammond, IN 46323 - Dr. Dan J. Yovich, 219-989-2354.

Iowa

Iowa Illinois Inventors, 12554 210th St. Davenport, IA 52804 - Norman Frye, 319-391-1663.

Kansas

Kansas Assoc. of Inventors, 1300 Kansas Ave., Great Bend, KS 67530 - Clayton Williamson, 316-793-1950 - Fax 316-793-1952.

Maryland

Capital Inventors Society, 2106 Salisbury Rd., Silver Springs, MD 20910 - Dr. John Boucher, 301-585-1885.

Massachusetts

Cape Cod Inventors Assoc., 1600 Falmouth Rd. Ste. 123, Centerville, MA 02632 - Steven Cressy, 508-428-8792.

Inventors Association of New England, 115 Abbot St., Andover, MA 01810 - Donald L. Gammon, 508-474-0488 - Fax 509-474-0488.

Worcester Area Inventors, 42 Shattuck St., Worcester, MA 01605 - Edith Morgan, 508-791-0226.

Michigan

The Entrepreneur Network, 1683 Plymouth Road, Ann Arbor, MI 48105- - Ed Zimmer, 800-468-8871 - Fax 313-663-9657.

Inventors Assoc. of Metro Detroit, 24405 Gratiot, East Pointe, MI 48021 - Peter D. Keefe, 810-772-7888.

Inventors Clubs of America, 524 Curtis Rd., E. Lansing, MI 48823 - Carl Preston, 517-332-3561.

Inventors Council of Michigan, 565 Mayer Ct., Lake Orion, MI 48362 - Tom Milgie, 810-693-3163.

Minnesota

Inventors' Network, 818 Dunwoody Blvd., Minneapolis, MN 55403 - 612-374-5234.

Minnesota Inventors Congress, 1030 E. Bridge St., Box 71, Redwood Falls, MN 56283 - Penny Becker, 507-637-2344. Monthly newsletter.

Society of Minnesota Inventors, 123 Maple Dr., Knollwood East, Mankato, MN 56001 - Franklin Wille.

Society of Minnesota Inventors, 20231 Basalt St., Anoka, MN 55303 - Paul G. Paris, 612-753-2766 - Fax 612-753-2766.

Mississippi

Delta Inventors Society, Box 257, Stoneville, MS 38776 - Gordon Tupper, 601-686-4041.

Society of Mississippi Inventors, Box 13004, Jackson, MS 39236 - Dr. William Blair, 601-982-6229 - Fax 601-982-6610.

Missouri

Inventors Association of St. Louis, Box 16544, St. Louis, MO - Robert Scheinkman, 314-432-1291. Monthly meetings.

Mid-America Inventors, 2018 Baltimore, Kansas City, MO 64108 - Ed Stout, 816-221-2442 - Fax 816-221-3995.

Montana

Yellowstone Inventors Association, 3 Carry Lynn, Billings, MT 59102 · WarrenT. George, 406-259-9110.

Lincoln Inventors Assoc., 92 Ideal Way, Brainard, NE 68626 · Roger Reyda, 402-545-2179 · Fax 402-545-2179.

Omaha Inventors Club, c/o SBA, 11145 Mill Valley Road, Omaha, NE 68114.

Nevada

Nevada Inventors Association, Box 9905, Reno, NV 89507 • Don Costar, 702-322-9636 · Fax 702-322-0147.

New Jersey

Inventrepreneurs' Forum, 813 Columbus Dr., Teaneck, NJ 07666 - Dr. Thomas M. Noone.

National Society of Inventors, Box 434, Cranford, NJ 07106 - Sheila Kalisher, 201-994-9282.

New Mexico

Albuquerque Invention Club, Box 30062, Albuquerque, NM 87190 - Dr. Albert Goodman, 505-266-3541.

New York

New York Society of Professional Inventors, 116 Steuart Ave., Amityville, NY 11701 - Phil Knapp, 516-598-3228 - Fax 516-598-3241.

United Inventors Assoc. of the USA, Box 23447, Rochester, NY 14692 -

Carol Oldenburg, 716-359-9310 - Fax 713-359-1132.

North Dakota

North Dakota Inventors Congress, Box 1530, Jamestown, ND 58401 - Arvid Brockman, 701-252-4830.

Ohio

Akron/Youngstown Inventors, 1225 W. Market St., Suite 231, Akron, OH 44313 - Ned Oldham, 330-864-5550.

Inventors Council of Dayton, 140 E. Monument Ave., Dayton, OH 45402 - George Pierce, 513-224-8513.

Inventors Council of Greater Lorain County, 1101 Park Ave., Elyria, OH 44035 - Henry B. Ferguson, 216-322-1540.

Inventors Network, 1275 Kinnear Rd., Columbus, OH 43219 - Rick Hagle, 614-470-0144.

Inventor's Society of Northwest, Ohio, 617 Croghan St., Fremont, OH 43420 - Mike Kingsborourgh, 419-332-2221.

National Inventors Hall of Fame, 80 W. Bowery, Suite 201, Akron, OH 44308 - Thomas B. Hollingsworth, 303-762-4463.

Ohio Inventors Association, 73 Maplewood Dr., Athens, OH 45701 - Ron Docie, 614-594-5200 - Fax 614-594-4004 - docie@docie.com.

Ohio's Thomas Edison Program, 77 S. High St., 25th Fl, Columbus, OH 43215-6108 - Kamal Alvi, 614-466-3887.

Yankee Ingenuity Programs, 623 Grant St., Kent, OH 44240 - Charles Clark, 330-673-1875.

Oklahoma

Invention Development Society, 8230 Southwest Eighth St., Oklahoma City, OK 73128 - Julian Taylor, 405-787-0145.

Oklahoma Inventors Congress, Box 27850, Tulsa, OK 74149 - Kenneth F. Addison, Jr., 918-245-6465 - Fax 918-245-2947.

Week-End Entrepreneurs, 12516 E. 37th St., Tulsa, OK 74146 - Dale A. Davis, 918-664-5831 - Fax 918-664-5831.

Oregon

Little Inventor Assoc., 3923 Lancaster Drive NE Salem, OR 97305 - Bill Nasset, 503-391-4464 - Fax 503-391-4887 - E-mail: patwiz@ inventorworld.com - http://

inventorworld.com,.

Pennsylvania

American Society of Inventors, Box 58426, Philadelphia, PA 19102 - Jay W. Cohen, 215-546-6601.

Northwestern Inventors Council, Gannon University, Erie, PA 16541 - Robert K. Jordon, 814-871-7619.

Pennsylvania Inventors Assocation, 10819 Wales Road, Erie, PA 16510 - Charles W. Duryea, Sr., 814-739-2928 - Fax 814-489-3572.

South Carolina

Carolina Inventors Council, 2960 Dacusville High Way, Easley, SC 29640 - Johnny Sheppard, 864-859-0066.

Inventors Assoc. of S. Carolina, 222 Terrace Way, Columbia, SC 29205 - Olivia Mixon.

Tennessee

Tennessee Inventors Assoc., Box 11225, Knoxville, TN 37939 - Dewey Feezell, 423-483-0151.

Texas

Amarillo Inventors Association, Box 15023, Amarilla, TX 79105 - Worth Hefley, 806-376-8726 - Fax 806-376-7753.

Austin Entrepreneurs & Inventors Organization, 1418 Fairwood Rd., Austin, TX 78722 - Tim Bigham, 512-246-7040.

Houston Inventors Assoc., 204 Yacht Club Lane, Seabrook, TX 77586 - Charles Mullen, 713-326-1795 - Fax 713-326-1795.

Network of American Inventors & Entrepreneurs, 11371 Walters Rd., Houston, TX 77067 - Wessle Cramer, 713-537-8277. Low cost patent work.

Texas Inventors Assoc., 4000 Rock Creek Dr., Suite 100, Dallas, TX 75204 - Tom E. Workman, 817-265-1540 - Fax 214-526-6725.

Utah

Intermountain Society of Inventors & Designers, 9888 S. Darin Dr., Sandy, UT 84070 - John Winder, 801-571-2617.

Vermont

The Inventors' Ally, Box 1527, Willington, VT 05363 - 802-464-8918.

Virginia

Assoc. for Science, Tech & Innovation, Box 1242 Arlington, VA 22210

- Dr. Mary E. Mogee, 703-759-5104.

Capital Inventors Society, 3212 Old Dominion Blvd., Alexandria, VA 22305 - Phillip Shaw, 703-739-0868.

Ch. 4 — Marketing Is Everything

Books & Directories:

The Great American Idea Book, Bob Coleman & Deborah Neville, W.W. Norton & Co., 500 Fifth Avenue, New York, NY 10110 (1993, $22.95). Guidebook to developing, protecting and marketing of all kinds of ideas, ranging from the arts (movies, books, music), to inventions, to business ideas. Provides practical advice and interesting histories of many present day inventors who were ignored, ridiculed and/or ripped off but who ultimately triumphed.

Guerrilla Marketing for the 90s, Jay Conrad Levinson, Houghton Mifflin Co., 2 Park St., Boston, MA 02108 - 800-225-3362 (1984, 226p, $11.95). Penny-pinching secrets for getting the most from your marketing dollars.

How to Make Big Money from Your Inventions & Patents, Steve S. Barbarich, U.S. Inventorship Books, 3862 Mission Ave., Carmichael, CA 95608 - 800-379-8726 (1993, 176p).

How to Invent Your Way to Wealth, L. Tony King, Knolls West Press, Box 2262, Wilmington, CA 90748 (1989, 160p). The author, who has brought 15 of his 20 patented inventions to commercial success, shares his insights.

$ *How to Turn Your Product Ideas Into Cash*, Dr. Vernon Brabham, Crafmark Products, Inc., Box 6308, Marietta, GA 30065 (1 hr. video, $21.95) Special price for Stand-Alone Inventors, $14.95, postage paid. Also free 3 page report, *"What your Should Know About Patents."*

Inventing & Patenting Sourcebook, Richard C. Levy, Ed., Gale Research Inc., 835 Penobscot Bldg., Detroit, MI 48226 - 800-877-4253 (1992, 1,022p., $79). A virtual encyclopedia of contacts and info.

Inventors' Resource Guide, United Inventors Association of the USA, Box 23447, Rochester, NY 14692 - 716-359-9310 - Fax 716-359-7732 ($9.95). Directory of services and companies of assistance to inventors.

Marketing Without A Marketing Budget, Craig S. Rice, Bob Adams, Inc., 260 Center Street, Holbrook, MA 02343 - 800-872-5627. Simple ideas for marketing your ideas on a shoe string.

Marketing Your Invention, Thomas E. Mosley, Jr., Upstart Pub-Dearborn Trade, 155 N. Wacker Dr., Chicago, IL 60606 - 800-621-9621, 800-245-2665, 312-836-4400 - Fax 312-836-1021 (1992, 222p, $21.95). Based on hundreds of invention evaluations, and sessions with inventors. Dispels myths and tells what inventors need to know to bring their inventions to market.

Marketing Your Services: For people who HATE to Sell, Rick Crandall, Select Press, Box 37, Corte Madera, CA 94976 - 415-924-1612 (1995, 308p, $15.95). Even though written from the viewpoint of selling services rather than products, many of the techniques are the same. Offers plenty of creative ideas.

NTC Publishing, 4255 W. Touhy Ave., Lincolnwood, IL. 60646 - 800-323-4900, 847-679-5500 - Fax 847-679-2494. Great source for the top books on marketiing, public relations, and sales promotion.

Only the Paranoid Survive : How to Achieve a Success That's Just a Disaster Away, Andy Grove, Bantam Doubleday Dell Pub, 666 Fifth Ave., New York, NY 10019 - 800-431-0725 (1996, $27.50). The CEO of Intel, the world's largest computer chip maker, shows how the ability to take advantage of changes in the marketplace to create a fabulous success.

Relationship Marketing, Regis McKenna, Addison-Wesley Publishing Co., Reading, MA 01867· 800-822-6339 (1991, 242p, $14). Secrets of the famous Silicon Valley PR guru on how to market in the Age of the Customer.

The 22 Immutable Laws of Marketing, Al Ries & Jack Trout, HarperBusiness, 10 East 53rd St., New York, NY 10022 - 212-207-7000 - Fax 800-822-4090 (1993, 143p, $12). Straight talking, hard hitting advice on what to do and what not to do in marketing.

That's a Great Idea!, Tony Husch &

Linda Foust, Ten Speed Press, Box 7123, Berkeley, CA 94707 - 800-841-2665, 510-559-1600 - Fax 510-524-1052 (1986, 228p, $9.95). How to create, evaluate, protect and sell new consumer products.

The Inventor's Handbook, Robert Park, Betterway Books-F&W Publications, 1507 Dana Ave., Cincinnati, OH 45207 - 800-289-0963, 513-531-2690 - Fax 513-531-4082. (1990, 230p, $14.95). How to put together a business plan to develop and market your invention.

Turning Your Great Idea into a Great Success, Judy Ryder, Perterson's, Box 2123, Princeton, NJ 08540 ($14.95). How to develop, license, protect and sell your new product idea.

Magazines & Newsletters:

Entrepreneur Magazine, 2392 Morse Ave., Irvine, CA 92619 - Rieva Lesonsky, Ed., 714-261-2325, 800-357-7299 - http://www. entrepreneurmag.com. Dozens of new business ideas, marketing and startup tips.

Commercial News USA, Export Awareness Div., U.S. and Foreign Commercial Service, ITA, Rm. 2106, The Dept. Of Commerce, Washington, DC 20230. Published 10x year though all U.S. Embassies reaching over 100,000 agents, distributors, buyers, in 140 countries. $395 buys a small ad.

Sales and Marketing Strategies & News, Hughes Communications, 211 W. State St., Rockford, IL 61101 - 800-435-2937, 815-963-4000.

Workshops & Courses:

National Innovation Workshops-*Making Inventions Pay*, Inventions & Innovation Div., U.S. Dept. of Energy, Mail Stop 5E-052, 1000 Independence Ave., SW, Washington, D.C. 20585 - Terry Levinson, 202-586-1478 - Fax 202-586-1605; Assoc. of Small Business Dev. Centers, 402-595-2387. This federally subsidized two-day seminar and workshop provides expert advice on "how to protect your ideas", "license your invention", and/or "market your product". The workshops tour from city to city.

California Invention Center, c/o Golden Gate University

536 Mission Street, San Francisco, CA 94105-2968 - 415-546-1997. Offers certification course on inventing.

MARKETING RESEARCH

Books:

Successful Market Research: The Complete Guide to Getting and Using Essential Information About Your Customers and Competitors, Edward L. Hester, John Wiley & Sons (1995, $17.95)

Catalogs & Directories:

Consumer Information Center, Box 100, Pueblo, CO 81002 - http://www.pueblo.gsa.gov. A good source for free, low-cost and hard-to-find reports and books on thousands of subjects paid for by your tax dollars through the US General Services Administration.

Gale Directory of Databases - Gale Research, 835 Penobscot Bldg., Detroit, MI 48226 - Kathleen Y. Marcaccio, Ed., 800-877-4253 - http//gale.com. Describes 5,200 online, specialized databases and 3,000 CD-ROM based sources. Tells where and how to access the databases and what you'll find when you do.

Off-the-Shelf Publications, 2171 Jericho Turnpike, Commack, NY 11725 - 516-462-2410. Bi-monthly catalog of private business reports, marketing studies and surveys covering a multitude of industries and marketing channels. Gives you the hard sales numbers and future trends you need to know.

Internet Resources:

Search Engines - http://search.com. Provides one stop access to hundreds of useful search engines and directories.

Gale Business Resources - http://gale.com. Integrates some 30 print volumes of Gale's business reference works with listings for some 200,000 U.S. companies drawn from the following Gale databases: *Ward's Business Directory of U.S. Private and Public Companies, American Wholesalers and Distributors Directory, Consultants and Consulting Organizations Directory, Brands and Their Companies* and others. Available only through subscribing public libraries and universi-

ties, but provides info and demo on the Web for free.

Markovits' Navigation Tools - http://www.algonet.se/~nikos/navigate.html. The place to get started when doing research on the Internet.

Telephone Directory - http:www.switchboard.com. Provides all the telephone listings in the US for both business and residencial.

Other On-line Resources:

America Online Inc., 8619 Westwood Center Dr., Vienna, VA 22182 - 800-827-6364. Access present and past newstories via the Knight-Ridder news service (keyword, MERCURY).

BRS Information Technologies, Maxwell On-line, Inc., 8000 Westpart Dr., McLean, VA 22102 - 800-955-0906. Strongest in medical and science databases, but also has business, news and education databases as well.

CompuServe, 5000 Arlington Center Blvd., Box 20212, Columbus, OH 20212 - 800-368-3343. Over 1700 databases, and 200 special interest forum: Patent searches (GO PATENT), Trademark searches (GO TRADERC), and Business Database Plus (Go BUSDB) that accesses articles from 450 publications.

DataTimes, 14000 Quail Springs Parkway, Suite 450, Oklahoma City, OK 73134 - 800-642-2525. Claims to be the largest full-text database of news stories.

Dialog Information Service, Inc., 3460 Hillview Ave., Palo Alto, CA 94304 - 800-334-2564. Claims to be the largest collection of databases in the world. Covers news, business, government, science, and more. Full text magazine and newspaper collections.

PRODUCT EVALUATION

Books:

Innovations: Evaluating New Products, Gerald Udell, Innovation Institute, Southwest Missouri State University, Route 2, Box 184, Everton, MO 65646 - 417-836-5671 (1995, 277p, $27). Describes a systematic approach for analyzing the market potential for a new product and accessing its strengths and weaknesses.

University Programs:

These programs provide business advice and marketability analysis for a fee. Some programs will team inventors with upper level business and marketing students to develop business plans, packaging, etc. Also, contact a college or university near you, as these programs are rapidly being adopted nationwide.

Wal-Mart Innovation (WIN) Network, Innovation Institute, Southwest Missouri State University, Route 2, Box 184, Everton, MO 65646 - 417-836-5671 - Fax 836-7666. Evaluates your idea or invention for a fee using 41 criteria. If considered marketable, refers your product for review and possible sale in Wal-Mart stores.

California Invention Center, c/o Golden Gate University, 536 Mission Street, San Francisco, CA 94105-2968 - 415-546-1997.

Center for Entrepreneurship, Wichita State University, 1845 Fairmount, Wichita, KS 67260 - Arleen Banowetz, 316-978-3000.

Inventors & Entrepreneurs Society, Purdue University, Box 2224, Hammond, IN 46323 - Dr. Dan J. Yovich.

Inventors Center of Michigan, Ferris State University., 1020 E. Maple, Big Rapids, MI 49307 - 616-592-3774.

Nevada Small Business Development Center, University of Nevada, Reno, NV 89557-0100 - 702-784-1717 - Fax 784-4337. Hosts inventor workshops.

Northwestern Inventors Council, Gannon University, University Sq., Erie, PA 16541 - Robert K. Jordan, 814-871-7619.

John F. Baugh Center Entrepreneurship, Baylor University, Box 98011, Waco, TX 76798 - Dr. Nancy Upton, 817-755-2265, ext 1.

Center for Entrepreneurship, 523 Zane Showker Hall, James Madison University, Harrisonburg, VA 22807 - 540-568-3227.

Association for Science, Technology & Innovation, Box 1242, Arlington, VA 22210 - Elizabeth Robertson, 703-352-6567.

Washington Small Business Development Center, Innovation Assessment Center, Washington State University, Box 644851, Johnson Tower 501, Pullman, WA 99164 - Stuart Leidner,

509-335-1576.

Wisconsin Innovation Service Center, University of Wisconsin, 402 McCutchan Hall, Whitewater, WI 53190 - Debra Malewicki, 414-472-1365 - Fax 414-472-1600 - malewicd @uwwvax.uww.edu.

INVENTION MARKETING FIRMS
Consumer Protection:

AIC Victims Advocate, 644 So. Trafton St., Tacoma, WA 98405-3050 - Linda J. Inman. Prepares class action law suits against fraudulent invention promotion companies.

Federal Trade Commission - 202-326-3650· http://www.ftc.gov/. Consumer reports on invention promotion firms and other info.

Inventor's Awareness Group, Inc., 1533 East Mountain Rd., Suite B, Westfield, MA 01089 - Robert G. Lougher, 413-568-5561 - Fax 413-568-5325. Consumer group for inventors that warns of disreputable firms and puts inventors in touch with legitimate organizations, agencies, companies and patent practitioners.

United Inventors Assoc. of the USA, Box 23447, Rochester, NY 14692 - Carol Oldenburg, 716-359-9310 - Fax 713-359-1132.

Books & Directories:

Inventor Assistance Source Directory, Battelle Pacific Northwest Laboratories, Innovative Concepts Program, Box 999, K8-11, Richland, WA 99352 - Dr. Robin Conger, Ed., 509-372-4328 - Fax 509-372-4369 - ipn_sii@pnl.gov. Inventor clubs and organizations that assist the individual inventor.

Wow! What a Great Idea. Now What?, Martin E. Smith, Rainbow Books, Box 430, Highland City, FL 33846 (1995, 69p, $9.95). How to Avoid Patent, Marketing & Invention Company Scams.

Pamphlets:

Invention Promotion Firms R. Woods, Consumer Information Center-5A, Box 100, Pueblo, CO 81002. Questions to ask before you hire a company to help sell your product or service. (Federal Trade Comm.#367B. ,$.50).

Marketing Services:

(Note: the listing of a company or service here is not necessarily an endorsement by the author, however these companies generally have a good reputation. Consult with an attorney before entering into any business arrangement.)

BLS Consulting & Management, 804 Queen Anne's Ct., Lancaster, PA 17601 - 717-898-4771 - Fax 717-898-1367. Marketing consultant with 25 years experience will help you detemine your market, locate salespersons, trade shows, and determine pricing, packaging and merchandising.

The HookTek - http://www.thehooktek.com/ Strictly performance (non-fee) based .

M&M Associates, Box 1020, 12424 Main St., Fort Jones, CA 96032 - Maggie Weisberg, Melvin Fuller, 916-468-2282 - Fax 916-468-2238. Creates teams, partnerships and "virtual" corporations of executives and inventors to develop and market inventions. Former founders of Inventors Workshop Int'l.

Popular Design Works, 851 Rambling Dr. Circle, West Palm Beach, FL 33414 - Richard A. Meyer, 407-795-0320. 30 years experience designing, manufacturing, marketing and licensing new products.

Professional Marketing Systems, Box 34022, Omaha, NE 68134 - Dr. Doug Brown, 800-805-2714.

Siler/Siler Ventures & Inventors Resource, Box 2405, Lake Oswego, OR 97035 - Buzz Siler, 503-635-6333. Consults with inventors, offers product development seminars, and does marketing. Does not require a contract or money up front. Guarantees satisfaction or no charge.

Venture Initiatives, 2639 Walnut Hill Lane, Suite 205, Dallas, TX 75229 - Geoffrey F. Walsh, 214-350-9771. Specializes in licensing and marketing consumer products and gadgets, such as the Parent Pager and ArtWatches.

Internet Marketing Services:

The Internet Invention Store - http://www.catalog.com/impulse. Showcases new inventions, offers marketing lists and ads.

Inventnet - http://www.inventnet.com

- 2433 E. Orange Thorpe, Suite 190, Fullerton, CA 92631 - Victor Lasvrov, 714-826-2843. Assistance for inventors and free advertising of inventions for sale.

Invention Tradeshows:

Although aimed at inventors seeking to license their inventions, these tradeshows are also useful places for meeting manufacturers, wholesalerers/retailers, venture capitalists and sources of marketing assistance.

Invention Convention, Invention Services Int'l Corp., Box 93669, Los Angeles, CA 93669 - Stephen Gnass, 800-458-5624 - Fax 213-962-8588.

InvenTech, Inventors Workshop International, 1029 Castillo St., Santa Barbara, CA 93101 - Arthur Tratner, 805-962-5722 - Fax 899-4927.

Yankee Invention Exposition - 203-597-9527 - Fax 203-597-8452.

Ch. 5 — Intellectual Property: Paid Protection

US Patent and Trademark Office and Libraries

The Commissioner of Patents & Trademarks, Patent & Trademark Depository Library (PDTL) Program, Crystal Mall, Bldg. 2, Rm. 306, USPTO, Washington, DC 20231 - 800-786-9199. Call for the location and phone number of the PDTL closest to you. Previously you had to travel to Washington, DC to do a patent search, or at least hire an agent there to do one for you. Not any more! Now nearly every state has a Patent & Trademark Depository Library that provides free access to patent collections stored on CD-ROMs.

Patent Maintenance Fee Inquiries - 703-308-5069. Call with patent number to find out if its maintenance fees have been paid, or if it has lapsed.

Register of Copyrights, Copyright Office, Library of Congress, Washington, DC 20559-6000 - Info Hot-line: 202-707-3000 - http://lcweb. loc. gov/copyright - Short Form applications, 202-707-9100.

Books & Software:

Patent It Yourself, David E. Pressman, Nolo Press, 950 Parker St., Berkeley, CA 94710 - 800-992-6656, 510-549-

1976 - http://www.nolo.com (1995, $39.95). Written by a patent attorney—a former patent examiner—this book shows you step-by-step how to search, prepare and submit a patent or trademark to protect your invention. Contains all the necessary forms. Also available as a software program.

Licensing—A Strategy for Profits, Edward P. White, KEW Licensing Press, 907 Linden Rd. Chapel Hill, NC 27514 - 800-833-0720, 919-929-7283 (1990, 289p,$30).

Marketing Your Invention, Thomas E. Mosley, Jr., Upstart Pub-Dearborn Trade, 155 N. Wacker Dr., Chicago, IL 60606 - 800-621-9621, 800-245-2665, 312-836-4400 - Fax 312-836-1021 (1992, 222p, $21.95). Based on hundreds of invention evaluations, and sessions with inventors. Dispels myths and tells what inventors need to know to bring their inventions to market.

Official Gazette of the United States Patent & Trademark Office: Superintendent of Documents, U.S. Gov't. Printing Office, Washington DC. 20402. Weekly listings of 2000+ newly issued patents and trademarks.

How to License Your Million Dollar Idea, Harvey Reese, The Inventor's Bookstore, 37 Seneca Road, Danbury, CT 06811, 203-797-8955, Fax: 203-792-1377 (233, $19.95)

Trademark, how to name your business & product, McGrath, Elias and Shena, Nolo Press, 950 Parker St., Berkeley, CA 94710 - 800-992-6656, 510-549-1976 - http://www.nolo.com. ($29.95).

You've Got An Idea..Now What?, Robert M. Sperry, Woodland Hills CA (1992, 126p). Former examiner of US Patent & Trademark Office.

Pamphlets:

Submitting An Idea, American Bar Association, 1155 East 60th St., Chicago, IL 60637.

Basic Facts about Patents; Basic Facts about Registering a Trademark; PTO Fee Schedule, Patent & Trademark Office, Crystal Park 3, Suite 441, Washington, DC 20231 - 800-786-9199 (Free).

Basic Facts About Trademarks, U.S.

Government Printing Office Superintendent of Documents, Mail Stop: SSOP, Washington, DC 20402-9328. Also lists patent and trademark depository libraries. 800-786-9199 (Free).

Associations:

Intellectual Property Owners, Inc. (IPO), 1255 23rd St. NW, Suite 850, Washington, DC 20037 - Herbert C. Wamsley, 202-466-2396. Keeps its members informed of changing information and laws about intellectual property, such as patents, trademarks, and licenses.

Intellectual Property Creators, 101 First St., Suite 425, Los Altos, CA 94022 - Paul Heckel, 415-948-8350 - http://www.best.com/~ipcCovers inventor and public policy issues

Patent Agents & Attorneys:

Attorneys and Agents Registered to Practice Before the U.S. Patent and Trademark Office, U.S. Patent & Trademark Office, Crystal Park 3, Suite 441, Washington, DC 20231 - 800-786-9199.

Patent Searches & Filings:

Greentree Information Services, Bethesda, MD - George Harvill, 301-469-0902. Recommended by successful toy inventor and author Richard Levy.

Intellectual Property Institute, 3639 Midway Drive, Suite 142, San Diego, CA 92110 · 619-222-1387 - E-mail: ipi@aol.com. Has attorneys and agents throughout the U.S. Can handle most searches and patent preparation by E-mail.

Inventors Workshop International, 1029 Castillo St., Santa Barbara, CA 93101 - Arthur Tratner, 805-962-5722. Founded in 1971. Offers workshops, patent services, including the international PatentSaver™ program. **Ask about special discount for Stand-Alone Inventors.**

Network of American Inventors & Entrepreneurs, 11371 Walters Rd., Houston, TX 77067 - Wessle Cramer, 713-537-8277. Low cost patent work.

Online Directory - http://pacificrim.net/~patents/resource.html. Directory of patent libraries, patent drawing services, patent attorneys and agents.

Trademark Searches:

Thompson & Thompson - 800-692-8833, 617-479-1600.
CompuMark U.S. - 800-421-7881.
Patent Search Workshops:
Creativity, Innovation & Productivity, RR1, Box 37, Highwood, MT 59450 - Fred E. Davison, 406-733-5031 - Fax 733-2039.   Do-It-Yourself-Patent workshops.

Patent & Trademark On-line Searches:

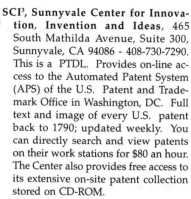 SCI[3], Sunnyvale Center for Innovation, Invention and Ideas, 465 South Mathilda Avenue, Suite 300, Sunnyvale, CA 94086 - 408-730-7290. This is a PTDL. Provides on-line access to the Automated Patent System (APS) of the U.S. Patent and Trademark Office in Washington, DC. Full text and image of every U.S. patent back to 1790; updated weekly. You can directly search and view patents on their work stations for $80 an hour. The Center also provides free access to its extensive on-site patent collection stored on CD-ROM.

CASIS CD-ROM (Patent & Trademark Office). Available at some libraries, this CD-ROM quickly searches by word all the categories to see if your prospective trademark is already registered.

CompuServe, 5000 Arlington Center Blvd., Box 20212, Columbus, OH 20212 - 800-368-3343. Patent search (GO PATENT) and Trademark search (GO TRADERC).

Internet Patent & Trademark Info Sites:

U.S. Patent Bibliographic Data Base - http://patents.cnidr.org:4242/. Free full text of patents from 1976.
Smart   Patents   -   http://www.zoom.com/smartpatents/. Provides complete text *and* drawings of patents in electronic form.
QPAT US - http://www.qpat.com/. Free front page abstract of patents since 1974.

These sites provide general information about patents, trade-

marks and helpful resources:

http://www./patents.com/index.htm. Oppendahl & Lawson patent law web server answers a multitude of questions about protecting intellectual property.
http://www.law.vill.edu/~rgruner/patent3.html. Patent law basics.
http://www.yahoo.com/text/governmetn/law/intellectural_property/patents/. Patent law basics.
http://www.naming.com/naming/icclasses.html. List of trademarks classes and sub-categories.

These sites offer information on their country's patent requirements.

United States Patent & Trademark Office - http://www.uspto.gov/.
Brazilian Patent Office· http://www.bdt.org.br/bdt/inpi/
Canadian Intellectual Property Office - http://info.ic.gc.ca/opengov/cipo/.
European Patent Office - http://www.epo.co.at/epo/.
Hong Kong Intellectual Property Office - http://www.houston.com.hk/hkgipd/
Japanese Patents http://www.epo.co.at/epo/patolis/
New Zealand - http://www.govt.nz/ps/min/com/patent/.
United Kingdom Patent Office - http://www.netwales.co.uk/ptoffice/
Various   Countries   -   http://www.questel.orbit.com/patnets/pt-dbs.html.

Patent Illustration:

Patent Art, 7318 Lightship Ct., Burke, VA 22015 - 703-644-4871.
Patent Drawing Services, San Diego, CA 92109 - 619-274-0223.
Patent Graphics, 4121 Monroe St., Toledo, OH 43606-2063· 419-471-0700.

Patent Infringement:

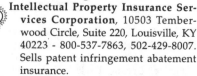 Intellectual Property Insurance Services Corporation, 10503 Temberwood Circle, Suite 220, Louisville, KY 40223 - 800-537-7863, 502-429-8007. Sells patent infringement abatement insurance.

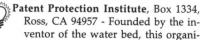 Patent Protection Institute, Box 1334, Ross, CA 94957 - Founded by the inventor of the water bed, this organi-

zation will put together the money to sue the "bad guys" in exchange for a share in the suit.

Products:

U.S. Patent Certificate, 1900 (L). Street NW, Suite 502, Washington, DC 20036 - 800-622-0677. ($124-$199). Show off! This company makes a beautiful metal and walnut wall plaque of your patent.

Other Services:

Faxpat, 1509-A Leslie Ave., Alexandria, VA 22301 - 800-866-1323 - FAX 800-666-1233. If you know the patent number you need a copy of, they will mail or fax it t you.

Venture Initiatives, 2639 Walnut Hill Lane, Suite 205, Dallas, TX 75229 - Geoffrey F. Walsh, 214-350-9771. Specializes in licensing and marketing your consumer products and gadgets, such as the Parent Pager and ArtWatches.

Ch. 6 — Financing your Invention

Books:

Financial Essentials for Small Business Success, Joseph Tabet & Jeffrey Slater, Upstart Pub-Dearborn Trade, 155 N. Wacker Dr., Chicago, IL 60606 - 800-621-9621, 800-245-2665, 312-836-4400 - Fax 312-836-1021 (1994, $19.95).

Finding Money for Your Small Business, Max Fallek, Dearborn Trade, 155 N. Wacker Dr., Chicago, IL 60606 - 800-245-2665, 312-836-4400 - Fax 312-836-1021 (1994, $19.95).

How to Write a Business Plan, Mike McKeever, Nolo Press, 950 Parker St., Berkeley, CA 94710 - 800-992-6656, 510-549-1976 - http://www.nolo.com (1992, $19.95).

Inc. Yourself, Judith H. McQuown, HarperBusiness, 10 East 53rd St., New York, NY 10022 - 212-207-7000 - Fax 800-822-4090 ($12).

Starting Your Own BIG Business with Venture Capital, William A. Gilmartin, Signum Research - Fax 602-595-8430. (1995, $24.95)

Financial Services:

ExpressChex, 2600 Senter Rd., Suite 8, San Jose, CA 95111 - 408-297-5532 - Fax 287-5564. Makes it possible for you to accept payment by check over the phone or fax.

!Solutions - 800-255-6643. Check the credit of companies and individuals you want to do business with through your computer.

American Business Information - http://www.abii.com/. Now you can find any business in the U.S. and order an in-depth business profile online that includes address and phone number, name of the owner or top decision-maker, number of employees, estimated annual sales, credit rating score for $3!

Funding Sources:

Grants and technical assistance from the US Gov't:

Energy & Non-Energy Related Inventions Program, Office of Technology & Innovation, NIST, Gaithersburg, MD 20899-0001 - George P. Lewett, 301-975-5500 - Fax 301-975-3839 - E-mail:innovate@enh.nist.gov. Provides grants of up to $100,000 for developing energy-related or energy-saving inventions and technologies, and also assistance for non-energy related inventions.

Information USA CDROM, InfoBusiness, 887 S. Orem Blvd., Orlem, UT 84058 - 800-657-5300, 801-221-1100 - Fax 801-221-1194. Information guru Matthew Lesko's database that gives you contact info on every federal grant, loan and financial assistance program. ($49.95, Windows).

Innovative Concepts Program, U.S. Dept. of Energy - Lesa Barnet, 202-586-1478 - Fax 202-586-1605. Grants of seed money to determine if your ideas are feasible for inventions that improve health conditions of industry, saves energy or improves efficiencies of factory operations, or helps the environment.

NTTC Inventions & Innovations Gateway - http://www.nttc.edu/invention.html.

Small Business Innovation Reseach (SBIR). Grants, Small Business Administration - 800-827-5722, 202-205-6450 - 800-697-4636 modem. Grants of up to $100,000 for feasibility studies for new technologies and up to $750,000 for their development.

Venture Capital:

Batterson Venture Partners L. L. C., 303 West Madision Street, Suite 1110, Chicago, IL 60606 - 312-269-0300 - Fax 312-269-0021 - E-mail: bvp@vcapital.com. Venture capital management firm providing equity capital to new or growing businesses with the potential to become major enterprises.

Castle Arch, 505 Pepperwood Court, O'Fallon, IL 62269 - 618-624-0165, voice/fax. Venture capital consultants who seek inventors.

Commercial Finance ONLINE! - http://www.cfonline.com/cgi-win/cfonline.exe/ Search engine helps you locate all types of financial services, and or list your needs for venture capital.

Silicon Valley Bank, 3003 Tasman Dr., Santa Clara, CA 95054 - Michael Field, VP, 408-435-9500. Private venture capital options for inventors.

Venture Capital OnLine - http://www.vcapital.com/ On the Internet listing service matches up money with startups and projects. Also, provides information and guidance on the venturing after capital.

Ch. 7 — How To Get It Manufactured

Directories of Manufacturers & Suppliers:

Thomas Register of American Manufacturers, Thomas Publishing Company, Thomas Publishing Co., Five Penn Plaza, New York, NY 10001 - 212-290-7277 - http://www.thomasregister.com - CompuServe: Go THOMAS. (33,000p., $225). The famous collection of oversized green books, 26 volumes, is found in most libraries and lists 140,000 companies under 48,000 product headings. - good starting place to find the company or product you are looking for. Now available on CD-ROM.

National 800 Directory, Business Edition - AT&T, 55 Corporate Dr., Bridgewater, NJ 08807 - 800-426-8686 - http://www.tollfree.att.net/ (1238p, $14.99). A quick and inexpensive way to find potential suppliers, vendors and manufacturers. Provides toll free telephone numbers to 160,000 companies listed by service

and product categories.Their web site allows you to download groups of phone numbers by product or service categories.

State Manufacturers Directory - Manufacturers' News, Inc., 4 E. Huron St., Chicago, IL 60611. Individual directories by state listing detailed data on manufacturers.

VendorHotline - Cy Stapleton - Fax 409-637-1480 - E-mail: hotlinecy@aol.com. Need a source to manufacture a printed item? Or do you need an unusual, hard to find product? Cy can tell you where to find them, or have them made, whether its playing cards, posters with pockets, pizza boxes or basketballs. Also, available on disk.

Industry Net - http://www.industry.net. On-line source of mfgs and suppliers.

Mfg Info - http://mfginfo.com/ Online database to manufacturers, suppliers, professional services, jobshops and used equipment.

Foreign Manufacturing Services:

Hong Kong Trade Development Council, 222 Kearny St., 4th Fl, Suite 402, San Francisco, CA 94108 - Marion, 415-677-9038 - Fax 421-0646 - http://www.tdc.org.hk. Source for referral to manufacturers in Hong Kong and China.

Business Opportunities Sourcing System (BOSS), Industry Canada, 235 Queen St., Ottawa, Ontario, Canada K1A 0H5 - 613-954-5031 - Fax 613-954-1894. Access contact information for 30,000 Canadian companies organized by products and markets served.

Doing Business in Hong Kong - http://www.hk.super.net/~rlowe/bizhk/bhhome.html. Provides a database of over 800 companies.

Feeco, Ltd. - Kim Shepard, 603-427-2460 - Fax 603-427-0457. Agent for sourcing manufacturers in the Far East. Offices in principal cities.

International Procurement Systems, Ltd. (IPS), 6 Fl., 13 Teh Wei St., Taipei, Taiwan 104 - George Arellano, 886-2-597-2213 - Fax 886-2-592-4476, 592-0010 - E-mail: ipssource@pristine.com.tw. Agent for sourcing manufacturers in the Far East. Product development consultation and mass-production cost analysis at no charge to Stand-Alone Inventors.

Global Yellow Pages - http://www.globalyp.com/world.htm. Phone directories from around the world.

Hong Kong Product Catalogue - http://www.hkguide.com.hk/~hkguide/product.html. Mfg. and traders, classified by product.

Mid-America Overseas - 708-766-5655. Freight forwarder lowers your cost for importing and helps you with handling customs and shipping procedures and paperwork. 10 offices nationwide.

Directories of Consultants & Experts:

Consulting Organizations Directory, Gale Research, 835 Penobscot Bldg., Detroit, MI 48226 - Janice McLean, Ed., 313-961-2242.

The Idea Engine, CyberKnight, Box 64, Spicewood, TX 78669 - 800-845-4332, 515-264-0224 - Fax 512-264-0581 - E-mail: info@goldmind.com. ($59.95, Mac/Windows). Software packed with "how-to" info on inventing and new product development, with over 2000 contacts for resources, parts and services.

Information USA CDROM, InfoBusiness, 887 S. Orem Blvd., Orem, UT 84058 - 800-657-5300, 801-221-1100 - Fax 801-221-1194 ($49.95, Windows). Information guru Matthew Lesko's database gives you contact info on thousands of *free* experts paid for courtesy of your tax dollar.

Who Knows What, Daniel Starer, Henry Holt & Co., 115 West 18th St., New York, NY 10011. (1994, 1239p). Concise descriptions and contact information on thousands of associations, magazines, directories, libraries, companies, databases, government offices are organized by topic. No matter what your subject of interest, from "abrasives" to "yarn", you can quickly locate the six to twelve best sources to contact next.

PROTOTYPE MAKING
Books & Videos:

Best of Design in Plastics, Douglas Cleminshaw, Rockport Book-F&W Publications, 1507 Dana Ave., Cincinnati, OH 45207 - 800-289-0963, 513-531-2690 - Fax 513-531-4082. (1989, 256p, $49.95).

The Design Of Everyday Things, Donald A. Norman, Doubleday (1988, 267p, $12.95). What makes a design good or bad? Case examples show why some products satisfy customers while others frustrate them.

Design for the Real World, Victor Papanek, Bantam Books, 666 Fifth Ave., New York, NY 10019 - 800-431-0725 (1973, 374p). Before anyone talked about the green revolution, before recycling was in, before socially conscious products became a buzz word, Victor wrote this book that says it all. Call it solutions for sane living, or inventing for a lasting tomorrow!

Lucite Acrylic Resins Design Handbook, E.I. du Pont de Nemours & Co., Wilmington, DE 19898. Information on how to cut, mold, bend acrylic plastic.

Reproduce Almost Anything, Cherokee Accessories, 2128 Farrol Ave., Union City, CA 94587 - 510-471-5770 voice/fax. ($43.55). Video and workbook teach basic silicone mold making for casting plastic parts.

The Millennium Whole Earth Catalog: Access To Tools For The Twenty-First Century, Howard Rheingold, Harper Collins Pub., 10 East 53rd St., New York, NY 10022 - 212-207-7000 - Fax 800-822-4090 (1994, 384p, $30.00). The current edition in a long line of venerable Whole Earth Catalogs continues teaching about new innovations in tools and worldly thinking.

The Way Things Work, David Macaulay, Houghton Mifflin Co., 2 Park St., Boston, MA 02108 - 800-225-3362 (1988, 384p, $29.99). Demonstrates how machines do what they do—from the simplest lever to the most sophisticated microchip—and how one invention leads to the next.

Trade Magazines:

Injection Molding, 55 Madison St., Suite 770, Denver, CO 80206 - Suzy Witzler, Ed., 303-321-2322.

Plastics World, 445 Broad Hollow Rd., Suite 21, Melville, NY 11747 - Mike McEnaney, Ed., 516-845-2700.

274 STAND ALONE, INVENTOR!

Parts & Tools Suppliers:
Mail Order Sources

AIN Plastics - 800-431-2451. Plastic sheeting, shapes, materials and tools.

Cole-Palmer Instrument Company, Chicago, IL - 800-323-4340. Scientific instruments.

Edmund Scientific, 101 E Gloucester Pike, Barrington, NJ 08007 - 609-573-6240. Scientific tools, gadgets, lens, lasers.

Enco Mfg. Co. - 800-860-3400. Huge selection of power tools and supplies.

Hysol Division, the Dexter Corp., 15051 E. Don Juliard Rd., Industry, CA 91749. Casting resins and other useful materials.

Industrial Arts Supply Company, 5275 West 36th St., Minneapolis, MN 55416. Wood working equipment and supplies.

Thomas Scientific, Swedesboro, NJ - 800-345-2100. Scientific apparatus and chemicals.

Wholesale Tool, Box 68, Warren, MI 48089 - 800-521-3420. Power tools, pumps, motors.

Prototype Making Services:

Industrial Designers Society of America, 1142 Walker Road, Great Falls, VA 22066 - 703-759-0100. Reference source to local designers who can help you make a working prototype.

3D Systems, 26081 Avenue Hall, Valencia, CA 91355 - 805-295-5600 - Fax 805-257-1200 - http://www.3dsystem.com. Within hours, creates a prototype or model of your product using computer controlled ultraviolet lasers that solidify a liquid plastic photopolymer.

Advanced Components Technology, Inc., 2865 Spring St., Redwood City, CA 94063 - Joe Hellerich, 415-365-2801. Precision sheet metal stamping, tooling, prototypes. Discounts for inventors.

Bob Reed, Pleasanton, CA - 510-485-0468 Voice/Fax. Good consultant for advice on new products that need pressure sensitive adhesives or can be manufactured using label technology.

Cherokee Accessories & Plastic Consulting, 4127 Bay St., Suite 226, Fremont, CA 94538 - Ben Ridge, 510-471-5770 Fax/ Voice.

Crown Mfg. Co., 37625 Sycamore St., Newark, CA 94560-3944 - 510-742-8800 - Fax 510-742-8500. Source for plastic injection molding.

Custom Urethane Engineering, Inc., 806 Prospect Ave., Osceola, Wi 54020 - 800-626-1663. Manufacturer of short runs of parts at low tooling cost.

E² Engineering, 10354 Bauer Rd., St. Louis, MO 63128 - 314-842-7714. Electronic and mechanical prototypes.

$ Hebert Engineering & Design Co., 307 Spring St., Manchester, CT 06040 - 860-647-1872 voice/fax. Light metals, plastics and composites prototypes. **10% discount for first-time Stand-Alone Inventor customers.**

Howell Consulting, 635 Yale Ct.,Des Plaines, IL 60016 - 847-296-2275 ·Fax 847-296-2757· E-mail: 75070.1454@compuserve.com. Rapid Prototyping. Full engineering services for automated manufacturing machines. Product development of cast and plastic parts.

Interplast, 1014 Front St., Greenville, OH 45331 - Mike McQuin, 800-367-6233 - Fax 513-548-3290. Good source for plastic injection molding.

$ Kelley Electronic Assembly, 2933 Pleasant Drive, Endwell, NY 13760 - 607-748-0639 voice/fax. Assembly and production of electro mechanical devices. **10% discount for Stand-Alone Inventor first-time customers.**

Plynetics, 627 McCormick St., San Leandro, CA 94577 - 510-613-8300 - Fax 510-632-6682. Rapid prototype making. Also, plastic injection molding. Branches in Portland and Chicago.

Progressive Engineering, 1213 W. Newport St., San Luis Obispo, CA 93405 - 805-541-0511. Plastic and metal prototypes.

Ch. 8 — How To Get Free Hype
Books:

The Publicity Manual, Kate Kelly, Maverick Mail Order Bookstore, 425 Cedar St., Box 909, Buena Vista, CO 81211 - Fax 719-395-8374 ($29). How to write compelling news releases that get printed.

Writing Effective News Releases, Catherine V. McIntyre, Piccadilly

Books, Box 25203, Colorado Springs, CA 80936 (1992, 176p, $17). How to get free publicity for yourself, your business or your organization.

Organizing Your Home Office For Success, Lisa Kanarek, Penguin Books USA, 375 Hudson St., New York, NY 10014 (1996, 160p, $8.95).

The Portable Office - Take Your Office on the Road Now and for the Future, Jefferson D. Bates & Stuart F. Crump, Acropolis South (1987, $16.95).

Trade Magazines & Newsletters:

Contacts Newsletter, 35-20 Broadway, Astoria, NY 11106 - 914-923-9400. Provides key media contacts by name, including magazine and newspaper editors, syndicated columnists, radio and TV talk shows.

Jack O'Dwyer's Newsletter & PR Services Report, 271 Madison Ave., Suite 600, New York, NY 10016 - 212-679-2471 (12x). Provides case histories of successful PR efforts and current info on media contacts and services.

Free Hype:

"Patents" Column, Box 11305, Tacoma Park, MD 20913 - Teresa Riordan, Ed., 301-589-0335 - Fax 301-589-0336 - E-mail: nypatent@aol.com. Syndicated column about newly patented inventions, appears weekly in hundreds of newspapers including the NY Times.

Inventors' Digest, 310 Franklin St., Boston, MA 02110 - Joanne Hayes-Rines, Ed-Pub., 800-838-8808, 617-367-4540 - Fax 617-723-6988 - E-mail: InventorD@ aol.com - http:// www.inventorsdigest. com. (6x yr, $22). "Patents Issued" column.

Media Contacts:

Bacon's Magazine & Newspaper Directories, 332 S. Michigan Ave., Chicago, IL 60604 - 800-621-0561 (1800p, 2 vol., $270). *The Magazine Directory* lists thousands of consumer magazines, trade journals and newsletters indexed by specific audiences or markets, such as advertising or medical. Each publication is described along with types of news releases they accept. The *Newspaper Directory* provides editors names and contact info for daily and weekly newspapers, news services and syndicated columns indexed by state and city. Bacon also publishes similar directories covering Radio-TV and Cable, plus the Media Calendar Directory that tells when editors are going to be doing special theme editions. Available on CDROM. (You can sometimes obtain last year's directories from an advertising or PR agency.)

All-In One Directory, Gebbie Press, Box 100, New Paltz, NY 12561 - 914-255-7560 ·http://www.gebbieinc.com/ ($85). 22,000 key media contacts in magazines, newspapers and radio/ TV broadcasting. Also available on disk ($95-$257).

Books In Print, R.R. Bowker, 121 Chanlon Rd., New Providence, NJ 07974 - 800-521-8110 (10 vol., 13,800p., $425). Lists by subject and title every book currently in print, as well as books about to be published. A good place to learn who the experts are in a given field who may write about your product in their next book. Also available on CD-ROM in some libraries.

Hudson's Subscription Newsletter Directory, The Newsletter Clearinghouse, 44 West Market St., Box 311, Rhinebeck, NY 12572 - 914-876-2081 ($128). 46 subject headings, 158 categories listing 4,247 newsletters. Includes title, publisher, editor and contact info and which invite press releases.

Magazines for Libraries, R.R. Bowker, 121 Chanlon Rd., New Providence, NJ 07974 - Bill Katz, Ed., 800-521-8110 (1212p., $139). Describes and rates the interests and strengths of popular magazines grouped by subject matter.

Media News Keys, Television.Index, Inc., 4029 27th St., Long Island City, NY 11101 - Timothy Hunter, Ed., 718-937-3990. Tells you who to contact in Radio and TV news media and talk shows to become a guest.

Newsletters in Print, Gale Research Inc., 835 Penobscot Bldg., Detroit, MI 48226 - John Krol, Ed., 800-877-4253 ·. (1500p., $185). Describes more than 10,000 newsletters covering a wide range of specialized interests.

NewsRelease, Box 239, Laurel, MD

20725-0239 - 301-498-1545 ($24.95). Provides addresses, phone numbers and fax numbers direct to the newsroom, to 500 newspaper, magazine, and television stations.

Oxbridge National Directory of Magazines, Oxbridge Communications, 150 Fifth Ave., New York, NY 10011 - 212-741-0231, 800-955-0231 - Fax 212-633-2938 - E-mail:info@ oxbridge.com (1000p, $495, CDROM - $750). Covers over 16,000 US and Canadian magazines, gives description, ad rates, editorial staff, publisher, and circulation. Also publishes directories of Newsletters, and College Media.

Power Media Selects, Broadcast Interview Source, 2233 Wisconsin Ave., NW, Washington, DC 20007 - Alan Caruba, Ed. Annual directory profiles the top U.S. radio, TV and print media contacts, including talk shows, leading syndicates, and major news dailies. Also publishes *PowerSources* newsletter.

Standard Rate & Data (SRDS), Standard Rate & Data Service, 3004 Glenview Road, Wilmette, IL 60091 - 614-486-0015. This multi-volume set provides current rates and data for advertising in nearly every magazine, newspaper and card deck in the nation. Publications are grouped by market. Besides being in most libraries, you can often obtain a used set from an advertising agency, as the SRDS is updated quarterly.

Writer's Market, Writer's Digest Books, F&W Publications, 1507 Dana Ave., Cincinnati, OH 45207 - 800-289-0963, 513-531-2690 - Fax 513-531-4082. (1002p). Provides information, on 4000 magazines and trade journals that pay for articles and stories. Many accept new product releases. Also, this is a good way to locate hard to find magazines that cover your area of interest.

Internet Directories:

Broadcast.Print Media E-Mail - http://www.armory.com/~leavitt/media.internet.html. Electronic mail addresses for many national and local newspapers, TV and radio stations, columnists, etc.

CMS Internet Catalogue of Newsletters - http://www.textor.com/cms/.

Describes 800 business newsletters, intelligence management reports and market surveys covering such areas as telecommunications, computing, pharmaceuticals, banking, finance, energy, legal, media and construction. Offers free sample issues.

INFOSEARCH - Broadcasting Links ·http://www.searcher.com/ links.html. An A-Z list of TV and radio stations with a Web presence.

Other Useful Hype Directories:

Directories in Print, Gale Research, 835 Penobscot Bldg., Detroit, MI 48226 - Charles B. Montney, Ed., 800-877-4253 - http://galenet.gale.com (2,155p., 2 vol., $270). Describes over 4,000 directories arranged, in 26 subject categories.

Directory of Directory Publishers, Directory Marketplace, Box 301, West Nyack, NY 10994. Lists 9,000 directory publishers worldwide and their titles.

Encyclopedia of Associations, Gale Research Inc., 835 Penobscot Bldg., Detroit, MI 48226 - Carol A. Schwartz, Editor, 800-877-4253 - http:// galenet.gale.com (1994, $340). Describes 22,400 associations, including trade, professional, non-profit, sports, hobby, fraternal and patriotic groups. Find out about associations of every size and subject ranging from the American Automobile Association (29 million members) to the Bald Headed Men of America (12,500 members).

National Trade & Professional Associations of the U.S., Columbia Books, Inc., 1350 New York Ave., NW, Washington, DC 20005. (475p, $60). 6250 entries provides description, current director, membership size, and annual meeting date.

Yearbook of Experts, Authorities & Spokespersons, Broadcast Interview Source, 2233 Wisconsin Ave., NW, Washington, DC 20007. Who better to promote the merits of your product than an expert in the field? Sometimes all it takes is making the right person aware of your new solution to an old problem.

Publicity Services:

Hollywood Duplicate Photo, Box 2670, Hollywood, CA 90028 - 213-466-7544. A source of low-cost quantity black and white 4x5 and 8x10 glossy photo prints for your publicity purposes.

Game-Show Placements, 7011 Willoughby Ave., Hollywood, CA 90038 - 213-874-7818, 213/874-0643 - gsp@ix.netcom.com. For $195 per spot, arranges for your product to be given away on TV game shows, such as *Jeopardy*.

News USA, 8300 Boone Blvd., Suite 810, Vienna, VA 22182· Richard D. Smith, Publisher, 703-827-5800 - Fax 703-827-5813. For a fee this company writes a news release about your product and includes it in a pre-printed syndicated column they send to all the newspaper editors, and Radio/TV news editors in the nation. Stories are often picked up and reprinted. Ask about a $100 discount.

Radio-TV Interview Report **(RTIR),** Bradley Communications Corp., 135 E. Plumstead Ave., Suite 102, Lansdowne, PA 19050 - 610-259-1070. Monthly newsletter read by news and programming directors, and talk show hosts, at 3,800 radio stations and TV shows. For a fee, they will do a write up in their newsletter about you and your invention. Often leads to free publicity and possible interviews on popular talk shows.

Wagner International Photos & Feature Photo Service, 62 W 45th St., New York, NY 10036-4208 - 212-944-7744 - Fax 212-944-9536. For a fee, takes a picture of your product and releases it to major photo news wires.

Ch. 9 — Merchandising Your Product

Books & Directories:

Great Packaging Design, and *International Brand Packaging Awards*, Rockport Book, F&W Publications, 1507 Dana Ave., Cincinnati, OH 45207 - 800-289-0963, 513-531-2690 - Fax 513-531-4082. (1995, 192p, $39.99). Gaining the competitive edge through packaging, plus directory of designers and sources.

Packaging Marketplace, Gale Research, 835 Penobscot Bldg., Detroit, MI 48226 - Joseph Hanlon, Ed., 313-961-2242. Directory of packaging manufacturers and sources.

Fundamentals of Packaging Technology, Walter Soroka, Institute of Packaging Professionals, 481 Carlisle Dr., Herndon, VA 22070 - 703-318-8970 (1995, 527p, $280).

Trade Magazines:

Good Packaging Magazine, 1315 East Julian St., San Jose, CA 95116 - 408-286-1661 - Fax 408-298-6757. Packaging equipment and suppliers.

Packaging Digest, 296 Schooleys Mtn Rd., Schooleys Mountain, NJ 07870 - 908-852-6560.

P-O-P Times, 7400 Skokie Blvd., Skokie, IL 60077 - 847-675-7400. Written for marketers and retailers who use point-of-purchase advertising, packaging and displays.

Trade Shows & Associations:

Westpack, Institute of Packaging Professionals, IOPP, Box 22373, Denver, CO 80222 - 800-417-1614, 303-743-9542 - Fax 303-727-4204. Exhibits of packaging materials, package design, containers, supplies and automated packaging machinery.

Pack Expo, Packaging Machinery Mfg. Institute, 4350 N. Fairfax Dr., Suite 600, Arlington, VA 22203 - 703-243-8555 - Fax 703-243-8556, 800-664-3976 - http://www.packexpo.com. Packaging machinery and supplies tradeshow.

Internet Resources:

Packaging Resource Pilot - http://www.packsource.com Source of suppliers, materials, education.

Services & Suppliers:

UPC Bar Code (Assignment). Council, Dayton OH - 513-435-3870. Assigns the machine-readable Universal Product Codes that uniquely identify your company and products.

PCS, Inc. - 201-BAR-CODE, 800-524-0599 - Fax 201-575-4718. Supplier of Bar Code film and art to be used for printing your packaging.

Altec Packaging, Inc., 1711 Junction Court, San Jose, CA 95112 - Steve Lang, 408-452-0505 - Fax 408-452-0542. Source for blister card packaging and equipment. 10% discount for Stand-Alone Inventor first-time customers.

Andex Corp., Box 887, 1911 4th Ave., N., Escanaba, MI 49829 - Maureen

Hughson, 800-338-9882, 906-786-6070. Mfg. of custom imprinted blister card packaging used for most small items to be sold in stores.

Central States Diversified Inc., 9322 Manchester Rd., Saint Louis, MO 63119 - 314-961-4300. Source for clear plastic acetate packaging and boxes.

Chiswick - 800-225-8708. General packaging, shipping supplies and ziplok bags.

Crafton Industries, 1011 Beecher St., San Leandro, CA 94577 - Jo Anne Santos, 510-632-7461. Mfg. of custom imprinted paper box packaging.

Dot (Clarke). Pkg. Co., 1500 Paramount Parkway, Batavia, IL 60510 - 800-323-6160, 312-879-0121. Source of blister cards, skin boards, display cards.

Fast Industries, Inc., 6850 N.W. 12th Ave., Fort Lauderdale, FL 33309 - 800-775-5345, 954-979-3278 - Fax 800-775-2064. Mfg. of "clip strips" for displaying small items by hanging them from store shelfs.

Freund Can Co., 194 West 84th St., Chicago, IL 60620 - 312-224-4230. Source for hard to find containers, cans, drums, bottles.

$ **Lee Packaging**, 555 Old County Rd., Suite 101, San Carlos, CA 94070 - 415-595-3394 - Fax 415-595-1114 - E-mail: LeePkg@ix.netcom.com. Designers and suppliers of custom and stock packaging materials. **Free 1-hour consultation for Stand-Alone Inventors.**

McCoy Label, 1250 Holm Rd., Petaluma, CA 94954-1172 - 800-327-5997, 707-778-1250 - Fax 707-762-1253. Source of low cost labels for use on packaging. Also, shelf talkers.

Northeast Polybag Co., 2 Northeast Blvd., Box 1460, Sterling, MA 01564 - 800-325-1045. Mfg. of polybags and packaging supplies.

Placon Packaging, 6096 McKee Rd., Madison, WI 53708 - 800-541-1535, 608-271-3162. Mfg. of blister and low cost "stock" clamshell display packaging, The Graphic Box Line.

Robinson Industries, 11320 E Main St., Huntley, IL 60142 - 800-874-7113, 847-669-5291. Mfg. of blister cards, skinboard, header and display cards, clamshells.

San Jose Label, 1920 Hartog Dr., San Jose, CA 95131 - Linda Kawasoki, 408-436-8221 - Fax 408-436-0696. Good source for hot stamped and flexi printing of labels for products and packages.

Servall Packaging Industries, 20550 S. Denker Ave., Torrance, CA 90501 - 310-533-5811 - Fax 310-533-6077. The largest thermoformer and packaging firm in the West offering package design, production, assembly and finished goods distribution.

Short Run Labels - 800-522-3583, 415-592-7683 - Fax 800-456-5575. Prints as few as 1000 labels at a time in a variety of stock sizes, shapes and styles suitable for packaging. Next-day turnaround.

SLM Manufacturing Corp. - 800-526-3708, 201-469-7500 - Fax, 201-469-5546. Mfg. of foldable clear, plastic PVC boxes for products, and blister card packaging.

Ch. 10 — Advertising and Sales Promotion

Books & Directories:

Adventures of a Verbivore, Richard Lederer, Pocket Books, Simon & Schuster, Inc., 1230 Avenue of the Americas, New York, NY 10020 - 212-698-7000 (1994, 277p, $21). Add pizzazz to your communications to get you and your product noticed.

The Copywriter's Handbook: A Step By Step Guide to Writing Copy That Sells, Robert Bly - 201-599-2276. Free ad hotline gives advice on copywriting and ad crafting.

Do-It-Yourself Advertising, Fred E. Hahn, John Wiley & Sons, 605 Third Ave., New York, NY 10158 (1993, 246p, $14.95). How to produce great ads, brochures, catalogs, and direct mail on a low cost budget.

Standard Rate & Data (SRDS), Standard Rate & Data Service, 3004 Glenview Road, Wilmette, IL 60091 - 614-486-0015. This multi-volume set provides current rates and data for advertising in nearly every magazine, newspaper and card deck in the nation. Publications are grouped by market. Besides being in most libraries, you can often obtain a set from an advertising agency as the SRDS is updated quarterly.

Magazines:

Advertising Age, 740 N. Rush, Chicago, IL 60611 - 312-649-5200,. The trade publication that covers the advertising industry.

Classified Communication, Box 4177, Prescott, AZ 86302 - Agnes Franz, Ed. ($29, 12x). Newsletter for small budget advertising shows how to write and place effective classified ads to sell your products.

Internet Resources:

The Advertising and Marketing Helper ·http://www.geocities.com/WallStreet/3584/. Links to web sites for ad agencies, direct marketing, PR, promotions, production companies.

Publishers' Yellow Pages http://www.morganprice.com/contents.htm. Directory of printers, printing supplies, mail services, copywriters, etc.

Services:

$ **Graphics International**, 20475 Bunker Hill Dr., Cleveland, OH 44126 - 216-333-9988 - Fax 216-333-9989. A line drawing of your product is often better than a photograph for use in newspaper ads, on sales sheets, for instructions on the back of packaging. This company can provide line art from a photo of your product. **Ask about special discount for Stand-Alone Inventors.**

Larry John Wright Advertising, 1045 E University Dr., Mesa AZ 85203-8054 - 800-821-5068, 602-833-8111 - Fax 602-969-2895 - www.ljwtub. Professional marketing videos, brochures, infomercials, press releases.

National Response Corporation, Santa Fe, NM - 505-424-6220. This company can place your classified ad nationally at greatly discounted prices in community newspapers, shoppers, computer networks.

PhotoLabels, 419 Eisenhower lane, So., Lombard, IL 60148 - 800-323-0776 - Fax 847-691-8188. Creates inexpensive self-adhesive full color labels from your slide or photo in quantities as low as 100. Quick way to create mockups and sales sheets for testing.

Portfolio - http://www.portfolio.skill.com. Source for professional copywriters, art designers, illustrators and photographers with branches in major cities.

Seattle Filmworks, Elliott Bay at Pier 89, 1260 16th Ave. W., Seattle, WA 98119 - 800-345-6967, 206-283-9074 - http://www.filmworks.com. Using their 35mm film processing service, you can get *both* prints and slides from the same roll. Slides are usually requested for use in color separations for printing brochures and packaging. They also offer inexpensive scanning of your photos onto a floppy disk. This allows you to add your images by computer directly to word-processing, or make computerized slide shows, sales presentations and much more.

Discount Printing Sources:

4P, 45278 Industrial Dr., Fremont, CA 94538 - 510-659-1900 - Fax 510-490-0818. For $495 will color separate one photo, prepare your layout and print 2000 4-c fliers! Also offers in-house photography of products for $95.

Apollo Graphics, PA - 800-522-9006. $695 buys 10,000 two sided, glossy 4-color sheets. Also, photography, typesetting and color seps, available.

Direct Press - 800-735-7666. A good source at a reasonable price for full color sales and catalog sheets in quantities of 5,000 - 10,000. They will photograph your product and design and typeset your sales sheet. Locations in major cities.

Joy of Printing, 1299 Old Bayshore, Suite 222, Burlingame, CA 94010 - 800-966-4569, 415-340-1640 - Fax 415-340-1549. Will print 2500 full color catalog sheets for $550. Includes photography, typesetting, and color sep.

Leesburg Printing Co., 1100 North Blvd. East, Leesburg, FL 34748 - 800-828-3348. Specializes in printing 8-to-32 page booklets and newsletters.

Miracolor, Service Web Offset Corp., 2500 S. Dearborn, Chicago, IL 60616 - 800-621-1567, 312/567-7000 - Fax 312-567-9121. Low cost full color printing of at least 50,000 copies, for brochures, catalog sheets, inserts.

Rapidocolor, 705 East Union St., West Chester, PA 19382 - 800-872-7436. Claims to be the world's fastest color printer for quanitities from 50 to 50,000 on paper or plastic.

U.S. Press, Box 640, Valdosta, GA 31603 - 800-227-7377, 912-244-5634. Low cost printing of 4-color catalog sheets, postcards. Free shipping with prepay.

Ch. 11 — How To Set Up Distribution

Directories of Vendors, Wholesalers & Distributors:

American Business Directories, 5711 S. 86th Circle, Omaha, NE 68127 - Publishes mailing lists and directories of specific types of companies and professionals, such as Auto Repair Shops, Dentists., compiled from the national Yellow Pages. Free catalog gives you counts and costs for various lists of professionals and trades. Ask about small test batches or pages. A useful marketing tool.

American Wholesalers & Distributors Directory, Gale Research Inc., 835 Penobscot Bldg., Detroit, MI 48226 - Deborah M. Burek, Ed., 800-877-4253 (1,745p., 1994). Lists 18,000 U.S. wholesalers and distributors covering all categories of business and industry.

Chain Store Guides, 3922 Coconut Palm Drive, Tampa, FL 33619 - Julia Bayzie, 800-274-6807, 813-664-6800 - Fax 813-664-6810. ($195-$995). Publishes various directories providing contacts, addresses, sales volumes and other information: Automotive, Drug Stores, Computer & Software Retailers, General Merchandise /Variety & Specialty Stores, Supermarkets, Home Furnishings, Hardware stores, etc. Also available on CDROM.

The Salesman's Guides, Reed Reference Publishing Co., 121 Chanlon Rd, New Providence, NJ 07974 - 800-223-1797 - Fax 908-665-3560. Publishes regional directories to store buyers selected by product, such as, "Sportswear Buyers".

Phelons Discount Stores, Chains & Jobbers Directory, Phelon, Sheldon & Marsan, Box 517 Fairview, NJ 07022 - 800-234-8804, 201-941-5515 - Fax 201-941-5512 ($175). Contacts and addresses of the buying offices for major store chains, mass merchandis-

ing centers, wholesalers and jobbers covering home improvement centers, drug stores, appliances, sporting goods, and discount stores.

Standard & Poor's Register of Corporations, Directors and Executives, - 800-221-5277. Provides data on over 45,000 corporations, including names, titles and functions of officers and executives, business classification, and annual sales.

Ward's Business Directory of US Private and Public Companies, Gale Research Inc., 835 Penobscot Bldg., Detroit, MI 48226 - 800-877-4253. Lists companies by their SIC (standard industrial classification), ranked by size, and gives main corporate office.

Directories on CD-ROM:

D&B MarketPlace CD-ROM, MarketPlace Information Corp., 460 Totten Pond Rd., Waltham, MA 02154 - 800-532-3775 - Fax 617-672-9290 - http://www.mktplace.com/home1102. ($249-$449). Allows your computer to instantly search and sort through over 18 million businesses by product and services and SIC code (standard industrial classification) down to 8 levels, or by location down to city level and 5 digit zip, and by company size (# of employees and/or sales volume). Information is from Dun and Bradstreet and includes key personnel and credit profiles. On screen searches and lists are included in the cost of the CD-ROM but printing labels or exporting the data, or credit info is additional. Its search categories are more reliable than PhoneDisc's yellow page categories, and it selects for the main buying offices—especially important when you are selling to chain stores! It was able to locate, for example, the main offices for the top 300 supermarket chains, and the top plastic injection molders within thirty miles. It could not however find magazines specific to a particular subject or readership such as Motorcycling.

PhoneDisc USA Business CD-ROM, Digital Directory Assistance, Inc., 6931 Arlington Rd., Suite 405, Bethesda, MD 20814 - 800-284-8353 ($59-$299). Although compiled from telephone directories and so not as up-to-date as *The MarketPlace CD-*

ROM, above, *PhoneDisc* nonetheless offers the best value around in obtaining mailing lists of businesses, professionals and residences. Within seconds for any of 12 million+ U.S. companies, you can locate entries by name, phone number, address or selected by products, services or SIC code. Similarly for locating any, of 90 million residential listings. There are no limits or additional charges for printing labels. *PhoneDisc* is also much faster and easier to use than any of the other telephone directory based products we tested. It's also a great way to see if a business name you wish to use is already in use somewhere in the nation. They also offer a Fax directory on disk listing 470,000 US fax numbers.

Directories on the Internet:

AT&T National 800 Directory, Business Edition - http://www.tollfree. att.net/ Lists toll free telephone numbers, to 160,000 companies listed by service and product categories. Numbers can be downloaded by groupings, such as "pet supply dealers".

Inter800 - http://inter800.com. Has some numbers that ATT doesn't list and visa versa.

Company Link - http://www. companylink.com/. Your starting point for research on 45,000 US companies cross-indexed to newswires, press releases, and addresses to headquarters.

BigYellow - http://s11.bigyellow.com/ first_visit.html. Telephone and address listings to over 16.5 million US businesses searchable by name and category.

BigBook - http://www.bigbook.com/. National telephone and address list of US businesses with street-level maps, customer voting, reviews.

Search Engines - http://search.com. Provides one stop access to hundreds of useful search engines and directories.

Trade Magazines:

Agency Sales, Manufacturer's Agents National Association (MANA), Box 3467, 23016 Mill Creek Rd., Laguna Hills, CA 92654 - Bert Holtje, Ed., 714-859-4040 - Fax 714-855-2973 ($37.50, 12x). Read by independent sales representatives who handle products on a commission-only basis. MANA also publishes a yearly directory arranged by category: from abrasives to home improvement to toys to woodworking ($93), and hosts a yearly convention.

Rep World, Box 2087, Sinking Spring, PA 19608 - Thomas C. Reinhart, Ed., 610-678-3361 (cir 15,000). For the independent manufacturers' representative.

Associations:

National Association of Wholesale Distributors, 1725 K Street, NW, Suite 710, Washington, DC 20006 - 202-872-0885. The largest association representing wholesalers and distributors in the nation.

Service Corps of Retired Executives (SCORE) - 800-827-5722. Offices in most metropolitan areas. Call for the office nearest you.

TRADESHOWS
Directories:

Annual Tradeshow Directory, Forum Publishing, 383 E. Main St., Centerport, NY 11721 (85p., $20). Describes 750 merchandise tradeshows by product and date. Published in September.

Directory of Trade Shows & Exhibits Schedule, Bill Communications, 633 Third Ave., New York, NY 10017 - Stan Itzkowitz, Ed., (700p., $130). Lists 18,000 meetings and provides site location, date, attendance size, key contacts. Published in January with supplement at midyear.

Trade Magazines:

Trade Show Week - 213-965-5300.
Trade Show Week Data Book - 908-665-2846.

Internet Resources

Tradeworld Exhibition Centre - http://www.tradeworld.co.uk/exhibitions/. Information on exhibitions, trade fairs, expositions and shows worldwide.

Services & Associations:

National Conferences Hotline - 407-791-0720.

LOCATING DISTRIBUTORS

In this section you will find references and key distributor contacts listed by specific market or industry.

GENERAL

Albee-Campbell, 806 Penn Avenue, Box 2087, Sinking Spring, PA 19608-9979 - 800-445-0586, 610-678-3361. Matches you up with manufacturer's reps who will sell your product.

Manufacturers Representative Profile (MRP), 2150 A Douglas Blvd., Suite 210, Roseville, CA 95661 - Roger Wilson, 916-784-2300 - Fax 916-784-2217. For around $5000 nation-wide ($730 regional), this company provides profiles on manufacturer rep agencies who match-up with your product distribution needs.

Oklahoma New Products Coalition, 4617 S. Quincy PL, Tulsa, OK 74105 - Thomas E. Mosley, Pres., 918-743-4933 - Fax 918-745-9815. Manufacturing firms seeking new products; mass merchandising services provided by former Wal-Mart buyers.

Z Industries, Suite 436, 3960 West Point Loma Blvd., San Diego, CA 92110 - 619-338-4397. Seeks products for distribution.

Listings By Market

AUTOMOTIVE MARKET

Trade Magazines:

For dealers of auto parts and accessories:

Aftermarket Business, 7500 Old Oak Blvd., Cleveland, OH 44130 - Larry Aylward, Ed., 330-891-2604 (cir 23,000).

Automotive Marketing, Chilton Co., 1 Chilton Way, Radnor, PA 19089 - Phil Katcher, New Products Ed., 610-964-4396 (cir 40,000).

Jobber-Retailer, Bill Communications, Inc., 633 Third Ave., New York, NY 10017 - Mike Maurigian, Ed., 330-867-4401.

Associations:

Association of Automotive Aftermarket Distributors, c/o Parts Plus, 5050 Poplar Ave., Suite 2020, Memphis, TN 38157 - 800-727-8112, 901-682-9090 - Fax 901-682-9098.

Automotive Merchandising News, Mortimer Communications, Box 1185, Fairfield, CT 06430 - Bill Mortimer, Ed., 203-384-9323.

Automotive Parts & Accessories Association, 5100 Forbes Blvd., Lanham, MD 20706 - Julian Morris, Pres., 301-459-9110 - Fax 301-459-8145.

Largest Retailers:

Grand Auto, 1400 North 4th St., Renton, WA 98055 - 206-251-7600 - Fax 251-7763 (123 Stores).

JC Whitney & Co., 1917-19 Archer Ave., Box 8410, Chicago, IL 60680 - 312-431-6102 (Mail order cataloger).

Northern Automotive Corp., Box 6030, Phoenix, AZ 85012 - 602-265-9200 - Fax 234-9200 (700 Kragens, Chucks, Checker stores).

PepBoys, 311 W. Allegheny Ave., Philadelphia, PA 19132 - 215-229-9000 (360 stores).

Western Auto Supply, 2107 Grand Ave., Kansas City, MO 64108 - 816-346-4000 (370 stores, 940 assoc. stores, sub. of Sears, Roebuck & Co).

Wholesalers & Distributors:

Kraco Enterprises, 505 E. Euclid Ave., Compton, CA 90224 - Brad Kraines, 310-639-0666 - Fax 310-603-2260.

Parts Inc., Sub. GKN/Parts Ind. Corp., 601 S. Dudley, Box 429, Memphis, TN 38101 - 901-523-7711.

COMPUTERS & ACCESSORIES MARKET

Free Hype:

High-Tech Hot Sheet, 220 Montgomery St., Suite 1098, San Francisco, CA 94104 - 415-421-6220. Contacts and tips for getting free hype in computer and hi-tech publications.

Trade Magazines:

Read by buyers at computer stores, VARs and other retailers:

Computer Reseller News, 600 Community Drive, Manhasset, NY 11030 - 516-562-5000.

Reseller Management, Box 7621, Highlands Ranch, CO 80126 - 303-470-4445.

Smart Computer & Software Retailing, 7025 Albert Pick Rd., Suite 200, Greensboro, NC 27409 - Lester Craft, Ed., 910-605-0121 - Fax 605-1143.

InfoWorld, Box 1172, Skokie, IL 60076 - 847-647-7925.

MacWeek, 301 Howard St., 15 Fl, San Francisco, CA 94105 - 415-243-3500 - Fax 243-3651.

PCWeek, Box 1770, Riverton, NJ 08077 - 609-461-2100.

Marketing Services:

DataSources, Box 5845, Cherry Hill, NJ 08034 - 609-354-4999 ($475). Comprehensive directory of the computer marketplace. Provides data and sourcing info on over 50,000 hardware, software and communications products and their manufacturers.

DP Directory, 525 Goodale Hill Rd., Glastonbury, CT 06033 - 203-659-1065. Low cost source for mailing labels to computer newspaper and magazine editors, hardware/software distributors, user groups, PC stores.

Electronic Representative's Directory, Harris Publishing Co., 2057 Aurora Road, Twinsburg, OH 44087 - 216-425-9000.

Tradeshows:

Comdex, Interface Group - 617-449-6600. The first and largest convention/tradeshow for computer hardware and software products.

Largest Computer Stores & Buying Groups:

ASCII Group, 7475 Wisconsin Ave., Suite 350, Bethesda, MD 20814 - 800-394-2724. Buying group of 1000 retailers and value-added resellers.

CompUSA, 14951 N. Dallas Pkwy, Dallas, TX 75242 - 214-383-4000 (55 super-stores).

Electronics Boutique, 1345 Enterprise Dr., West Chester, PA 19380 - 215-430-8100 (300 stores).

Radio Shack, Ft. Worth, TX - 817-390-3011. (7106 stores).

Software City, 1415 Queen Anne Rd., Teaneck, NJ 07666 - 800-222-0918, 201-833-8510.

Largest Mail Order Dealers:

Inmac, 2465 Augustine Dr., Santa Clara, CA 95054 - 800-547-5444. Publishes monthly catalog with 2700 computer supplies and accessories.

MicroWarehouse & MacWarehouse, 1720 Oak St., Box 3013, Lakewood, NJ 08701 - 800-255-6227, 908-367-0440. 181 page catalog of software and hardware.

CONSUMER ELECTRONICS MARKET

Free Hype:

The Gadget Guru, Andy Pargh - 615-356-9595. Syndicated writer and contributing correspondent to the NBC *Today* show.

Tradeshows:

Consumer Electronics Show, Electronic Industries Association - 703-907-7600. Electronic gizmos from TV's to robot lawn mowers. Held in Las Vegas, Chicago.

Largest Consumer Electronics Dealers:

Circuit City, 9950 Maryland Dr., Richmond, VA 23233 - 804-527-4000.

Highland Superstores, Inc., 909 N. Sheldon Ave., Plymouth, MI 48170 - 313-451-3200.

Cosco Price Club, 1809 120th Ave., NE, Kirkland, WA 98033 - 206-828-8100. 89 super stores.

Radio Shack, 1800 One Tandy Center, Ft. Worth, TX - 817-390-3011. 7,106 stores.

The Sharper Image, 650 davis St., San Francisco, CA 94111 - 800-344-4444, 415-445-6000 - Fax 800-552-2525. Carries a wide selection of the latest electronic gizmos and high tech consumer goods.

Service Merchandise, Box 25130, Nashville, TN 37202 - 800-251-1212. Catalog sales and 390 stores of home accessories and consumer electronic products.

Venture Initiatives, 2639 Walnut Hill Lane, Suite 205, Dallas, TX 75229 - Geoffrey F. Walsh, 214-350-9771. Specializes in licensing and marketing consumer and other products and gadgets, such as the Parent Pager and ArtWatches

EDUCATIONAL MARKET

Trade Magazines:

The Educational Marketer, Box 7430, Wilson, CT 06897 - Glenn J. Sanislo, Ed., 203-834-0033.

Stores & Retailers:

Edmund Scientific, 101 E Gloucester Pike, Barrington, NJ 08007· 609-573-6240. Mail order dealer of scientific and educational items.

The Nature Company, Box 188, Florence, KY - 800-227-1114 - http://www.natureco.com. Catalog sales and 114 retail stores carrying ecological and educational products.

Rockville Creative Learning -

800-588-9880. Mail order dealer of children's educational products.

Associations & Tradeshows:

School and Home Office Products Association Annual Show, SHOPA - 513-297-2250.

Museum Store Association, 501 S. Cherry St., #460, Denver CO 80222-1325 - 303-329-6968

ENVIRONMENTAL MARKET

Books & Directories:

Access EPA (Doc. # PB95-255782). - 800-553-6847. Lists information sources and contacts of the Environmental Protection Agency (EPA).

Trade Magazines:

Alternative Energy Retailer, Box 2180 Waterbury, CT 06722 - John Florian, Ed., 203-755-0158.

Electrifying Times, 636 Deschutes Road, Bend, OR 97701 - 503-388-1908 - Fax 360-693-4408 ($10, 3x). Coverage of electric autos, new propulsion technology and sources.

Internet Resources

Alternative Entery Sources - http://solstice.crest.org/online/aeguide/. Hydrogen power.

Global Recycling Network - http://grn.com/grn. Helps businesses around the world recycle resources, surplus mfg. goods and machinery.

Energy Yellow Pages - http://www.gridwise.com/. Renewable energy companies and organizations.

Recycler's World - http://www.recycle.net/recycle. Publications, organizations and money-making ideas.

Solar Energy - http://www.netins.net/showcase/solarcatalog/.

Contacts & Associations:

U.S. Department of Energy, Terry Levinson, Director, Inventions & Innov., 1000 Independence Ave. EE 521, 5E052, Washington, DC 20585 - 202-586-1478 - Fax 202-586-1605 - http://www.eren.doe.gov/. Info on energy saving, pollution control, etc.

California Recycling Market Development Zones, 8800 Cal Center Dr., Sacramento, CA 95826 - Christy Porter, 916-255-2628. Provides funding, engineering and tech and marketing assistance.

Electric Car Conversion, 5106 Ustick Rd., Modesto, CA 95358 - Michael Parker, 209-988-2487.

Energy Conversions, Inc., 6411 Pacific Highway East, Tacoma, WA 98424 - Paul Jensen, Pres., 206-922-6670 - Fax 206-922-2258.

Energy Related Inventions Program, Office of Technology & Innovation, NIST, Gaithersburg, MD 20899-0001 - George Lewett, 301-975-5500 - Fax 301-975-3839 - E-mail:innovate@enh.nist.gov. Provides grants of up to $100,000 for developing energy related or energy saving inventions and technologies.

Florida Energy Office, Department of Community Affairs, 2740 Centerview Drive, Tallahassee, FL 32399-2100 - Edward A. Cobham Jr., Comm. Asst. Consult., 904-488-2475 - Fax 904-488-7688.

Georgia Energy Resources, Governor's Ofc., 100 P Street N.W. Suite 2090, Atlanta, GA 30303-1911 - Elizabeth S. Robertson, Program Manager, 404-656-3887 - Fax 404-656-7970.

Illinois Recycling Association, 9400 Bormet Drive Suite 5, Mokena, IL 60448 - Mindy B. Solomon, Executive Director, 708-479-3800 - Fax 708-479-4592.

Industrial Materials Exchange, 6401 Congress Ave., Suite 200, Boca Raton, FL 33487 - 407-995-7455. Matches unwanted industrial materials with companies that could use them. (Check in Yellow Pages under Industrial Materials Exchange, Recycling, or Waste Exchange for organizations and companies near you. Another person's waste and landfill could be just the material you need!)).

New Mexico State Energy & Minerals, 2040 South Pacheco St., Santa Fe, NM 87505 - Michael McDiarmid, Engineer, 505-827-5948 - Fax 505-827-5912.

Pacific Northwest Laboratories, 65 Centennial Loop, Eugene, OR 97401 - 541-484-4493. Free information on environmental cleanup technologies.

Rhode Island Solar Energy Assoc., 42 Tremont Street, Cranston, RI 02920-2543 - Domenic Bucci, President, 401-942-6691.

Rhode Island State Energy Office, 275 Westminster St., Providence, RI 02907 - Janice McClanaghan, Energy

Program Mgr., 401-277-3370 - Fax 401-277-1260.

Sandia Laboratories - 505-845-0011. Free information and expertise on solar energy.

Triad Energy Resources, Inc., 4418 Carver Rd., Modesto, CA 95356 - 209-527-0607 - Fax 209-527-1279. Utilizing agricultural by-products, such as waste feed.

Utah, Office of Energy Services, 324 South State Suite 230, Salt Lake City, UT 84111 - Denise E. Beaudoin, Info. Specialist, 801-538-8690 - Fax 801-538-8660.

EXPORTING
Books & Directories:

How to Export (Free) and *Sources of Aid and Information for U.S. Exporters* ($35), Washington Researchers, 918 16th St., NW, Washington, DC 20006.

Export Profits: A Guide for Small Business, Jack S. Wolf, Upstart Pub-Dearborn Trade, 155 N. Wacker Dr., Chicago, IL 60606 - 800-621-9621, 800-245-2665, 312-836-4400 - Fax 312-836-1021 (1992, $19.95).

The Export Yellow Pages, USWest Marketing Resources, - 800-288-2582.· http://export. uswest.com - Superintendent of Documents, Washington, DC 20402 - 202-783-3238.Free yellow page directory listing for companies in the US, Canada and Mexico who want to export their products or services Free copy.

World Buyers' Guide to Unusual & Innovative Products, Emit Publications, Box 134, Katong, Singapore 9143 - Ismeth Emir, 2951414 7433307.

Worldwide Trading Partner Locating System, Applied Technologies Int'l, 391 Taylor Blvd., Suite 180, Pleasant Hill, CA 94523 - 510-680-0200 ($495). CD-ROM for windows gives contacts for 300,000 importers, distributors, manufacturers, agents, reps wholesalers and exporters, in 150 countries.

Export Magazines & Card Decks:

Commercial News USA, Export Awareness Div., U.S. and Foreign Commercial Service, ITA, Rm. 2106, The Dept. Of Commerce, Washington, DC 20230. Published 10x year though all U.S. Embassies reaching over 100,000 agents, distributors, buyers, in 140 countries. $395 buys a small ad.

Export Today Magazine, Box 28189, Washington, DC 20038 - Leah Young, Ed., 202-737-1060 (cir 38,000). Free to companies that export. Provides information on marketing, finance, insurance, transportation., for U.S. businesses.

Import/Export Executive Card Deck, Simon Direct, F-4 Brier Hill Court, East Brunswick, NJ 08816 - 908-651-7559. Free card pack advertising various companies and services that may assist you in exporting your invention.

International Marketing Digest, Butterworth-Heinemann, 225 Wildwood Ave., Box 4500, Woburn, MA 01801 - 617-928-2500 - Fax 617-933-6333.

International Marketing Resource Guide, William A. Delphos, Ed., Int'l Product Management, US Postal Service, 475 L'Enfant Plaza, SW, Washington, DC 20260 - 800-456-3600, ext 667 (1994, 335 p). This compact reference contains useful info on doing business with a number of countries, along with phone numbers to free expert assistance.

Passport, WorldPost Services, The US Postal Service, Box 23793, Washington, DC 20026-3793. Free quarterly newsletter explains new mail services from the US post Office to help you do business overseas.

US/Latin Trade, Box 3000, Denville, NJ 07834. Free magazine for companies desiring to export.

World Trade Magazine, Box 3000, Denville, NJ 07834. Free to individuals who import or export.

Internet & On-line Export Resources:

1st WorldWide Yellow Pages - http://www.worldyellowpages.com/. Companies, products and services from countries around the world.

Stat*USA - http://www.stat-usa.gov/stat-usa.html A Service of the U.S. Department of Commerce provides information on export & international trade and business leads & procurement opportunities.

Trade America - 405-624-3319, voice - 405-624-3577. Computer bulletin board that provides trade leads, referrals and other export information.

Tradexpress International - http://www.trade-express.com/ Listing service on the Net for buying and selling. Also, gives contact info for international export/import companies and manufacturers.

TradePort - http://tradeport.org. Free web site that helps companies increase their export sales.

Export Services:

U.S. Dept. Of Commerce, Trade Opportunity, Attn.: DIBA 266, Washington, DC 20230 - 202-482-2753. Automated telephone information services, such as ELVIS, Export License Voice Information System, which give taped replies to questions on obtaining export licenses and directs callers to export experts. Also compiles the National Trade Databank that provides info on foreign tradeleads, economic conditions.

American Export Register, Thomas Publishing Co., Five Penn Plaza, New York, NY 10001 - 212-629-1130. Provides free listings and paid ads for US companies looking for overseas customers. Sent to buyers, in 180 countries.

Center for International Trade Development, 90 West Fir, Suite 201, Clovis, CA 93611 - 800-344-3812. Free assistance to small businesses in California through the Community College system. Call for similar programs near you.

Export Hotline - 800-872-9767. Sponsored by *Business Week* magazine and other companies, provides over 5,000 market-research reports, covering 78 countries and 50 industries. It also offers information how to connect with potential customers.

Export Opportunity Hotline - 800-243-7232. Trade specialists of the Small Business Foundation of America consult by phone and give referrals to experts in your area.

Global Vision - Susan Khrystal, VP, 800-701-9029. Hosts *Direct from the USA* overseas catalog expos, where they will promote your products for a set fee.

Scott Allen Export Sales, 267 Fifth Ave., Suite 714, New York, NY 10016 - Janet Brandt, 212-213-2040. Offers mailing lists of English speaking importers, distributors, and buyers in varous countries. $72 each.

Showcase USA, Sell Overseas America, 2512 Artesia Blvd., Redondo Beach, CA 90278 - Michael Spivak, New Products Editor, 310-376-8788 (cir 33,000). Helps bring together exporters in the U.S. with buyers in other countries.

GIFTS & NOVELTIES (See also section on Toys)

Books:

Fad Money, How To Make Money From Fads, Crazes & Trends, Howard J. Klein - Franklin Watts, Inc., 730 Fifth Ave., New York, NY 10019 (1979). Provides case studies of fad creators who succeeded and those who failed and suggests the reasons why. Shows how to launch a fad item, and when to bail out.

How To Create Your Own Fad & Make a Million Dollars, Ken Hakuta, Morrow Press. (1988). From the man known as "Dr. Fad", who brought to America's youth such creations as the Wacky Wall Walker, here is sound advice on how to launch your own "fad" ideas.

Directories:

The Gift & Decorative Accessory Buyer's Guide, 51 Madison Ave., New York, NY 10010. Lists 30,000 manufacturers, importers, distributors, manufacturers, and vendor sources serving the gift industry.

Trade Magazines:

G S B: Gift & Stationery Business Magazine, Gralla Publications, 1515 Broadway, New York, NY 10036 - Joyce Washnick. Ed., 212-869-1300 (cir 32,000).

Gift Digest, Market Place Publications, 170 World Trade Mart, 2050 Stemmons Frwy, Dallas, TX 75258 - Misty Smiler, Ed., 214-747-4274.

Gifts & Decorative Accessories, 51 Madison Ave., New York, NY 10010 - Marie Stock, New Products Ed., 212-689-4411 (cir 34,000).

Giftware News, Box 5398, Deptford, NJ 08096 - Anthony De Masi, Ed., 609-227-0798 (cir 45,000).

Souvenirs & Novelties, Kane Communications, 7000 Terminal Sq., Suite 210, Upper Darby, PA 19082 - Sandy

Meskow, Ed., 215-734-2420.

Associations & Tradeshows:

National Merchandise Show, Thalheim Expositions, Inc., 4200 Bayview Rd., Box 4200, Manhasset, NY 11030 - 516-627-4000. Giftwares, novelties, housewares.

New York International, George Little Management, Inc., Two Park Ave., Suite 1100, New York, NY 10016 - 800-272-7469, 212-686-6070. Greeting cards, desk accessories, gifts. Other gift shows held in major cities: Chicago, Washington, Boston, San Francisco.

Souvenirs & Novelty Trade Assoc., 7000 Terminal Sq., Suite 210, Upper Darby, PA 19082 - 215-734-2420. Publishes *Souvenirs & Novelties* magazine.

Largest Gift & Novelty Stores:

Spencer Gifts, Inc., 6826 Black Horse Pike, Pleasantville, NJ 08232 - 609-645-3300. 500 retail stores.

The Summit Corporation, 10500 American Rd., Cleveland, OH 44144 - 216-252-8800. 368 Carlton Cards stores.

Things Remembered Inc., 5340 Avion Park Dr., Highland Heights, OH 44143 - 216-473-2000. 700 stores.

W. H. Smith Retail, 3200 Windy Hill Rd., Suite 1500W, Marietta, GA 30067 - Michele Gelernter, Buyer, 404-952-0705. 350 stores located in hotels and airports.

Mail Order & Catalog Retailers:

Hanover House, 340 Poplar St ., Hanover, PA 17331-2358 - 717-637-6000.

Johnson Smith Co., 4514-19th St. Court East, Box 25500, Bradenton, FL 34206 - 813-747-2356 - Fax 813-746-7896. The original company that started it all, from "whoopee cushions", to "itching powder", to novelties and gadgets of all kinds.

Lilian Vernon Corp, 2361 Central Park Ave, Yonkers, NY 10710-1215 - 914-961-8044. Housewares, notions, gifts.

The Smithsonian Catalogue, 7955 Angus Court, Springfield, VA 22153 - 800-322-0344.

Starcrest Products of California, 3660 Brennan Ave., Perris, CA 92370 - Joie Hill, 215-430-1000. Housewares, notions, gifts.

Taylor Gifts, Inc., 355 E Conestoga Rd., Wayne, PA 19087-2508 - 610-688-3046. Gifts, travelers aids.

Wholesalers & Distributors.

Giftware Online, 3010 LBJ Freeway, Ste. 1435, Dallas, TX 75234 - 800-234-5318, 214-488-8296 - Fax 214-488-9367 - http://www.giftonline.com/. Internet site for gift stores to search for products and order from manufacturer's online catalogs. This is a secure site. You will need an access code by calling the 800#.

Miles Kimball Company, 41 W 9th Ave., Oshkosh, WI 54901-6051 - 414-739-7796. Nationwide jobber of unusual gifts and housewares.

Russ Berrie & Co., Inc., 111 Bauer Dr., Oakland, NJ 07436 - 201-337-9000.

Telecom Corp., 1545 W. Mockingbird Lane, Dallas, TX 75235 - 214-638-0638.

GOVERNMENT & MILITARY MARKET

Books:

Selling to Uncle Sam: How to Win Choice Government Contracts for Your Business, Clinton L. Crownover & Mark Henricks, McGraw-Hill, 1221 Ave. of the Americas, New York, NY 10020 - 800-262-4729 - http://www.osborne.com/ (1992).

Internet Resources:

General Services Administration (GSA). - http://www.gsa.gov. The main gateway for most purchases by the federal government.

Information Database - http://lib-www.ucr.edu/govpub/. Federal, state, and local resources searchable by keyword.

Marketing Services:

Military Ads, USA, AdsUSA, 7303 Broadway, Lemon Grove, CA 92045 - 800-262-8923, 619-280-2985. One stop ad placement service for all 240 military base newspapers.

HARDWARE-HOME IMPROVEMENT

Books & Directories:

Builder-Buyer's Guide, Hanley-Wood, Inc., 655-15th St. NW Suite 475, Washington, DC 20005 (Mar, $10). Lists the products of 1500 manufacturers.

Sweets General Building & Renovation

Catalog File, Sweet's Group, 1221 Avenue of the Americas, New York, NY 10020 - 212-512-6566. A vast collection of catalogs from thousands of manufacturers organized and bound into a 28 volume set covering every type of building component. Here you will find everything from sound proofing materials to escalators to skylights.

Trade Magazines:

Builder, Rick Schwolsky, New Products Ed., and *Building Products*, Paul S. Kitzke, Ed., 655 15th St., NW, Suite 475, Washington, DC 20005 - 202-383-8350 (cir 189,000).

Building Design & Construction, 1350 E. Touhy Ave., Des Plaines, IL 60018 - Susan Casson, New Products Ed., 847-635-8800 (cir 79,000).

Building Supply Home Centers, Cahners Publishing Co., Box 5080, Des Plaines, IL 60017 - Rod Sutton, Ed., 847-635-8800 (cir 46,000).

Do-It-Yourself Retailing, 5822 W. 74th St., Indianapolis, IN 46278 - Marlena Elkins, New Product Ed., 317-297-1190 (cir 70,000).

Hardware Age, Chilton Co., One Chilton Way, Radnor, PA 19089 - Janet Baldwin, New Products Ed., (cir 71,000).

National Home Center News, Lebhar-Friedman, Inc., 425 Park Ave., New York, NY 10022 - Diane Fristachi, New Products Ed., 212-756-5151 (cir 52,000).

Tradeshows:

The Builders Show, National Association of Home Builders - 202-822-0200.

Construction & Building Products Show, Professional Program Management - 716-834-9431, 800-222-4465. New products, supplies and services for commercial building, design, maintenance and renovation.

National Hardware Show, Association of Expositions & Seminars - 203-325-5099.

Largest Home Centers & Distributors:

Builders Square (Div. Of K-Mart), 9725 DataPoint Dr., San Antonio, TX 78229 - 210-616-8000 (183 stores).

Home Base, 140 Orangefair Ave., Fullerton, CA 92632 - 714-441-0171 (87 stores).

Home Depot, 2727 Paces Ferry Rd., Atlanta, GA 30339 - 404-433-8211 (250 stores).

Payless Cashways, Inc., 2300 Main St., Box 419466, Kansas City, MO 64108 - 816-234-6000 (196 stores).

Wholesalers:

Hardware Wholesalers, Inc., Box 868, Ft. Wayne, IN 46801 - 219-749-8531.

Servistor Corp. Box 1510, Butler, PA 16003 - 412-283-4567.

HEALTH CARE INDUSTRY

Trade Magazines:

Health Foods Business, Howmark Pub. Corp., 567 Morris Ave., Elizabeth, NJ 07208 - Ging Geslewitz, Ed., 908-353-7373.

Healthcare Technology & Business Opportunities, Biomedical Business International, 1524 Brookhollow Dr., Santa Ana, CA 92705 - 714-755-5757 - Fax 714-755-5707. Source of health related patents and technologies for sale or license, and distributors seeking products.

Medical Products Sales, 1419 Lake Cook Rd., Deerfield, IL 60015 - Bill Briggs, Ed., 847-945-0345 (cir 24,000).

Novicom, Inc., 20000 Mariner Ave., Suite 480, Torrance, CA 90503 - 310-793-4141 - Fax 310-793-4138. Publishes a number of trade magazines describing new products for Dental Surgery, Chiropractic, Physical Therapy, Plastic Surgery, Podiatric, and Orthodontic.

Proofs, Box 3408, Tulsa, OK 74101 - Mary E. Good, Ed., 918-835-3161 (cir 6,000). Trade magazine for dentist supplies dealers.

Associations:

Health Industry Distributors Assoc., 225 Reinekers Lane, Suite 650, Alexandria, VA 22314 - 703-549-4432 - Fax 549-6495 Distributors of medical and health care equipment.

Internet & On-line Resources:

ABLEDATA - 301-589-3563, modem - gopher://val-dor.cc.buffalo.edu. Database describing over 22,000 products to assist people with disabilities.

MediSource - http://www.medisource.com/msource/. Medical equipment marketplace, medical yellow pages, and medical information.

Marketing Services:

DP Directory, 525 Goodale Hill Rd., Glastonbury, CT 06033 - 203-659-1065. Low cost source for mailing labels to editors of medical and health magazines, and newspaper columns.

National Institute on Disability and Rehabilitation Research, US Dept. of Education, c/o Jim Leahy, RERC on Technology, Evaluation and Transfer Center for Assistive Technology, University at Buffalo, Buffalo, NY 14214 - 716-829-3141. Free evaluation and assistance in developing and marketing inventions that assist people who have handicaps.

OFFICE PRODUCTS INDUSTRY

Trade Magazines:

Access Centers Magazine, 2082 Lincoln Ave., Suite G-3, Altadena, CA 91001 - Wayne Snyder, Ed., 818-794-2573 (Cir 10,000). Copyshops, office-supply stores, mailbox franchises, instant print shops.

Industry Report, Business Products Industry Association, 301 N. Fairfax Street, Alexandria, VA 22314 - Simon de Groot, New Prod Ed., 800-542-6672, 703-549-9040 - Fax 703-683-7654 (22x, cir 10,000). Trade magazine provides product information for retailers of office supplies, equipment. A good place to publicize and advertise your new office product.

Managing Office Technology, 1100 Superior Ave., Cleveland, OH 44114 (110K cir).

The Office Dealer, Box 150, Georgetown, CT 06829 - Brian Lewis, Ed., 215-628-7716 (cir 20,000). Trade magazine for retailers and wholesalers of office machines and supplies.

OfficeWorld News, 1905 Swarthmore Ave., Lakewood, NJ 08101 - Kim McCabe, Ed., 908-785-1919.

Associations & Tradeshows:

Business Products Industry Association (BPIA), 301 N. Fairfax St., Alexandria, VA 22314 - 800-542-6672, 703-549-9040 - Fax 703-683-7654. Formerly called NOPA, National Office Products Association, BPIA represents office products and furniture dealers, reps, wholesalers and manufacturers. It offers industry meetings,

research and statistics, tradeshows and publishes annual directory and buyers guide, and trade magazine.

International Business Products Convention, Business Products Industry Association (BPIA). - 800-542-6672. Largest tradeshow.

National Stationery Show, George Little Management, Inc. - 914-421-3200.

Largest Stores:

Each of these companies has a specific buyer for types of office supplies and merchandise such as paper goods, computers. Call before sending samples.

Office Depot, Inc., 2200 Old Germantown Rd., Delray Beach, FL 33445 - 407-278-4800 (500+ stores).

Staples/Office Depot Inc., 100 Pennsylvania Ave., Framingham, MA 01701 - 800-333-3330 - 508-370-8500 - Fax 508-370-8955 (1000+ stores).

OfficeMax, Inc., 3605 Warrensville Center Rd., Shaker Heights, OH 44122 - 216-921-6900 - Fax 216-491-4040. (468 stores).

Independent Stationers, Inc.,(dba Office Plus), 9900 Westpoint Dr., Suite 116, Indianapolis, IN 46256 - 317-845-9155 - Fax 317-842-9437(Buying group of 240 dealers).

Point Marketing & Procurement, Inc., 4141 Bienville St., New Orleans, LA 70119 - 800-41-POINT - 504-486-6659 - Fax 504-488-7221. (Buying group of 507 dealers).

UDI Corp., 90 Tapley St., Box 5064, Springfield, MA 01101 - 800-541-4834 - Fax 413-732-3333. (International buying group of 1300 dealers).

Mail Order/Catalog Retailers:

Quill, 100 Schelter Rd., Lincolnshire, IL 60069 - 800-789-1331 - 708-634-6690 - Fax 800-789-8955.

Reliable HomeOffice, Box 1501, Ottawa, IL 61350 - 800-869-6000 - Fax 800-326-3233

National Wholesalers:

SP Richards Co., 6300 Highlands Pkwy., Box 1266, Smyrna, GA 30081 - 770-436-6881 - Fax 770-433-3570. (42 branch outlets).

United Stationers, Inc., 2200 E. Golf Rd., Des Plaines, IL 60016 - 847-699-5000 - Fax 847-699-0891. (44 branch outlets).

PET MARKET

Trade Magazines:

Pet Age, 20 E. Jackson Blvd., Chicago, IL 60604 - Karen MacLeod, Ed., 312-663-4040 (cir 18,000).

The Pet Dealer, 567 Morris Ave., Elizabeth, NJ 07208 - Gina Geslewitz, Ed., 908-353-7373 (cir 17,000).

Pet Product News & P S M (Pets, Supplies & Marketing), Fancy Publications, Inc., Box 6050, Mission Viejo, CA 92690 - John Chadwell, Ed., 714-855-8822 (cir 19,000, bi-m).

Veterinary Product News, 1483 Chain Bridge Road, Suite 202, McClean, VA 22101 - Lynn E. Densford, Ed., 703-448-0336 (cir 43,000).

Associations & Tradeshows:

Pet Industry Distributors Association, 5024-R Campbell Blvd., Baltimore, MD 21236 - 301-931-8100.

Pet Industry Joint Advisory Council, 1710 Rhode Island Ave., NW, Washington, DC 20036 - 800-553-7387, 202-452-1525.

Major Retailers & Distributors:

Petco, Inc., 9151 Rehco Rd., San Diego, CA 92121 - 619-453-7845 - Fax: 619-453-6585 - E-mail: petco.com. (219 stores, including 113 superstores)

PetSmart, Inc., 10000 N. 31st Ave., Ste. C100, Phoenix, AZ 85051 - 602-944-7070 - Fax 602-395-6502 - http://www.petsmart.com. (110 stores, in 19 states).

For Pets Only, 1903 Hillhurst Ave., Los Angeles, CA 90027-2711 - 213-664-4211

Pet Wharehouse - 800-443-1160 (Mail order catalog.)

R.C. Steele, 1938 Transit Way, Box 910, Brockport, NY 14420 - 800-872-3773 (Mail order catalog).

SENIORS MARKET

Associations:

AARP, American Association of Retired Persons, 601 E St. NW, Washington, DC 20049 - 202-434-2277.

ProMatura Group, 428 North Lamar Blvd., Oxford, MS 38655 - Margaret A. Wylde, 601-234-0158 - Fax 601-234-0288. Has info on the American Society on Aging award program for products that make life more livable for people of all ages and abilities.

Senior Net - http://www.seniornet.org

Books:

The Age Wave: How The Most Important Trend Of Our Time Will Change Your Future, Ken Dychtwald, Bantam Books, 666 Fifth Ave., New York, NY 10019 - 800-431-0725 (1990, 400p, $9.95). Business and life style opportunities of an aging America.

Direct Marketing, Direct Selling & The Mature Consumer, Marjorie J. Caballero, Ed., Greenwood Publishing Group, 88 Post Rd., W, Box 5007, Westport, CT 06881 - 203-226-3571 - Fax 222-1502 ($55).

Magazines:

Creative Retirement, 1502 Augusta, Suite 415, Houston, TX 77057 - Elizabeth Armstrong, Ed., 713-974-6903 (cir 35,000).

Selling to Seniors Newsletter, 8204 Fenton St., Silver Spring, MD 20910 - Frank Cavaliere, Ed., 301-588-6380.

Contacts & Services:

Abledata - 800-227-0216. Database of over 20,000 assistive devices to help disabled individuals. You can see if your idea is new or not.

Center of Assistive Technology and Aztech, Inc., University of Buffalo, Occupational Therapy, 515 Kimball Tower, 3435 Main St., Buffalo, NY 14214 - 800-628-2281, 716-829-3141 - Fax 716-829-3217. Non profit group works with you to turn your prototype assistive device into a commercial product.

Senior Ads USA, AdsUSA, 7303 Broadway, Lemon Grove, CA 92045 - 800-262-8923, 619-280-2985. Provides one stop ad placement in all magazines, newsletters and newspapers serving seniors.

SPORTING GOODS INDUSTRY

Trade Magazines:

Action Sports Retailer, 31652 Second Ave., South Laguna, CA 92677 - Sada Valov, Ed., 714-499-5374 (cir 14,000). Trade magazine for the retailer of outdoor sports equipment and fashions, including volleyball, snowboarding, surfing and skateboarding.

Golf Pro Merchandiser, 7 W. 34th St., New York, NY 10001 - David Chmiel, New Products Ed., 212-630-3750 (cir 12,000).

Golf Product News, 15-22 Fair Lawn

Ave., Fair Lawn, NJ 07410 - Kim Post, Ed., 201-796-6031 (cir 19,000).

Inline Retailer, 2025 Pearl St., Boulder, CO 80302 - Dave Kingsbury, New Products Ed., 303-440-5111 (cir 5,000). Skating equipment retailers.

Outdoor Retailer, 31652 Second Ave., South Laguna, CA 92677 - Wendy Geister, New Products Ed., 714-499-4591 (cir 14,000). For retailers selling backpacking, climbing, camping, hiking and skiing equipment.

Sporting Goods Business, 1515 Broadway, 32nd Fl, New York, NY 10036 - Andrew Gaffney, Ed., 212-869-1300 (cir 29,000). Trade magazine for retailers, wholesaler jobbers, independent reps and manufacturers.

The Sporting Goods Dealer, 2 Park Ave., New York, NY 10016 - Michael Jacobsen, Ed., 212-779-5556 (cir 30,000).

Largest Stores:

United Merchants Corp., 2525 E. El Segundo Blvd., El Segundo, CA 90245 - 310-536-0611 (152 *Big 5 Sporting Goods* stores).

Herman's Sporting Goods, 2 Germak Dr., Carteret, NJ 07008 - 908-541-1550 - Fax 969-1550 (125 stores).

TOYS & HOBBIES (See also section on Gifts & Novelties)

Books:

Design and Sell Toys, Games & Crafts, Filis Frederick, Chilton Book Company, Chilton Co., 1 Chilton Way, Radnor, PA 19089 (1979). The former toy and game designer for Mattel, Cadillac and Transogram Toys explains what makes a successful toy, how to create and manufacture toys, and how to market the toy industry.

From Workshop To Toy Store, Richard C. Levy, Fireside Books, Simon & Schuster, Rockefeller Center, 1230 Avenue of the Americas, New York, NY 10020 - 212-698-7313 (1990). A fascinating inside look at how toy inventors develop, sell and cash in on their ideas.

Game Inventor's Handbook, Stephen Peek, F&W Publications, 1507 Dana Ave., Cincinnati, OH 45207 - 800-289-0963, 513-531-2690 - Fax 513-531-4082. (1993, 192p, $18.95).

ASTM F:963, Voluntary Safety Standard for Toys, American Society for Test-

ing and Materials, 1916 Race Street, Philadelphia, PA 19103 - 215-299-5585.

Directories:

Playthings Buyers Guide, Geyer-McAllister Pub., 51 Madison Ave., New York, NY 10010 - 212-689-4411. Annual special issue of *Games, Playthings Magazine* that contains lists of toy manufacturers, sales reps, designers suppliers and toy inventors.

Trade Magazines:

Game Developer, Miller Freeman, 600 Harrison St., San Francisco, CA 94107 - 800-642-9619, 415/905-2200 - Fax 415-905-2234. Bimonthly magazine for software and arcade game inventors. ($39.95).

Playthings, Geyer-McAllister Pub., 51 Madison Ave., New York, NY 10010 - Frank Reysen, New Products Ed., 212-689-4411 (cir 15,000). Trade magazine for mass merchandisers of toys, electronic games and hobbies. Publishes annual special issue, *Buyers Guide*, which contains list of toy manufacturers, sales reps, designers suppliers and inventors.

Small World, Earnshaw Publications, Inc., 225 W. 34th St., Suite 1212, New York, NY 10001 - Thomas Hudson, Ed., 212-563-2742 Covers toys, nursery furniture and children's accessories.

Toy & Hobby World International, Box 704, Clinton, CT 06413 - Christopher Byrne, Ed., 203-669-6150 (cir 18,000). Trade magazine for the toy & hobby retailer.

The Toy Book, and *The Licensing Book*, 264 W. 40th St., 7th Fl, New York, NY 10018 - Chantal Tode, Ed., 212-575-4510. Monthly new product updates for toy distributors.

Toy Business, 10711 Burnet Rd., Suite 305, Austin, TX 78758 - Kathleen M. Carson, Ed., 512-873-7761.

Pamphlets:

TMA Guide to Toys & Play, Box 866, Madison Square Station, New York, NY 10159 - 800-851-9955. Free safety booklet.

Toy Inventor/Designer Guide, Toy Manufacturers of America, Inc., 200 Fifth Ave., Suite 740, New York, NY 10010. Free brochure tells how to manufacture or license your toy ideas.

Associations:

American Toy Export Association, Robert Urquiola, Ex. Dir., c/o Kraemer Mercantile Corp., 200-5th Ave., Rm. 1303, New York, NY 10010 - 212-255-1772. .

National Association of Doll and Stuffed Toy Manufacturers, Ralph Katz, Adm., 200 E. Post Rd., White Plains, NY 10601 - 914-682-8900.

Toy and Hobby Wholesalers Association of America, William MacMillan, Ex. Dir., Box 955, Marlton, NJ 08053 - 609-985-2878.

Toy & Game Inventors of America, 5813 McCart Ave., Ft. Worth, TX 76133 - Bruce Davis, 817-292-9021 - Fax 817-346-8697. Toy invention evaluation $50; includes book *Invent a Toy and Get Rich!*, and list of toy sales agents.

Toy Manufacturers of America, Inc. (TMA), 200 Fifth Ave., Suite 740, New York, NY 10010. The trade association for the American toy industry, provides business services to over 260 US manufacturers and importers of toys.

Education:

Fashion Institute of Technology, Toy Design Dept., 227 West 27th St., New York, NY 10001 - 212-760-7700. Offers a BA degree in Toy Design.

Marketing Services:

Excel Development Group, 1721 Mount Curve Ave., Minneapolis, MN 55403 - Andrew Burton, 612-374-3233 - Fax 612-377-0865 - http://www.keystroke.com/exceld. Toy sales agent since 1982.

Invention Incubator, 29 Cummings Park, Suit 422, Woburn, MA 01801 - 617-933-8824. Arthur Venditi, former toy and game developer with Parker Brothers, and his partner Mike Trunfio, claim to have licensed over 100 products, including: Home Alone™ board game, Ren & Stimpy™ electronic LCD game, NERF™ balls and planes, Merlin™ᵛ electronic game system.

Tradeshows:

American International Toy Fair, Toy Manufacturers of America, 200 Fifth Ave., Rm. 740, New York, NY 10010 - 212-675-1141 - Fax 212-645-3246.

Toys, games, electronics, sporting goods. Held in February in New York City at the **Toy Center,** 200 Fifth Ave., this is the biggest and the most difficult to attend toy tradeshow. Showroom access to the larger manufacturers, such as Mattel, is by appointment only. However, concurrently at Javits Convention Center, 1107 Broadway, you can easily visit exhibit booths of smaller toy and game manufacturers.

Chicago Model Hobby Show, 2400 E. Devon, Des Plaines, IL 60018 - 312-299-3131. Radio controlled cars, planes and such.

Consumer Electronics Show, - 202-457-4919.A variety of products, and entertainment.

Dallas Toy Shows, Dallas Market Center, 2100 Stemmons Freeway, Dallas, TX 74207 - 800-325-6587. Held Spring and Fall.

Game Manufacturers Association Trade Show, Tropicana Hotel, Las Vegas - 214-247-7981.

Greater Toy Center, 200-5th Ave., Rm. 303, New York, NY 10010 - 212-675-4633. Houses the showrooms and sales offices of all the major toy companies.

Hobby Industry Convention & Trade Show, Hobby Industry Association of America, 319 E. 54th St., Elmwood Park, NJ 07407 - 201-794-1133.

Pacific Northwest Toy Association Show, Box 66900, Seattle, WA 98166 - 206-242-4462.

Toytech, Penta Hotel, New York - 212-513-7878.

Western States Toy & Hobby Show, 11100 Valley Blvd., Suite 340-20, El Monte, CA 91731 - 818-442-1635. Held in Spring.

Largest Retailers:

Each of these companies does over $1 billion dollars in annual sales.

Child World, Inc., Sub. of Trefoil Capital Investors, L.P., 25 Littlefield St., Avon, MA 02322 - 508-588-7300.

Kay Bee Toy Stores, 100 West St., Pittsfield, MA 02101 - 413-499-0086 - Fax 499-3739. 1244 stores.

Toys R Us, Inc., 395 W. Passaic St., Rochelle Park, NJ 07662 - 201-262-7800. 540 stores.

Wholesalers:

Felix V. Bass & Co., 611 Delsea Dr., Westville, NJ 08093 - 609-848-8800.

MW Kasch Co., 5401 W. Donges Bay Rd., Mequon, WI 53092 - 414-242-5000. 4500 accounts; toys, hobbies and school supplies.

Ch. 12 — Mail Order, Direct & Internet Marketing
MAIL ORDER MARKETING
Books:

The Golden Mailbox: How To Get Rich Direct Marketing Your Product, Ted Nicholas, Enterprise Dearborn, (1992, $39.95).

How I Made $1,000,000 In Mail Order, E. Joseph Cossman, Fireside Press, Simon & Schuster, Rockefeller Center, 1230 Avenue of the Americas, New York, NY 10020 - 212-698-7313 (1992, $13).

How to Start and Operate a Mail Order Business, Julian L. Simon, McGraw-Hill, 1221 Ave. of the Americas, New York, NY 10020 - 800-262-4729 - http://www.osborne.com/ (1965).

The Lazy Man's Way to Riches, Joe Karbo, 17105 S. Pacific St., Sunset Beach, CA. The book that started it all for many future mail order millionaires.

The Greatest Direct Mail Sales Letters of All Times, Dick Hodgson, Dartnell Corp., 4660 N Tavnswd Ave., Chicago, IL 60640 - 312-561-4000 (1987).

Direct Marketing Success Stories, Bob Stone, NTC Business Books, 4255 W. Touhy Ave., Lincolnwood, IL. 60646 - 800-323-4900, 847-679-5500 - Fax 847-679-2494. From one of the pioneers of the industry.

Trade Magazines:

Catalog Age, 911 Hope St., Bldg. 6, Stamford, CT 06907 - Kathleen Joyce, Ed., 203-358-9900.

Catalog Marketer, Lori Boyko, Ed., 522 Forest Ave., Evanston, IL 60202 - 847-866-1890.

Direct, Box 4949, Stamford, CT 06907 - Laurie Petersen, Ed., 203-358-9900 (cir 43,000).

Direct Marketing, Hoke Communications, 224 Seventh St., Garden City, NY 22530 - Mollie Neal, Ed., 516-746-6700 (cir 10,000).

Direct Marketing News, 1200 Markham Road, Suite 301, Scarborough, Ontario M1H 3C3 Canada - Cheryl Sandys, Ed., 416-439-4083 (cir 6,000).

Who's Mailing What!, North American Publishing, 401 N. Broad St., Philadelphia, PA 19108 - Denison Hatch, Ed., 215-238-5300 (cir 1500).

What's Working In Direct Marketing & Fulfillment, 11300 Rockville Pike, Suite 1100, Rockville, MD 20852 - 301-816-8950.

Shop At Home Catalog Directory, 2080 S. Holly St., Box 221050, Denver, CO 80222 - 800-315-1995. Free catalog describes hundreds of other catalogs of consumer, scientific, hobby and other interests.

Directories:

$100 Billion Dollar Directories - Publishers Services, 2163 Fulton Ave., No.1, Sacramento, CA 95825 ($70). Lists 3,550 mail order companies, 2,560 catalog houses and 4,450 buyers, showrooms and mass merchandising companies.

National Directory of Catalogs, Oxbridge Communications, 150 Fifth Avenue, Suite 302, New York, NY 10011 - 212-741-0231, 800-955-0231 - Fax 212-633-2938 - E-mail:info@oxbridge.com ($345). Describes over 9,000 catalogs organized by 78 product areas. Also, available on CDROM.

National Directory of Mailing Lists, Oxbridge Communications, 150 Fifth Avenue, Suite 302, New York, NY 10011 - 212-741-0231, 800-955-0231 - Fax 212-633-2938 - E-mail:info@oxbridge.com ($295). Describes 33,000 available mailing lists covering 200 different categories of audiences — from concrete contractors to sporting goods store owners to golfers.

SRDS Direct Mail List Rates & Data, Standard Rate & Data Service, 3004 Glenview Road, Wilmette, IL 60091 - 800-323-4588. Directory of thousands of mailing lists available and the firms who sell them. Describes lists of specific kinds of companies, professionals and consumers—such as people who like to scuba dive, or work on old cars!

Who's Who in Catalog Showroom Mer-

chandising - CSM Communications, 195 Smithtown Blvd., Nesconset, NY 11767 ($295). Lists 2200 catalog showrooms indexed by type of product.

Internet Resources:
Catalog Mart - http://catalog. savvy.com/ This site offers access to hundreds of catalogs by subject.

Mailing Lists:
See also section on Distribution for related resources, particularly the *D&B MarketPlace CD-ROM* and *PhoneDisc USA Business CD-ROM.*
American List Counsel - 800-252-5478 ($150 min. order for basic lists. Good selection of response/consumer lists, such as mail order buyers of LL Bean, subscribers to Sunset Magazine, etc).
Ed Burnett-Database America - 800-223-7777.
Compilersplus - 800-431-2914 ($95 min. for basic lists).
National Demographics & Lifestyles - 800-525-3533. Provides *The Lifestyle Selector* that allows you to locate individuals grouped together by their lifestyles, such as: income, hobbies/interests, age, etc.
The SpeciaLists - 800-888-3462 ($200 min. order). Good selection of professions broken down to the "specialty" level such as greenhouse builder, golf club pro, medical engineer.
Wholesale Mailing Lists - 800-553-2123.

Software:
Mailer's Software, 970 Calle Negocio, San Clemente, CA 92673 - 800-800-6245 - Fax 714-492-7086. Source for direct marketing software to assist you in tracking orders, preparing mass mailings, checking for address corrections, pre-sorting for postal discounts, and converting databases.

Mail Order/Catalog Companies:
Note: Individual M/O companies are also listed under specific categories in the previous section Ch. 11, "Distribution".
Starcrest Products of California, 3660 Brennan Ave., Perris, CA 92571 - 909-943-2011.
Tilberry Direct Marketing, 20717-F Highway 99, Lynwood, WA 98036 - 206-776-2120. Sales rep looking for products for 80 major catalog accounts.

MARKETING ON THE NET
Books & Directories:
Guerrilla Marketing On-line, Jay C. Levinson & Charles Rubin, Guerrilla Marketing Library, Houghton Mifflin Co., 215 Park Ave. South, New York, NY 10003 - 800-225-3362 (1995, $12.95). Like the other "guerrilla" books, the authors show how to get the most marketing response at the lowest cost. Shows the various ways of using the Net, such as E-mail, Gopher sites, newsgroups. Also offers plenty of clever ideas on how to motivate customers to visit your "virtual store" and get them to buy.
The Internet Business Companion, David Angell, Addison-Wesley Publishing Co., Reading, MA 01867 - 800-822-6339 (1995, 242p, $19.95).
Marketing on the Internet, Jill H. & Matthew V. Ellsworth, John Wiley Sons, 605 Third Ave., New York, NY 10158 (1995, 404p, $24.95) - http://www.oakridge.com/orr.html. Takes a hands-on approach with lots of examples of how to set up a business on the World Wide Web.
What's on the Web, Eric Gagnon, Ed., Internet Media Corp., 3052 Railroad Vine, Fairfax, VA 22031 - 703-255-6569 - Fax 703-255-7237 - htp://www.jumpcity.com/ (1996, $23.95) A review of only the best WEB sites on the Internet. Saves an enormous amount of time finding what you need.
The Internet Yellow Pages, Harley Hahn, Osborne McGraw-Hill, 2600 Tenth St., Berkeley, CA 94710 - http://www.osborne.com/ (1996, $29.95). An encyclopedic synopsis of thousands of resources accessable on the Internet.

Magazines & Newsletters:
The Internet Business Journal - Michael Strangelove, Ed., 613-241-0982 - E-mail: mstrange@fonorola.net. Monthly newsletter. $75 for small businesses. Offers free FAQ (frequently asked questions). report on advertising on the Internet.
Internet Business Advantage - 800-223-8720. Monthly newsletter. ($59).
Internet World, Meckler Corp., Box 713,

Mount Morris, IL 61054-9959 - 800-632-5537 - E-mail:meckler@jvnc.net. (12x, $14.97).

The Internet World Response Deck, 117 W. Hicheltorena, Santa Barbara, CA 93101 - 800-266-3353, 805-966-3353 - Fax 805-963-1143 - E-mail: mktgbb@aol.com. A free card deck with assorted offers from companies serving internet marketers.

On-line Access Magazine, 900 N. Franklin St., Suite 700, Chicago, IL 60610 - Alan Rosenthal, Ed., 312-573-1700 - Email: 70324.343 @compuserve.com. (Semi-montthly, $19.80).

Internet Resources:

Yahoo - http://www.yahoo.com. A great place to begin getting information on everything on the Internet, nicely arranged by subject areas.

Netscape - http://www.netscape.com - The company that launched the web as we know it today. Good source of web page design and free software.

Web Digest for Marketers - hjttp://www.mid.net/NET/PM-1995/95-08/95-08-03/0013.html. - Searchable database of the best marketing sites on the net. Or, try www.advert.com.

Internet Directory of Network Marketers - http://www.he.net/~image/nwm/people.html. List of network marketers with contacts & product info. Free listings.

Marketing on the Internet 1 - http://www.oakridge.com/orr.html.

Marketing on the Internet 2 - http://tig.com/IBC/White/Paper.html.

The Internet Advertising Resource Guide - http://missouri.edu/internet-advertising-guide.html.

Internet Commercial Use Strategies - http://pass.wayne.edu/business.html. A good place to begin for anyone wishing to start a business on the Net.

Search Engines - http://search.com. Provides one stop access to hundreds of useful search engines and directories.

Internet Marketing Companies:

These organizations operate "Web Malls" or other net advertising services to help you market your new product .

101 A Internet Promotion Service - http://www.kwik-link.com/c/ promote.htm. Promote and market your business on the internet free in 40 directories.

Ad Home - http://www.adhome.com/. Free listing on their directory of your company. Also for fee placement service to put your ad on relevant Web sites.

BigBook - http://www.bigbook.com/. BigBook offers every business in the U.S. an opportunity to maintain a detailed listing in their directory free of charge.

Free Classified Ads - http://www.freeclassifieds.com/

Giftware Online, 3010 LBJ Freeway, Ste. 1435, Dallas, TX 75234 - 800-234-5318, 214-488-8296 - Fax 214-488-9367 - http://www.giftonline.com/. Internet site for gift stores to search for products and order from manufacturer's online catalogs. This is a secure site. You will need an access code by calling the 800#.

Innovators Network Directory - http://www.innovatorsnet.com/. Find products. Free yellow pages!

Internet Shopping Network - http://www.internet.net/. From the same people who bring you the Home Shopping Network on cable TV.

NetSearch - http://www.ais.net:80/netsearch/ Free directory listing to lead users to your company.

ABI Net Yellow Pages - 402-593-4593 - http://www.abii.com. Free basic listing with American Business Information.

Sparkys Web Site Service - http://CyberZine.ORG. For $10 per month, they will build a basic web page for selling your wares.

Yellow Pages Online - http://www.ypo.com/. Easy-to-use yellow page directory with over 18 million listings. Web site design and service, free basic listings.

YelloWWWeb Pages - http://yellowwweb.com/freyel.html.Include your business listing for free, on and off the net.

Internet Service Providers (ISP):

These companies provide you with a way to hook your computer on to the internet, and get an E-mail address. A flat monthly rate gets you unlimited access. Before you sign on, make sure they can provide you with a local access number so you don't have to pay toll charges.

AT&T WorldNet - 800-222-0400, x487 - http://www.att.com/. Offers current phone users a free E-mail address and 5 free hours a month access to the net, or unlimited access for $19.95.

Delphi - 800-695-4005.

Digital Express Group - 800-969-9090.

MCI Network - 800-550-0927.· http://www.mci.com/.

NetCom - 800-501-8649.

Sprint - 800-877-4646 - http://www.sprint.com/.

Other On-line Services:

Each of these on-line services offer a wide variety of marketing tools, such as classified ad sections, web pages, and specialized information groups (SIGs) through which you can promote and sell your products.

America On-line Inc., 8619 Westwood Center Dr., Vienna, VA 22182 - 800-827-6364.

CompuServe, 5000 Arlington Center Blvd., Box 20212, Columbus, OH 20212 - 800-368-3343.

Prodigy Services Co., 445 Hamilton Ave., White Plains, NY 10601 - 914-448-2496.

TV & RADIO MARKETING

Books & Directories:

How to Make Big Money On TV, Craig Daugard, Upstart Pub-Dearborn Trade, 155 N. Wacker Dr., Chicago, IL 60606 - 800-621-9621, 800-245-2665, 312-836-4400 - Fax 312-836-1021 (1996, 178p, $16.95). The author is an inventor with 25 patents to his credit whose products have sold on the home shopping TV. Shows how to test your product on the air, how to do an infomercial, how to approach the big home shopping networks.

Eicoff on Broadcast Direct Marketing, Al Eicoff, NTC Business Books, 4255 West Touhy Ave., Lincolnwood, IL 60646 - 800-323-4900, 847-679-5500 - Fax 847-679-2494. (1988, 191p, $29.95). Textbook classic on how to make TV and radio advertising ring your cash register in sales.

Or Your Money Back, Alvin Eicoff, Crain Books, 740 Rush St., Chicago, IL 60611 - 312-649-5250. First hand account of how the author used direct marketing on TV to launch many successful products.

SRDS Radio & TV Stations, Standard Rate & Data Service, 3004 Glenview Road, Wilmette, IL 60091. Provides contacts arranged by geographic market.

Trade Magazines:

Infomercial Marketing Report, 11533 Thurston Circle, Los Angeles, CA 90049 - Steve Dworman, Pub., 310-472-5253 - Fax 310-472-6004. ($395, 12x) Lots of contacts and inside info on companies in the business of marketing on TV.

Response TV, Avanstar Communications, Inc., 201 E. Sandpoint Ave., Suite 600, Santa Ana, CA 92707 - Jack Schember, Ed., 714-513-8400 (cir 18,000).

Trade Shows:

Sell Your Product On Television Hunt, 11533 Thurston Circle, Los Angeles, CA 90049 - Sandee Richardson, 310-472-5253 - Fax 310-472-6004. - Produced by the publishers of Infomercial Marketing Report, during this three day event you will meet with key buyers from 10-15 of the major direct response television marketing companies to review your product. Costs $1700-$2200.

Associations:

Cabletelevision Advertising Bueau, 757 Third Avenue, New York, NY 10017 - 212-508-1200. - One stop source for information and contacts for advertising on Cable networks. Publishes Cable TV Facts ($8) and other directories.

National Infomercial Marketing Assoc. (NIMA), 1201 New York Ave., NW, Suite 1000, Washington, DC 20005 - 202-962-8342.

Home Shopping Networks:

The Golf Channel, 7580 Commerce Center, Orlando, FL 32819 - 407-363-4653.

Home Shopping Network, Box 9090, Clearwater, FL 34618 - 813-572-8585.

QVC Network, Goshen Corp., 1365 Enterprise Dr., West Chester, PA 19380 - 610-701-1000.

Value Vision, 6740 Shady Oak Rd., Minneapolis, MN 55344 - 612-947-5200.

Infomercial Producers & Shows:

These companies are always looking for new products to market that have a high markup and perceived value. They will produce the ad, buy the air time and take the lion's share of the profits.

American Telecast, 16 Industrial Blvd., Paoli, PA 19301 - David Savage, 610-430-7800.

Gunthy-Renker, 4550 Eclectic Ave., Suite 200, Palm Desert, CA 92260 - 619-773-9022. Producers of "Personal Power".

Impact Television & Marketing, 100 Larkspur Landing Circle, Larkspur, CA 94939 - Bill Seidel, 415-331-9095 - Fax 415-464-8099. Producer of "Preview 2000".

National Media Corp., 1700 Walnut Street, Philadelphia, PA 19103 - 215-772-5000. Producer of "Jet Stream Oven", "Juice Tiger", "Amazing Discoveries".

Positive Response Television, 14724 Ventura Blvd., 6th Fl., Sherman Oaks, CA 91403 - 818-380-6900 - Fax 818-380-6966 - E-mail: askmike@aol.com. Producers of "Amazing Discoveries".

Power Media Marketing Group, 150 E. Olive Ave., Suite 305, Burbank, CA 91502 - 818-557-8318.

Premier TV Products, Inc., 23 Vreeland Rd., Florham Park, NJ 07932 - Terry Robinson, 201-377-7500.

The Regal Group, 355 Lexington Ave., 18th Fl, New York, NY 10017 - 215-643-6300.

Talk America, attn: New Products, 510 Congress St., Portland, ME 04101 - 207-775-5007 x3064. Seeks unique, mass appeal products for sale.

USA Direct, 12701 Whitewater Dr., Minnetonka, MN 55343 - 612-945-4000.

Video Production Studios & Services:

DigiVideo Productions, 444 E Grant Rd., Suite 108, Tucson, AZ 85715 - 602-321-4546, 800-636-DIGI. Creates 30 second ad using digital video for $495-$2,995.

New Day Marketing, 1819 Cliff Dr., Suite F, Santa Barbara, CA 93109 - Vickki Schuman Hunt, 805-965-7833 - Fax 805-965-1284. Researches and buys TV ad space and tracks the re-sults for direct selling of your product.

These companies offer "complete packages". For a set price they will script, direct, shoot an ad, run it on selected cable stations, and take the orders for you.

Larry John Wright Advertising, 1045 E University Dr., Mesa AZ 85203-8054 - 800-821-5068, 602-833-8111 - Fax 602-969-2895 - www.ljwtub.com. Free television test marketing. 1 and 2 minute direct response TV commercial produced for $2,995. Includes 800 number and credit card set-up.

TV Ad Partners, 180 Weidman Rd., Suite 214, Manchester, MO 63021 - 314-230-0300.

800 Telephone Order Taking Services:

These companies can handle high volume telephone orders for your company and process credit card orders.

CSC, Communication Service Centers - 800-251-3030.

Mattrix Marketing - 800-453-4003. Has 400 operators.

Sterling Communications - 800-783-7546.

The Product Line ·· 303-671-8000. Has 100-400 operators.

Ch. 13 — Selling Your Invention as a Promotional Advertising Product and Premium

Trade Magazines:

Business-Incentive Strategies, Miller Freeman, Inc., 1 Pennsylvania Ave., New York, NY 10019 - 212-714-1300 (Circ. 40K). Written for executives who use premiums and travel incentives to increase retailer and consumer sales, or employee productivity and safety awareness.

The Counselor, The Advertising Specialty Institute, NBS Inc., Bucks County Business Park, 1120 Wheeler Way, Langhorne, PA 19047 - Catherine S. Holnick, Ed., 215-752-4200. Written exclusively for promotional advertising products distributors and suppliers listed with the Advertising Specialty Institute. *Kaleidoscope* section features new products from outside (non ASI). manufacturers. Arn Bernstein, new products editor.

Incentive, Bill Communications, Inc.,

355 Park Ave., South, 5th Fl, New York, NY 10010 - Judy Quinn, New Products Editor, 212-592-6449 - Fax 212-592-6459 (Circ 40K). For executives who use incentive and promotional merchandise in their sales and marketing programs.

Insider, Impact Advertising, Inc., 1546 Main St., Dunedin, Fl 34698 - Jill South, Ed. ($40, Qrtly). For distributors and resellers of promotional advertising products.

Potentials In Marketing, 50 S. Ninth St., Minneapolis, MN 55402 - 800-328-4329, 612-333-0471 - Fax 333-6526. Magazine for executives who use ad specialties and premiums to increase sales.

Promotional Products Business, Promotional Products Association International., 3125 Skyway Circle North, Irving, TX 75038 - Tonya McMurray, New Prod Ed., 214-252-0404 (cir 6,000). Formerly called *Specialty Advertising Business*, it's written exclusively for distributor and supplier members.

Associations :

Advertising Specialty Institute, (ASI). 1120 Wheeler Way, Langhorn, PA 19047 - 800-546-1343. This listing organization is a clearinghouse for manufacturers and distributors of promotional advertising products. Services include: publishing directories of listed manufacturers and distributors, catalogs of products, sourcing of products, credit reporting, web page on the Internet. There is a $185. charge to have your company listed in their printed indexes.

Impact Group, 1546 Main St., Dunedin, FL 34698 - 800-222-6228, 813-736-6228 - Fax 813-734-8368. A competitor to ASI. Publishes buying guides, directories, catalogs and co-op mailings showcasing advertising promotional products. An effective method of getting your product seen by buyers of such items.

Promotional Products Association International (PPAI), 3125 Skyway Circle North, Irving, TX 75038 - 214-252-0404. Formerly called the Specialty Advertising Association International, it sponsors seminars, annual tradeshows and educational programs and materials; and pub-

lishes the *Promotional Products Business* magazine.

Advertising Specialty Association for Printers (ASAP), Box 5882, Katy, TX 77491 - George Duckworth, Pres., 713-855-8522. Offers manufacturers a free listing in directory.

Marketing Services:

Charles A. Hoffman Associates, 2903 N.E. Rose Tree Dr., Jensen Beach, FL 34957-4759 - 407-334-4937 - Fax 407-334-9371. Marketing consultant to the promotional advertising industry will exhibit your products at the PPAI Dallas show for a fee. Also can supply mailing labels of Promotional Advertising products distributors/jobber firms. **(Ask for special offer: 3,000 of the largest firms for $75).**

Sales and Marketing Merchandising, Hughes Communications, 211 W State St., Rockford, IL 61101-1111 - 815-963-4000. This card deck goes out to thousands of Sales and marketing executives who may find your product just the ticket for their next promotion.

Tradeshows:

National Premium Incentive Show, Hall-Erickson, Inc., 150 Burlington Ave., Calrendon Hills, IL 60514 - 312-850-7779.

Premium Incentive Show, Miller Freeman, Inc., 1515 Broadway, Box 939, New York, NY 10108 - 800-950-1314.

PPAI Show, Promotional Products Association International, 3125 Skyway Circle North, Irving, TX 75038 - 214-252-0404.

Top Promotional Advertising Products Distributors:

HA-LO Advertising Specialties, 5980 Touhy Ave., Niles, IL 60714 - 847-647-2300 - Fax 647-5999. $91M, 500 reps, 12 offices.

Herman Marketing, 1400 N. Price Rd., St. Louis, MO 63132 - 314-432-1800 - Fax 432-1818. $97.3M, 25 reps, 18 offices.

K-Products Inc., 1520 Albany Place SE, Orange City, IA 51041 - 712-737-4925 - Fax 737-2408. $77M, 45 reps, 1 office.

Swingster Marketing Services, 10450 Holmes Road, Kansas City, MO 64131 - 816-943-5000 - Fax 943-

5172. $70M, 43 reps, 2 offices.

Brown & Bigelow, 345 Plato Blvd. E, St. Paul, MN 55107 - 612-293-7000 - Fax 293-7277. $68M, 650 reps, 3 offices.

Creative Concepts in Advertising, 31535 Southfield Rd., Beverly Hills, MI 48025 - 810-258-0000 - Fax 258-1339. $65M, 32 reps, 4 offices.

JII Sales Promotion Associates, 110 South 2nd St., Red Oak, IA 51566 - 712-623-5531 - Fax 712-623-5749. $62M, 1100 reps, 12 offices. Conshocton, OH.

The Vernon Company, One Promotion Place, Newton, IA 50208 - 515-792-9000 - Fax 792-690. $61M, 650 reps, 12 offices.

Geiger Brothers, Box 1609-Mt. Hope Ave., Lewiston, ME 04241 - 207-783-2001 - Fax 207-783-6418. $60M, 500 reps, 23 offices.

Newton Manufacturing, 1123 First Avenue East, Newton, IA 50208 - 515-792-4121 - Fax 792-6261. $50M, 1575 reps, 1 offices.

Ch. 14 — How To Set Up Your Virtual Office

Books:

101 Home Office Success Secrets and **Organizing Your Home Office For Success,** Lisa Kanarek, Penguin Books USA, 375 Hudson St., New York, NY 10014 (1996, 160p, $8.95). Filled with business strategy details for successful home-office entrepreneurs.

AMACOM, American Management Association, 135 West 50th St., New York, NY 10020. Publishes a wide variety of books on managing a startup business, developing products and marketing.

Entrepreneur's Small Business Catalog, - 800-421-2300 - Fax 714-851-9088. Carries 200 start-up guides, books and software to help you succeed in a business of your own.

Government Giveaways for Entrepreneurs and *Lesko's Info-Power II,* Matthew Lesko, Information USA - 800-862-5372, 800-879-6862. ($37.95). Thousands of sources of information and assistance to start your business.

Homemade Money - Barbara Brabec, Betterway Books-F&W Publications,

1507 Dana Ave., Cincinnati, OH 45207 - 800-289-0963, 513-531-2690 - Fax 513-531-4082. ($19.95). The "home business bible" that tells you how to select, start, manage, market and multiply the profits of a business at home.

The Office Equipment Adviser, What to Buy for Business, Inc., Box 22857, Santa Barbara, CA 93121 - 800-247-2185. (1993, 512 p, $27.95) Advice on which brands of faxes, copiers, printers, etc., are the best to buy.

The Portable Office - Take Your Office on the Road Now and for the Future, Jefferson D. Bates & Stuart F. Crump, Acropolis South (1987, $16.95).

The Whole Work Catalog, New Careers Center, Box 2193, Boulder, CO 80306 ($1). Large selection of entrepreneurial books.

Books that Inspire:

Fireside Press, Simon & Schuster, Rockefeller Center, 1230 Avenue of the Americas, New York, NY 10020 - 212-698-7313. Publishes a number of top titles, including: *Awaken The Giant Within,* Anthony Robbins, (1992), *How To Win Friends and Influence People,* Dale Carnegie, (1981), *Psycho-Cybernetics,* Maxwell Maltz, (1975),

Think And Grow Rich - Napoleon Hill, Napoleon Hill Foundation,1440 Paddock Dr., Northbrook, IL 60062-6811 - 847-998-0408 (1989).

Magazines:

Entrepreneur Magazine, 2392 Morse Ave., Irvine, CA 92619 - Rieva Lesonsky, Ed., 714-261-2325, 800-357-7299 - http://www.entrepreneurmag.com. Provides info on starting and promoting your own small business.

In Business Magazine, 419 State Ave., Emmaus, PA 18049 - Jerome Goldstein, Ed., 215-967-4135 (cir 10,000). For individuals who want to succeed in business on their own. Articles cover marketing, management, staffing and raising funds.

Home Office Computing, 411 Lafayette St., New York, NY 10003 - Bernedette Grey, Ed., 612-633-0578 - Fax 633-1862. Not just about computers, this great magazine covers a wide range of information, advice and resources for small businesses and startups.

National Home Business Report, Box 2137, Naperville, IL 60567 - Barbara Brabec, Ed., 708-717-0488 ($18/yr). Marketing and promotion tips, vendor sources, and articles on running and developing a business.

Gov't. Resources:

Small Business Administration, Answer Desk & SBA Publications, Box 30, Denver, CO 80201-0030 - 800-368-5855, 800-827-5722 - http://www.sbaonline.sba.gov/. Huge resource that can be somewhat intimidating but offers expert advice, assistance and even funding. (Ask for SBA Form 115A for list of available books and publications).

Service Corps of Retired Executives (SCORE) - 800-827-5722. An organization sponsored by the Small Business Administration of over 13,000 volunteer business executives who provide free help in writing business plans, developing export markets, and general business counseling. Call for location of the SCORE office nearest you.

Small Business Institutes (SBIs) These are organized through the SBA on over 500 university and college campuses nationwide. On-site management counseling is provided by senior and graduate students guided by faculty advisors. Contact your local university.

Small Business Development Centers (SBDCs). Sponsored by the SBA in partnership with state and local governments and universities to provide counseling and training to businesses. Check with your local university and chamber of commerces for one near you.

Internet Resources:

American Assn of Home-Based Businesses - http://www.aahbb.org/

Business on the Web - http://euro.net/innovation/WelcomeHP.html

Krislyn's Strictly Business Sites - http://www.krislyn.com/sites.html. A starting place for finding all kinds of helpful business pages on the Web.

Small Business Advancement - http:/

/www.sbanet.uca.edu/. Large on-line business library, free software.

Small Business Help Center - http://www.kciLink.com/sbhc/

Small Business Resource Center - http://www.retailadvz.com/. Provides discussion groups, business bookstore, and a fee-fased Biz-Therapist program that gives expert advice from on-line advisers.

Other On-line Associations & Groups:

America Online Inc., 8619 Westwood Center Dr., Vienna, VA 22182 - 800-827-6364. Hosts Microsoft's **Small Business Center** (keyword: MSBC).

CompuServe, 5000 Arlington Center Blvd., Box 20212, Columbus, OH 20212 - 800-368-3343. Provides *Business Database Plus* (Go BUSDB). that contains thousands of articles from over 450 business publications, and the forums *Working From Home* and *Entrepreneurs*.

Prodigy Services Co., 445 Hamilton Ave., White Plains, NY 10601 - 914-448-2496. Hosts *The Home Office and Entrepreneurs' Bulletin Board* (jump HOME BUSINESS BB: jump: ENTREPRENEURS EXCHANGE BB). gives direct access to other individuals running homebased businesses and to the editors of *Home Office Computing* magazine.

COMPUTING

Computer Hardware:

ComputerShopper Catalog, One Park Ave., 1 Fl., New York, NY 10016 - 212-503-3500 - Fax 503-3995. A one-stop resource for shopping by mail for hardware and software.

Dell Computing - 800-449-3355. Mail order vendor of computers with a reputation for very fast pcs, impeccable service and in your home repair guarantee.

PC Potential - 800-581-9866. Mail order vendor of hardware and software.

Raceway Computers - 800-240-0055. Mail order vendor of hardware and software.

Software:

Arts & Letters Express, Computer Support Corp., Dallas, TX 75244 - 214-661-5429. Free test-drive version of desktop publishing software and a fully-functional version of their drawing program with clip art.

MYOB Mind Your Own Business, Bestware - 800-851-1812 - Fax 201-586-2200. An all-in-one business accounting, management, scheduling, order entry, purchasing, report generating and form making package for Windows or Mac. Trial version for $10.

Nebs Business Training Software - 800-225-6380. CD-ROM multimedia programs for basic business training, such as, "How To Start You Own Business", "How to Advertise Your Business" and "How to Finance your Business" ($49.95 ea).

PrintMaster Gold, Micro Logic Software - 800-888-9078 - Fax 800-933-0571. Inexpensive ($19.95). but complete publishing system for Windows. Create brochures, signs, ads, labels, package designs.

QuickBooks - 800-781-6999. Highly popular bookkeeping program that handles invoicing and accounts receivable, check writing and accounts payable. Trial version for $10.

Seriff - 800-489-6719. For $6.95 shipping/handling receive fully functioning lite versions of desktop publishing software for Windows.

Shareware:

Shareware is software that you can try for free and then buy only if you decide to continue using it.

For Windows/DOS - www.shareware.com.

For Mac - http://wwwhost.ots.utexas.edu/mac/main.html.

Ask for free catalogs:

Reasonable Solutions - 800-876-3475.
Software Labs - 800-569-7900.
MEI/Micro Center - 800-634-3478.
Walnut Creek CDROM - 800-786-9907.

INSURANCE:

Don't assume your home owners or renters insurance will automatically cover losses to your home office equipment. Or the loss of your business software! Here are options. Also, before you sell your first product, get product liability insurance.

Books & Pamphlets:

Product Liability: Design & Mfg. De-fects, Shepards, McGraw-Hill, Inc., Box 35300, Colorado Springs, CO 80935 - 700-525-2474 - http://www.osborne.com/. Advice on warning labels, packaging and such to avoid product liability.

Insuring Your Business, Insurance Information Institute - 800-331-9146.

Product Safety Up Date, National Safety Council, 444 N. Michigan Ave., Chicago, IL 60611 - 800-621-7619.

Services:

Aetna Life & Casualty Insurance, 151 Farmington Ave., Hartford, CT 06156 - 203-683-3648 - Fax 683-3746. Provides product liability insurance, and home office equipment insurance.

Boston Computer Society/Utica Insurance - 800-933-1914, ext.4821.

Intellectual Property Insurance Services Corporation, 10503 Temberwood Circle, Suite 220, Louisville, KY 40223 - 800-537-7863, 502-429-8007. Patent infringement abatement insurance in case you need to sue to protect your patent.

Safeware - 800-848-3469. Provides special insurance for your computer equipment and software in case of fire, theft or accident.

LAW:

Books:

Inc. Yourself: How To Profit by Setting Up Your Own Corporation, Judith H. McQuown, Harper Collins Pub., 10 East 53rd St., New York, NY 10022 - 212-207-7000 - Fax 800-822-4090 (1992).

The Legal Guide for Starting and Running a Small Business, and *The Limited Liability Corporation,* Nolo Press, 950 Parker St., Berkeley, CA 94710 - 800-992-6656, 510-549-1976 - http://www.nolo.com. Two good books for covering your legal assets. Call and ask for their free catalog that lists dozens of useful self-help law and business management books and software.

OFFICE: Space
Business Incubators :

Business Incubators Directory - International Venture Capital Institute, Inc., Baxter Associates, Box 1333, Stamford, CT 06904 ($19.95). Lists 650 companies.

Incubators of Small Business - Office of Private Sector Initiatives, Small Business Association, 1441 L. Street, NW, Suite 317, Washington, DC 20416. Free Lists 170 public and private incubators.

Executive Suites:

InterOffice Management - 703-934-6090. Rents a part-time offices at any of their 27 executive offices, in 12 major cities; includes receptionist service, voice mail and use of a conference room and office suite.

Virtual Offices:

Kinkos - 800-2-KINKOS - http://www.kinko.com. Provides copying services, computers, mail box suites, faxing, and teleconferencing rooms. 860 locations nationwide and international.

Mail Boxes Etc. - 800-949-6660. Provides a business address with suite numbers. They can also receive and send faxes for you.

OFFICE: Supplies

Beaver Prints, 305 Main Street, Bellwood, PA 16617 - 814-742-6063 - Fax 814-742-6063. Imprinted business cards in full color from stock art designs, 500 for $49. (Special offer $29). Also, color brochures, post cards, letterheads, mailers, newsletters.

The Container Store 800-733-3532. Innovative office and home shelving, filing and organizing furniture and accessories.

Laserwave Graphics - 800-653-2131. Creates and typesets a custom logo for your company with layout for Business Card, Letterhead and envelope for $99.

Nebs - 800-225-6380 - Fax 800-234-4324. Request their free *Small Business Start-up Catalog* or their *Manufacturers & Wholesalers Success Reference Guide*, a mail order source for every type of preprinted business form, including: labels, invoices, stationery, business cards and checks.

Quill - 800-789-1331 Fax 800-789-8955. Excellent mail order source for office supplies & equipment. Same day shipping and the best customer service around.

PHONE SERVICES:
800 Numbers:

Office Depot Business Services 800-800-5243. Sets your company up with a low cost 800 number.

AT&T - 800-222-0400, x487 - http://www.att.com/. Offers $20 month 800 number (plus calls).

Discount Long Distance:

MCI Preferred - 800-727-555 - http://www.mci.com/.

Sprint -   800-877-4646 - http://www.sprint.com/.

Interlink Communications Inc., Box 272846, Tampa, FL 33688 - Fax 813-960-8006. At 10 cents a minute, currently the lowest cost flat rate long distance service.

Phoenix Network - Mark Poeschel, 800-800-3773 - Fax 800-775-0366. Provides discount flat rate per minute long distance calling in the US and for international calling.

Fax Mail Services:

Delrina - 800-670-8777. Service can receive and/or broadcast thousands of faxes at a time for your company.

Voice Mail Services:

American Voice Mail - 800-347-2861 x837.

Afterword

Thank you for reading this book. I hope that you will contact me and give me your reaction. Did you like it? What did you get out of it? What helped the most? What other topics do you need covered? Just give me any feedback you have, and I'd really appreciate it. When I do the next edition, I want to pick up on new developments, and update everything. I hope to have a longer list of Stand-Alone Inventors with their success stories, and I'd like to include yours.

Meanwhile, good luck venturing your idea. Please let me hear from you at P.O. Box 2277 Sunnyvale, CA 94087. Fax 408/739-4351; E-mail: bobmerrick@aol.com.

ABOUT THE AUTHOR

Bob Merrick has been successfully developing and marketing his own inventions for more than twenty-five years. He does this as head of Merrick Industries, Inc., a six-employee company in Sunnyvale, California. The company does no manufacturing in house; rather, it outsources all production, and concentrates on marketing. Merrick maintains that simplicity is the key element in all of his inventing, and the reason for its success. His retail products are sold nationally in such stores as Office Depot, Staples and OfficeMax. Merrick Industries also conducts business-to-business marketing of promotional advertising products.

Robert G. Merrick

Frequently, Merrick is an invited guest speaker at government and university-sponsored seminars and workshops. He is also in demand as a consultant.

Merrick's background includes a BA degree in communications from the University of California at Berkeley, four years active duty as a naval officer, including a tour as an adviser in Vietnam, six years as advertising manager at Fairchild Semiconductor Corp., and three years as a partner in the Hal Lawrence Advertising and Public Relations agency in Palo Alto. He served 10 years as a founder and director of Pioneer Federal Savings and Loan of San Jose. In addition to running his company, he is active in real estate development and management. He was president of the non-profit California Inventors Council and a delegate to the White House Conference on Small Business.

He is married, has three grown children, and lives in Monta Vista, CA.